The Oral Performance in Africa

edited by

Isidore Okpewho

The Oral Performance in Africa

edited by

Isidore Okpewho

The Oral Performance in Africa

Edited by

Isidore Okpewho

Spectrum Books Limited
Ibadan. Owerri. Kaduna

Spectrum Books Ltd.
Sunshine House
Second Commercial Road
P. M. B. 5612,
Oluyole Estate
Ibadan, Nigeria

in association with
Safari Books (Export) Ltd.
Bel Royal House,
St. Helier
Jersey, Channel Islands
U. K.

ISBN 978-246-009-5

Printed by Intec Printers Limited, Ibadan

CONTENTS

PREFACE

THE contributions here have been selected from a list of papers presented at the Sixth Ibadan Annual African Literature Conference, held at Ibadan University July 27 - August 1, 1981, on the subject "The Oral Performance in Africa". The authors were given the opportunity to revise their papers in the light of discussions held during the conference and some editorial suggestions made by me. A few changes have been incorporated and the papers, while remaining essentially as they were presented at the conference, may be taken as products of the well-considered judgement of their authors rather than as raw materials hurriedly trussed up for the nonce.

It would be fair to say that our expectations of the conference were to a large extent satisfied and that the entire experience was rewarding. Participants came from as far away as Kenya, Malawi, Ghana, Britain and the United States of America. Our discussions were punctuated throughout with evening interludes befitting the subject of the conference — a performance of Yoruba hunter's poetry *(ijala)* by world-renowned troupe led by Alabi Ogundepo; a modern poetry reading by up and coming poets like Kofi Anyidoho and Niyi Osundare; a drama production by Femi Osofisan, easily the star of the post-Soyinka generation of playwrights; a showing of John Pepper Clark's *Tide of the Delta,* a documentary film of an Ijo festival drama depicting scenes from the Ozidi Saga; and other attractions.

The discussions were equally enriching. There was an atmosphere of good-humoured confrontation between certain groups tagged "the SOAS connection" and "the Madison connection". A fair number of the participants at the conference either came from or had studied at the London University School of Oriental and African Studies or the University of Wisconsin at Madison; to a large extent the difference in exposure and outlook between the British and American traditions was a boon to that search for a balance between ethnography and analysis which it was hoped the conference would encourage. Other influences at the conference — Ibadan, Ife, Legon, etc. — played a more or less accommodating role. On the whole the exchanges were incisive and illuminating.

I would like to thank the various persons and bodies that have made possible the publication of this book. First, the Department of English at Ibadan University must be saluted for providing a yearly forum for the discussion of various issues in African literature and culture. Inaugurated in 1976 by Professor Michael J. C. Echeruo, then Head of Department, these annual conferences have endeavoured to attract scholars from various countries and disciplines, and, we hope to publish selections of this kind, on a more regular basis. I am immensely grateful to the Nigerian Federal Ministry of Education and the Federal Department of Culture, whose chief executives — at that time Dr Ihechukwu Madubuike and Dr Garba Ashiwaju, respectively have long been personally committed to the development of traditional cultures of Nigeria in particular and Africa in general and did not hesitate to provide generous financial support towards the cost of hosting the 1981 conference. Thanks are also due to UNESCO for its more recent but very generous financial assistance in this regard. Finally, I wish to thank the contributors for responding so promptly to my editorial queries, despite the great distances separating me from most of them.

I regret to say that, because of production costs which ultimately affect the price of the book, it has not been possible for us to publish the original African texts in every instance — particularly those texts appended to three of the papers and substantial passages in others — or to indicate tone marks and diacriticals in the original texts that are published. Otherwise, everything possible has been done to ensure that the essential value of these contributions has not been impaired.

Ibadan Unversity
October 1989

Introduction: The Study of Performance

Isidore Okpewho

ONE of the most programmatic statements made in contemporary folklore research comes from Bronislaw Malinowski. In his study of Trobriand oral narratives he was struck by how much was lost in the reduction of the oral text to print and the subsequent analysis of the material divorced from the context that gave it life in the first place. The father of modern ethnography was moved to stress the need for a rehabilitation of that context for a proper understanding of the meaning of the text. Said he of the Trobriand "fairy tales" (*kukwanebu*):

> The text, of course, is extremely important, but without the context it remains lifeless. As we have seen, the interest of the story is vastly enhanced and it is given its proper character by the manner in which it is told. The whole nature of the performance, the voice and the mimicry, the stimulus and the response of the audience mean as much to the natives as the text; and the sociologist should take his cue from the natives. The performance, again, has to be placed in its proper time-setting — the hour of the day, and the season, with the background of the sprouting gardens awaiting future work, and slightly influenced by the magic of the fairy tales. We must also bear in mind the sociological context of private ownership, the sociable function and the cultural role of amusing fiction. All these elements are equally relevant; all must be studied as well as the text. The stories live, in native life and not on paper, and when a scholar jots them down without being able to evoke the atmosphere in which they flourish he has given us but a mutilated bit of reality.[1]

The fieldwork of Malinowski and his contemporaries (notably A.R. Radcliffe-Brown) was more or less a reaction against the then prevalent tendency on the part of comparative ethnologists (especially Sir James George Frazer) to make sweeping cultural

1

statements, without much basis in empirical evidence, about societies they had no experience of. Frazer, for one, never visited any of the "primitive" societies whose mythologies he wrote so learnedly about; but Malinowski believed that only first-hand experience of a society and careful study of the various forms and aspects of its cultural life would qualify us to make categorical statements about any one aspect of its cognitive system. The burden of his mission, as revealed by the above extract, is to emphasize the study of the proper social setting of a cultural act (e.g. storytelling) as an aid to a reliable understanding of its meaning and effectiveness.

This concern for empirical data marked the victory of pragmatism over intellectual romance.[2] Malinowski's mission was in the centre of a new movement which sought to replace the abstractionist tone of studies in human and social attitudes with a concrete demonstration of how these phenomena were realized in actual situations. As a cardinal aspect of behaviour, language was seen as one of those areas whose study, long subjected to speculative discussions about origins and diffusion, was overdue for the empiricist revolution. In this connection Malinowski did make a contribution. In an early paper he proposed that language could best be studied within the "context of situation" in which it was actually used;[3] he also undertook a detailed linguistic investigation of Trobriand agricultural life.[4] Though he was less a linguist than a "parlist",[5] his contextualist zeal was supported by more linguistically oriented anthropologists like Edward Sapir, who proposed that lingusists "must become increasingly concerned with the many anthropological, sociological, and psychological problems which invade the field of language."[6]

Such proposals gave birth, after World War II, to disciplines like ethnolinguistics, sociolinguistics, and psycholinguistics designed to explore the varied ambience of speech behaviour. Perhaps no scholar in these disciplines has done more in recent times to proselytize the contextual approach than Dell Hymes, who in various publications has recommended the title "Ethnography of Speaking"[7] for the study of language within specific social situations; he has also used the phrase "enthnography of communication" to locate this study within wider behavioural and cognitive system of the community and, echoing Malinowski, emphasized "the need to investigate the use of language in contexts of situation."[8]

2

The stress on *situation* has consequently favoured the study of *performance* over competence and so re-ordered the traditional scale of interests in linguistic studies—i.e., in the relationship, long established by Ferdinand de Saussure, between the abstract system of a language (*langue*) and the peculiar realizations of it in actual speech (*parole*). This was a welcome change, because it ultimately aimed at representing social man in a creative capacity within the context of a system of signs recognized by his community. A feeling for that system does indeed persist. Thus, in a seminal study, Arewa and Dundes have examined a whole spectrum of Yoruba proverbs in terms of "how and when they (are) employed in particular situations" relating to traditional child-rearing among the Yoruba.[9] Ben-Amos is also a notable advocate of the contextual approach.[10] In his study of Bini oral narrative performances[11] he has been inclined to see generic distinctions of the tales only within the system of classification recognized by the Bini themselves, and in his general study of ethnic systems of communication he has lamented that "in our zeal for scientific methodology, we have abandoned the cultural reality and striven to formulate theoretical analytical systems."[12] The functionalist concern remains. But to the extent that scholars have given some attention to the dynamic process by which the system is actualized, they may justly be credited with highlighting its creative potential. In a more recent statement on the subject of performance, Ben-Amos has pointed to these dynamic possibilities and even to their implications for conventional interest in linguistic research:

The contextual approach in folklore narrows the perspective of sociolinguistics somewhat, focusing not on the entire network of culturally defined communicative events, but upon those situations in which the relationship of performance obtains between speakers and listeners. It concentrates on those utterances which transform the roles of speaker and listener to those of performer and audience. The nature of this transformation is one of the main analytical tasks for the study of the communicative process of folklore. The discovery of the attributes of speech and behaviour change reporting into narrating, stating fact into stating proverbs, inquiring into riddling, and describing this transition as it happens is one of the main objects of the study of folklore in context.[13]

This focus of interest on performance as a subject deserving of an attention beyond the limited purview of the fixed communicative model of society has certainly appealed to a leading ethnographer of communication like Hymes. In a notable paper, he would seem to be taking some leave of the situational concern to concentrate on performance as an activity "emergent . . . or arising within" its social context. "The concern," he tells us of his textual analyses, "is with performance, not as something mechanical or inferior, as in some linguistic discussion, but with performance as something creative, realized, achieved, even transcendent of the ordinary course of events." After exploring the various progressive stages through which performance could usefully be analyzed, he is convinced of a fundamental "distinction between knowledge'what'and knowledge'how', or, more fully, between assumption of responsibility for knowledge of tradition and assumption of responsibility for performance. Much that has been published, I think, has neglected or confused this difference, treating tradition as something known independent of its existence as something done." Investigations into tradition as a system by way of analyses of content and structure are, Hymes argues, relevant; but there is the inherent danger of overlooking or even distorting "something essential to the peoples who shaped the traditions, the shaping of the performances in which tradition was made manifest, through which it was communicated and made part of human life. Consider the virtual absence of serious stylistic analysis of native American Indian traditions and of individual performers, of the literary criticism, as it were, that should be a first concern and a principal justification of the study of such traditions."[14] This statement is significant not only for the preference shown for *parole* over *langue,* in effect a devaluation of the modish efforts in structural linguistics; not only for suggesting that a tradition may be less important than the individual historical moments that gave life to it; but indeed for the admirable prospects of a re-unification of the arts (literary criticism) and the social sciences (ethnography).

Hymes' point about the lack of interest in performance has been echoed by Kirshenblatt-Gimblett, who laments that "in accounts of storytelling, we generally find information about the broad cultural context of the tales and occasionally an indication or general description of the major types of storytelling occasions. Very rarely do we come across accounts of actual narrative events."[15] While this is true, I think we should give some credit to efforts being made to correct the situation. In a useful essay, Ben-Amos has drawn attention to two notable Bini performers. Even though the study does not provide detailed analyses of actual performances, it does make an effort to give us an insight into the creative personalities of the artists.[16] Toelken's portrait of Yellowman, his Navaho informant, is equally effective in this regard.[17] Basgoz's discussion of performances by his Turkish narrator, Mudami, of the same tale before two separate audiences, perhaps updates Albert Lord's well-known monitoring of a Yugoslav *guslar* as a brilliant exposé of art in "context of situation".[18]

The significance of audience-oriented studies like Basgoz's is that they are squarely within the territory of aestheticist enquiry. There is no longer an interest in tradition as a sacrosant body of data nor of society as an aggregate of interests. Rather, there is a clear identification of two separate components of society and a portrait of how the narrator, by negotiating his creative skill cautiously around their respective sensibilities, endeavours to hold his ground on each occasion. It is partly this interaction of sensibilities between narrator and audience that encourages Tedlock, in his study of American Indian "ethnopoetics", to recommend that their narratives should be treated more as "dramatic poetry" than as analogues of written prose fiction.[19] One does feel that, with this aestheticist interest in the dramatic subtleties of the relationship between artist and audience on specific occasions, studies in *performance* are well on their way to achieving full maturity. Editions of oral narrative performances by Toelken, Clark, Tedlock, and Seitel[20] have—through their respective identifications of the narrator's varied levels of intonation, the audience's reactions, and other contingencies at the scene of the performance—helped this process in no small way.

In this study of the oral performance, will the collaboration between sociological and literary interests ever realize its full potential? One gets the impression that, whatever concessions the "ethnography of performance" (to use Bauman's felicitous phrase)[21] makes to the interests of art, it is in the final analysis unwilling to abandon its home base in sociological investigations. There is something of a grammatical curiosity, if not exactly a Freudian slip, in Hymes' view (see above) of performance as "arising within" a social context, not "from" it; even when he pushes this view to incorporate performance as "transcendent of the ordinary course of events", it is doubtful that for him this implies the liberty of art to look beyond the barriers of a particular social setting. The same goes for Bauman. Although in his epoch-making essay "Verbal Art as Performance" he claims to have made use of insights from a variety of disciplines, including literature, where he had an "earlier training",[22] his arguments belong squarely within the field of sociolinguistics or, to put it more generously, of the ethnography of communication. "A performance-centred conception of verbal art," he tells us, "calls for an approach through performance itself. In such an approach, the formal manipulation of linguistic features is secondary to the nature of performance, per se, conceived of and defined as a mode of communication."[23] Nobody denies the communicative imperative in any art; but to consider the manipulative skills of an artist a secondary order of investigation is a bit of a tall order for many a literary scholar.

One of the more significant issues in performance studies is that of the "emergence" of performance elements or qualities. There is a particularly interesting treatment of the issue by Bauman in his discussion of Sherzer's study of verbal arts among the Cuna Indians.[24] Sherzer has worked out an impressive model of relations, for all kinds of performance, between (a) event, (b) act, (c) role, and (d) genre. Such a model accounts for what, within the context of Cuna traditional life, would be considered a "conventional performance", e.g. a chief (c) delivering a chief's (d) curative chant (b) in a congress (a). But then Bauman cites two cases of personal correspondence from Sherzer to him, reporting violations of such a model of conventional performance. In one of them, little girls whom Sherzer used as linguistic informants once launched into a ritual chant normally done by adult men; in another, a young man would sit in a hammock meant for a chief and chant, at any time of the day, a chant traditionally done by a chief only in the evening, "just for the fun of it". Bauman uses the term "optative performance" to describe such violations, considering them instances of "playful imitation" and "creative manipulation".[25] I wonder if Bauman or Sherzer ever considered what would have happened to those little girls or young men if a Cuna elder or chief were to catch them usurping hallowed roles. They would, I guess, not want to be caught doing such things, and my feeling about their actions is that whereas aesthetically speaking they may be a success, sociologically speaking they are a failure.

The point being made is that, although there is clearly room for co-operation between the two disciplines in the study of the oral performance, an aestheticist model is not exactly the same thing as a sociological model. When a literary scholar investigates an oral narrative event, he should of course explore the social circumstances as an aid to contextual insight, but he is really more interested in probing the aesthetic basis for the effectiveness of the devices used in the performance. Let us take an example. In my fieldwork among Aniocha storytellers in Bendel State, Nigeria, I encountered one who claimed that his box-harp (*opanda*) had a spiritual origin.[26] In my reading of the Sunjata story collected from the Gambian Mandinka, I find a narrator who claims his guitar (*kora*) has a spiritual origin.[27] In my reading of ancient Greek heroic narratives, I find Hesiod claiming that the Muses gave him a wand (*skeptron*) for use in singing heroic songs.[28] Faced with these similar phenomena from three distinct cultural settings, the literary scholar of performance is inclined to explore, not so much the environment of belief or religion in the respective societies, as the basis of such a claim before an audience. The judgment he reaches is ultimately an aestheticist one—that the performer is simply trying to impress or to *affect* his audience as to the authoritativeness of his art. Even when he investigates a performance squarely set within ritual or religious premises and thus more amenable to sociological analysis, he will explore the aesthetic basis of its appeal or effectiveness, a task which I have set at least one of my students.[29]

Why have I opted for a structural reading in the claims of art to spiritual attachment? Literary scholars have long been content to explore the aesthetic distillate in a body of cultural data, not in disregard of the local setting of these data but in the conviction that in art the urge to please or affect quite often is — to quote Hymes while recalling Sherzer's correspondence to Bauman — "transcendent of the ordinary course of events". Japanese *Haiku* verse appeals to an African reader precisely because it abounds in elements that transcend the ordinary course of Japanese life. I would like to believe that foreign ethnographers researching African folklore find the material attractive enough to their foreign sensibilities to deserve serious study. If they do, it can only be because it transcends the boundaries of African life. Otherwise, if they are here simply to indulge a curiosity for the exotic, then they can hardly expect anyone, least of all their African colleagues, to take their work seriously.

The above arguments are by no means intended to polarize the interests of literature and sociology, though some of the more recent statements in this connection may leave that impression.[30] It simply seems to me that, for any fruitful collaboration to exist between the two disciplines in the study of the oral performance, we need to recognize not only the discrete contributions that they would make to the enterprise, but also the areas of tension which must be reconciled. Alan Dundes has, in a notable paper, recommended a coalition of insights from linguistics, literature and anthropology in the analysis of an oral performance.[31] But such a feat requires a scholar of true specialist competence in these areas, not one who would gloss over the salient issues with an amateurish sweep. Sadly, the tendency these days towards disciplinary atomism has turned most of us into amateurs in some areas of folklore research. I think that one could observe, without any malice, that one danger in ethnographic research — the kind, for instance, that urges us to base our classification of folklore genres only on the systems recognized by individual communities — is that it aids this atomism by representing every society as unique unto itself and reducible to an inventory of usages that are unlikely to be duplicated anywhere. It is perhaps in recognition of this danger that a well-known anthropologist was to lend his support to structural studies and to state: "Inventory making for its own sake, however diligently pursued, must ultimately reach the point where there is nothing further to do".[32]

I suggest that we have come far enough in cultural scholarship for ethnographers to heed this warning. In our study of the oral performance, a true collaboration between literature and sociology will come about in at least the following way: on the one hand, the literary scholar cannot afford, in his study of an art form in which there is more immediate dialogue between artist and context, to give the kind of token acknowledgment to that context that traditionally characterizes the study of written literature; on the other hand, the ethnographer of performance may reflect that the concept of "emergence" implies the liberation of his scholarly vision from the narrow constraints of the sociological model, towards the recognition of structural continuities.

8

The contributions which literature can make towards a fruitful understanding of the nature and results of the oral performance are adequately represented in this collection of essays, written mainly by scholars who have come to the subject with a background in literature. They are no less convinced, than their sociologically oriented colleagues, of the usefulness of going out to the field to observe the situation and reporting it with due loyalty, but the character of their commitment may be seen in the assumption of the title *Oral Literature* as a more representative description of their field of study. In many of these essays we find a combination of fieldwork insights and critical concepts and approaches which cut across cultural boundaries.

Performers and performances

The essays in this first section are basically ethnographic portraits of the artists who recreate the traditions of oral performance as well as sample performance situations.

Edris Makward, who wittily refers to himself here as "an amateur griot", gives us very useful sketches of two Senegalese Wolof griots: one a male, Anchou Thiam, the other a female, Haja M'Bana Diop. The picture of a female griot is particularly enlightening because students of the oral art of the Western Sudan are more familiar with the names of male performers like Mamadou Kouyaté and the inimitable Kélé Monson Diabaté than with those of females. But more than that, Makward's essay is significant for what it tells us about the relationship between the "traditional" and the "modern" in the performances of the griots. Part of the appeal of the oral traditions of this region to scholars is the witness which they bear to a great artistic heritage as well as the historical and other subjects that they treat. This region is also the scene of tremendous socio-political ferment, and some of the griots here are really more interested in celebrating this contemporary picture than in nostalgically evoking the figures of the past. This is essentially the difference Makward sees between Anchou and M'Bana: the one a wistful defender of "the tradition of the 'true griot' ", taking his subject exclusively from bygone days; the other a modish and enthusiastic celebrator of the notable figures of the new Senegal, like Leopold Sédar Senghor, erstwhile president of the country.

Chukwuma Azuonye's paper is a detailed, meticulous portrait of the art of the oral epic among the Ohafia Igbo of south-eastern Nigeria as seen through the work of its most distinguished practitioner, Kaalu Igirigiri (recently deceased). The rigour of Azuonye's ethnographic research can be seen in the frequent statistical references, and in the care with which he documents the original Igbo words for the ideas expressed by his informants. This study gives us a good picture of an artist who has a thorough knowledge of the history of his people and whose wisdom and ethnocentric pride are conveyed by the vividness of the tales. One of the virtues of this study is the way Azuonye tries to put Kaalu in the proper context of the artistic tradition, in terms of his relationship to both his forebears and his contemporaries in song. With particular reference to the latter, we can discern an atmosphere of well-intentioned competitiveness in the criticisms made of Kaalu by his rivals; not only does he respond to them in good measure, but he is concerned enough about his reputation as an artist to improve upon his mode of performance. The vitality of Kaalu's tradition of art is also demonstrated by his inclusion of material from very recent experience, most notably the Nigerian civil war. Notable also are the sensitive aestheticist insights which Azuonye brings into the portrait of Kaalu: the careful analysis of "the internal patterns of variation which occur in the individual singer's renderings of particular tales on different occasions"; the detailed consideration of the four major aesthetic principles on which the Ohafia artist operates; the survey of the various "voices" discernible in Kaalu's narrative performance; and so forth. The paper is a solid contribution to that marriage between ethnography and literary criticism which Hymes recommends.

Mvula's discussion of the *gule wamkulu* among the Chewa of Malawi gives us a vivid picture of an actual performance. In this very methodical treatment we are first introduced to the incidence and functions of the performance in Chewa society: the relationship of the masqueraders to actual figures and elements in the society; the educational value of the performance in teaching accepted norms of behaviour; its psychological value in giving both performers and audience a forum for releasing tension by behaving "out of the norm"; and so on. Next we are told about the elaborate pre-performance organization and chores: procuring materials for masks and drums; the individual initiation and collective editing of songs to be performed; purification rites to protect the arena and performers from evil spirits and influences; the announcement of the forthcoming event by animal-figures baying on the eve; and the structural arrangement of performers and audience in the arena.

The rest of the paper is devoted to a description of an actual performance which is a bustling combination of mime, song and dance to the accompaniment of well-modulated drum music. One of the most striking aspects of this discussion deals with the interaction of performers and audience which invests the bare text of a song with vivid meaning. Of a song about a barren wife's pleas to her absent husband we are told: "The *nyolonyo* (performers) sing the song solemnly and sorrowfully to portray the sadness of the woman in the picture. They sit down facing each other so that the audience sees the family situation . . . The performance of the *nyolonyo* hypnotizes the audience so that they also act the situation which the *nyolonyo* are singing." There is, however, one problem which the contextual approach to the study of oral literature frequently poses, and it stands out prominently in a mixed-grill performance such as the *gule wamkulu* where a whole range of social issues from public morality to family relationships is treated. "These sketches," Mvula tells us, "might occasionally be linked with a common theme, but they are mostly acts of various themes within the given performance occasion." Assuming we were to predicate our generic classification of the songs on Chewa views alone, as Ben-Amos would urge, how would Mvula's statement above help us?

From performance to print

Whatever the analytical methods used, our first task is to ensure that we have a proper record of the performance in our published texts. Gordon Innes is well known for his edition and translation of several Gambian Mandinka epics,[33] but in his present contribution he wonders whether he has in his translations succeeded in conveying the full impact that these epics have in their original language and setting. He has recognized three "modes" of vocalization (what Azuonye calls "voices") on which the performance is borne: the *speech* mode, a "free-form" narrative style in which the careers of the heroes "are described in the sort of language that a man might use to recount some personal experience"; the *song* mode, used for the singing of songs which occur occasionally in the story;

11

and the *recitative* mode, used in chanting the praises of the heroes, which are often couched in formulae of fixed diction and high emotive value. For Innes the crux of the translator's problem is how to translate these formularized praises so as to convey the high sense of pride which the original inspires in native Mandinka listeners, and here he doubts he has succeeded in conveying to the English reader the "emotive force" of these formulae. He is particularly impressed by Niane's translation of the Sunjata epic which he considers more as a "literary recreation" than as a translation of the original text of a performance, but which he judges — despite the purist reservations of professional folklorists — to be "extremely successful . . . in the difficult aim of conveying to the reader something of the feeling of a bard's performance".

We salute Innes' concern as an honest desire "to secure for the best in the oral literature of Africa its rightful place in world literature", but I suspect he has been over-cautious in his efforts not to violate the ethnic integrity of the oral literature. My paper "Towards a Faithful Record", which rests mainly on my own fieldwork in the oral narrative, addresses itself partly to this problem of translation. My experience has been that even within the general run of the narrative cast in the so-called speech mode, there is usually a high poetic afflatus which frequently erupts into supportive proverbs of emotional and poetic intensity. Besides, the narrative performances are mostly done to musical accompaniment which adds much to the poetic value of the vocalization at any level. "The story," if I may quote an earlier observation, "is a song, and its poetry consists more in the fervid process of making, than in any qualities we may recognize when the hands are resting and the voice is still."[34] It would therefore seem to me that, without taking undue liberties with the recorded text, it is the duty of a translator to represent in his version as much of the poetry as he felt at the event and as the audio-visual apparatus has been able to capture. Not only that, a faithful representation of the performance should incorporate as much of its intrinsic and extrinsic elements as possible to enable us to form the right sort of judgements about the art and culture. While giving credit to the earlier contributions of Clark and Tedlock in this regard, I append a sample text to demonstrate how I think an oral narrative performance should best be represented.

Text and context

The first two essays in this section are audience-oriented studies of the narrative, comparable in one way or another to the work of Ilhan Basgoz. They are also significant as explorations in oral literary theory based on fieldwork done by the authors' colleagues as well as themselves.

The difference between Sekoni's study and that of Basgoz is that, while Basgoz discusses the ways in which the audience's tastes and interests dictate the performer's choice of details in his narration, in Sekoni we see the ways in which the narrator-performer manipulates the sensations of the audience. Oral literary scholarship is full of unproven clichés about voice, gesticulation, histrionics, dress and other factors — devices which the performer employs outside of the tale to ensure the success of his enterprise.[35]

But Sekoni reaches into the very structure of the tale to explain what he considers an even greater insurance of the success of the narration: "the performer must align the images constituting his story in such a manner that he moves the sensation of his audience back and forth on a spectrum of expectancy that can be characterized on the one extreme by activation, in the middle by stabilization, and at the other extreme by depression." It is on this model that Sekoni analyzes the two Yoruba stories which he uses for his study.

More significantly, the paper illustrates that stress between the sociological and aestheticist approaches which I pointed to earlier. Sekoni believes that in a narrative performance the narrator's "transfer of cognitive experience" to the audience is inseparable from his manipulation of their responses. But his attention to the aesthetic relationship between artist and audience leaves little room for an exploration of the relevance of the cognitive component of the narrative experience. "While the nature of communication or the exchange of ideas in oral narrative-performance may be similar to other processes of communication in which the communicator transfers some message to the listener, the additional factor of entertainment or the creation by narrators of a product that is pleasant to experience by the listeners, calls from the narrator and the audience, as well as the student of verbal art, a special attention to the composition and delivery of the product itself in contradistinction to the message or the cognitive aspect of the narrative."

Perhaps we can now understand the independence from the search for a social-communicative model that Ben-Amos and Goldstein recognized in context-oriented studies of verbal art, when they saw the latter as "focusing not on the entire network of culturally defined communicative events, but upon these situations in which the relationship of performers obtains between speakers and listeners."[36]

In "The Oral Performer and His Audience", however, I show one area in which we can attempt to marry aestheticist and sociological insights. J. P. Clark has done an immense service to African oral literary studies by his edition of *The Ozidi Saga,* in which he has incorporated contextual elements like interpolations by "spectators" and the overall dialogue of intentionalities between artist and audience in an oral narrative event. What I have done here is to examine, as carefully as I could, those running commentaries by spectators—in many ways related to what Babcock describes as "metanarrative"[37] or Basgoz as "extra-constructional elements of the performance"[38]—so as to see how they help or bend the creative process of performance and how they underline the emotional stresses within the narrative event. The recognition of these stresses then leads me to query the old assumptions about social harmony or the communalistic instinct in traditional creativity. To justify or disprove my hunches I would, I am aware, have to undertake a larger sociological probe of the Ijo and perhaps demonstrate more convincingly that the circumstances of this particular performance could be considered sufficiently representative of the festival atmosphere back in the delta; but I should like to see my essay as one possible way of establishing "social structure" as an "emergent quality" of performance in at least one of the senses that Bauman has pointed out.[39]

Elizabeth Gunner's study of the Zulu *izibongo* is an attempt to bring some fresh insights into the much discussed topic of formulae in the composition of oral poetry. Exploring the wide variety of formulae occurring in Zulu praise poetry, she is able to show them in their dual capacities as ensuring stability and facilitating manipulation. Focusing on their significance in the context of performance, she makes a point which has not been heard often enough in studies of southern African poetry: "I would suggest that formulae lines or part lines serve both as recognition cues for an audience and as mnemonics for bards. Also the fact that for-

14

mulae are widely known and in some cases carry considerable affective charge, makes them particularly suitable as starting points for expansions likely to hold an audience's attention in a solo performance situation.''

Avorgbedor's contribution is a welcome event in African oral literary discussion, uniting as it does a variety of disciplinary approaches—psychoanalysis, ethnomusicology, and linguistics—in the treatment of oral poetic expression. In this paper the song is put into the proper perspectives not only of the basic human responses that go into accommodating it, but also of various contextual factors like the movement of the singer through the audience and even the physical effects at the scene of the performance that give meaning to the text. For instance, when the singer sings a piece to one spectator, then moves on to repeat the piece to the next spectator, the text assumes a fresh dimension and meaning for the first spectator. This is because the increased distance between him and the singer—which consequently reduces the intensity of sound from the singer's voice and musical accompaniment—frees the spectator from the overwhelming presence of the singer and thus enables him to concentrate more on the text of the song. For that spectator, therefore, the second delivery of the song is not so much a repetition, as a fresh encounter requiring a different emotional and mental response. Avorgbedor also cites a situation in which a proverb relating to the turtle and the eagle is sung in the presence of an actual sculpture depicting these creatures. ''The visual memory of the sculpture,'' we are told, ''will help concretize the text into a more permanent and affective whole.'' This is, no doubt, a welcome illustration of a point Finnegan once made of the text of the oral performance, that ''the bare words can*not* be left to speak for themselves''.[40]

Rassner's ''Narrative Rhythms'' is a stimulating contribution to the debate initiated many years ago by Claude Levi-Strauss—in the first volume of his *Mythologiques*—on the isomorphism between myth and music. Inspired on the one hand by structural studies of the folktale under the influence of Harold Scheub at Madison (where Rassner studied) and on the other by contact with musicologists at Yale (where he taught), the paper endeavours to see the disposition of images in the sequential development of a Kenyan *ngano* (tale) in terms of rhythmic patterning in music, within the context of the audience's perception of the narrative performance. What we have in this paper, therefore, is something of a combination of the approaches of both Sekoni and Avorgbedor. The relationship with Sekoni (who was Rassner's contemporary at Madison) can be seen in Rassner's view of the audience's mode of reception of the episodes of a tale: "An audience feels a performance through rhythm; aesthetic enjoyment is made up of this multiplicity of excitements and moments of respite, of expectations disappointed or fulfilled beyond anticipation." This somewhat agrees with Sekoni's division of a narrative-performance into moments of activation, stabilization, and depression; Rassner further agrees with Sekoni in arguing that this manipulation of images "induces an affective response from an audience and enhances the communication of 'message' ". But he goes further than Sekoni in trying to identify the smaller and larger units—which he calls respectively "micro-rhythms" and "macro-rhythms"—into which the images that constitute the message are organized. All this discussion is aimed at demonstrating that the communication between artist and audience proceeds very much in the manner of a musical experience: "Symbols become rhythmic in their repetition and variation. Repeated symbols are like accents in a musical beat; they become narrative rhythms. The simplest structure in music is the beat; certain beats are accented, and this in turn creates rhythm. In the *ngano,* symbols arise as accented beats from the mass of *ngano* details. Because of their importance or uniqueness to the *ngano,* they are remembered by the audience and developed by the performer." In his obsession with aprioristic mental structures, Lévi-Strauss has become notorious for his disregard of the interests of "contingencies" like the audience.[41] Rassner's paper opens up further possibilities for a revision of Lévi-Strauss' position.

Radical perspectives

This volume of contributions ends with Mbye Cham's paper, a ground-breaking study which sees the affinities between traditional and modern culture (oral narrative and film) in the context of a commitment to revolutionary action. It is essentially an analysis of the cinematic art of the Senegalese marxist-socialist writer Sembène Ousmane who, by incorporating the themes and structure of the oral narrative in his films, sees "himself as the equivalent of the griot in the society of today." A comparative dissection of Sembène's film *Mandabi* and two trickster tales (one Ashanti. one

16

Wolof) — the use of the structural concept "image-set" recalls Rassner, Cham's colleague in their Madison days—shows how Sembène has employed the repetitive structure not simply to lyrical effect but indeed to drive home the message about the exploitative "whims and tricks of bureaucratic and other social wolves who manage a world in which the likes of Ibrahima Dieng are not only struggling misfits, but also fair game." In tracing the affinities between *Mandabi* and the oral tradition, Cham invites critics to see the modern African film as rooted in traditional modes and consciousness — with the same degree of recognition accorded modern African literature written by Soyinka, Kourouma, P'Bitek, etc. — "rather than limping off to Hollywood or to Europe to seek models".

Conclusion

This selection of essays cannot claim to have covered all areas of discussion on the subject of the oral performance in Africa—we have simply tried to explore some of the major dimensions in which the phenomenon can be understood both in its own terms and in terms of its relevance to culture and society. We have started by taking an ethnographic look at the phenomenon from the point of view of the performers and their work; we have moved on to query some of the ways in which that work may best be represented in print for proper appreciation; next, we have tried to read the text of the performance back into the circumstances from which it derived; and finally, we have tried to see the past in the context of the future, not only in terms of creative adaptation but also of critical standards. On the whole it would be fair to say that, although these essays have been written mostly by scholars with a background in literary criticism, they have demonstrated a concern for contextual factors and present needs, not unlike that felt by their counterparts in the social sciences.

The need for co-operation between the two approaches can hardly be overstated, but the obstacles are just as remarkable. Not the least of these is established disciplinary prejudice, of a more or less defensive kind, which we may illustrate with two brief encounters from the literary side. In one of our discussions during the conference from which these papers emanated, one participant remarked: "Let us deny ourselves the use of the term 'folklore' as a description of the subject of our study." Despite the mist of understanding surrounding the use of that term, some of us who took courses in "folklore" during our graduate days are not often driven to see it as automatically antagonistic to the interests of "oral literature". But, in the minds of many, the term "folklore" conjures up images of material culture and arcane customs which are somewhat outside the immediate province of literary concerns; nobody in the discussion openly questioned the plea of that participant.

The second experience was related to me by a colleague in one of our Nigerian universities who had been supervising some honours essays in Oral Literature. When it was found he had too many students registered with him, his head of department moved a couple of the students over to another lecturer. On looking at the ethnographic introduction presented by one of these students (who was writing on funeral poetry in his community), the new lecturer rejected the work on the grounds that it was sociology, not literature.

We hope tnat in time such prejudices will disappear. In presenting this book we share with Bauman and others the noble mission of operating "at an intellectual level beyond the boundaries which separate academic disciplines, sharing an interest in the aesthetic dimension of social and cultural life in human communities."[43]

NOTE

1. Bronislaw Malinowski, *Myth in Primitive Psychology* (New York: Norton, 1926) p. 24.
2. See Edmund R. Leach, "The Epistemological Background to Malinowski's Empiricism," *Man and Culture: An Evaluation of the Work of Bronislaw Malinowski,* ed. Raymond Firth (London: Routledge and Kegan Paul, 1957) pp. 119—37.
3. See Malinowski, "The Problem of Meaning in Primitive Language," *The Meaning of Meaning,* ed C.K. Ogden and I.A. Richards (London: Kegan Paul, 1923). pp. 296—336.
4. Malinowski, *Coral Gardens and Their Magic II: The Language of Magic and Gardening* (London: Allen and Unwin, 1935).
5. Raymond Firth, *Symbols: Public and Private* (London: Allen and Unwin, 1973). p. 143
6. Edward Sapir, "The Status of Linguistics as a Science." *Selected Writings of Edward Sapir,* ed. David G. Mandelbaum, (Berkeley: Univ. of California Press,

1949), p. 166. **Paper first appeared in** *Language, 5* (1929), 207—14.

7. See Dell Hymes, "The Ethnography of Speaking" *Anthropology and Human Behaviour, T. Gladwin and W.C. Sturtevanteds (Washington,* D.C.: Anthropological Society of Washington, 1962).

8. See J. Gumperz and D. Hymes, eds. *The Ethnography of Communication. Special Publication of American Anthropologist,* 66/6, part 2 (1964) p. 2.

9. E. Ojo Arewa and Alan Dundes, "Proverbs and the Ethnography of Speaking Folklore" *The Ethnography of Communication,* pp. 70—85.

10. See Dan Ben-Amos. "Toward a Definition of Folklore in Context " *Journal of American Folklore,* 84 (1971) pp. 3—15.

11. See Ben-Amos, *Sweet Words: Storytelling Events in Benin* (Philadelphia: In-

12. Ben-Amos (ed.) *Folklore Genres* (Austin: Univ. of Texas Press, 1976). Cf. Ben-Amos "Introduction: Folklore in African Society" *Forms of Folklore in Africa,* ed. Bernth Lindfors (Austin: Univ. of Texas Press, 1977), pp. 1—34.

13. Dan Ben-Amos and Kenneth S. Goldstein (eds.) *Folklore: Performance and Communication* (The Hague: Mouton, 1975), pp.4.

14. Dell Hymes, "Breakthrough into Performance" *Folklore: Performance and Communication,* pp. 11—74.

15. Kirshenblatt-Gimblett Barbara, "A Parable in Context: A Social International Analysis of Storytelling Performance" *Folklore: Performance and* Communication, p. 107.

16. Ben-Amos, "Two Bini Storytellers" *African Folklore,* ed. Richard Dorson

17. Barre, Toelken, "The 'Pretty Languages' of Yellowman: Genre, Mode, and Texture in Navaho Coyote Narratives" *Folklore Genres,* ed. Dan Ben-Amos, pp. 145—70.

18. See Ilhan Basgoz, "The Tale Singer and His Audience" *Folklore: Performance and Communication,* pp. 143—203. *See also* Albert B. Lord "Avdo Mededovic. Guslar" *Slavic Folklore: A Symposium,* ed. A.B. Lord (Philadelphia: American Folklore Society, 1956), pp. 122—32. Some of the work done here in Ibadan under my supervision may be cited. Kingsley A. Ude's Master's Thesis "Ukwa Ufiem: The Artist and His Enviroment" 1981) and Edwin Okoiruele's Honours Essay. "Chief Omobuarie Igberaese: Portrait of an Artist" 1982) are in the holdings of the Department of English, University of Ibadan.

19. Dennis Tedlock, "Toward an Oral Poetics" *New Literary History,* 8 (1977) pp. 513.

20. Toelken, "The 'Pretty Languages' of Yellowman" J.P. Clark *The Ozidi Saga* (Ibadan: I.U.P. and O.U.P., 1977). Tedlock, *Finding the Center* (Lincoln: Univ. of Nebraska Press, 1978). Peter Seitel, *See So That We May See* (Bloomington: Indiana Univ. Press, 1980).

21. Richard Bauman, *Verbal Art as Performance* (Rowley, Mass.: Newbury House, 1977), p. 13.

22. Ibid., p.vii.

23. Ibid., pp. 8—9.

24. Ibid., pp. 31—35.

25. Ibid., p. 34. Compare Arewa and Dundes' discussion of the manipulations of the Yoruba proverb, "One should not say in jest that his mother is fainting," loc. cit., 74.

26. Isidore Okpewho, *Myth in Africa* (Cambridge: Cambridge University Press, 1983), pp. 58—59.

27. See Gordon. Innes, (ed.) *Sunjata: Three Mandinka Versions* (London: School of Oriental and African Studies, 1974), p. 41.

28. See Hesiod, *Theogony*, 30—32.

29. See Yomi Akeremale, "Function and Aesthetics in Folklore: Ritual Poetry — A Case Study of Aiyelala from Okitipupa". Honours Essay, Department of English, University of Ibadan. 1980.

30. See introduction to Jacobs Melville and John Greenway (eds.) *The Anthropologist Looks at Myth* (Austin: Univ. of Texas Press, 1966). See also my rejoinder in "The Anthropologist Looks at the Epic" *Research in African Literatures* 11 (1980), pp. 429—48. Reviewing Robert Layton's *The Anthropology of Art* in the London *Times Literary Supplement* of January 15, 1982, Raymond Firth remarks on anthropology's "uneasy relationship with aesthetics". Though in general terms he welcomes a collaboration between the two fields, he is no less emphatic on the traditional dichotomy between them "the *anthropology* of art should primarily be concerned with the human relations of the art rather than with its aesthetic qualities."

31. Alan Dunde's, "Texture, Text, and Context" his *Interpreting Folklore* (Bloomington. Indiana Univ. Press, 1980), pp. 20—32.

32. Edmund R. Leach, Foreword to *Sexual and Asexual Pursuit: A Structuralist Approach to Greek Vase Painting*, Herbert Hoffmann. Occasional Paper No. 34 of the Royal Anthropological Institute, London, 1977.

33. *Sunjata: Three Mandinka Versions* (1974). *Kaabu and Fuladu: Historical Narratives of the Gambian Mandinka* (1976). *Kelefa Saane: His Career Recounted by Two Mandika Bards* (1978). All titles published by the School of Oriental and African Studies, London.

34. Isidore Okpewho, *The Epic in Africa* (New York: Columbia Univ. Press, 1979), p. 66

35. See E.B. Uwatt, "Beside the text: Paranarrative Elements in Efik Oral Performance." Masters thesis, Univ. of Ibadan, 1982.

36. *Folklore: Performance and Communication*, p. 4.

37. See Barabara A. Babcock, "The Story in the Story: Metanarration in Folk Narrative" In Richard Bauman *Verbal Art as Performance*, pp. 61—79.

38. Basgoz, "The Tale-Singer and His Audience," p. 143.

39. See Bauman, *Verbal Art as Performance*, pp. 42—45.

40. Ruth Finnegan *Oral Literature in Africa* (Oxford: Clarendon Press, 1970), p. 15. With Avorgbedor's comments on *halo*, compare Kofi Awoonor's useful study, *Guardians of the Sacred Word: Ewe Poetry* (New York: Nok Publishers. 1974),

41. See especially Claude Levi-Strauss, *The Savage Mind* (London: Weidenfeld and Nicolson, 1966). p. 29.

42. K.K. Ruthven *Myth* (London: Methuen, 1976), p. 82

43. Bauman, *Verbal Art as Performance, p. 3.*

Part One

Performers and Performances

Two Griots of Contemporary Senegambia

Edris Makward

I

AS AN introduction to this presentation of two Wolof griots of Senegal, it is still appropriate to repeat the famous statement of Djibril Tamsir Niane: "The word of our griots, carriers of tradition, deserves more than contempt."[1] Tamsir Niane was referring to the widely held tendency to identify "griots" with that "caste of professional musicians" who live on the backs of others. Many of these professionals do perform in the recording studios of Dakar, Abidjan and other capitals, and they consider themselves as 'stars' whose most trifling utterances must be rewarded with cash.

Naturally, I would agree with Tamsir Niane that though such griots do prosper unscrupulously in the cities of modern Africa, they certainly are not authentic representatives of the old griot tradition of the Western Sudan. However, this authentic tradition has fortunately not yet completely disappeared from the villages and the cities of the Western Sudan. One of these great authentic voices is without doubt Djeli Mamadou Kouyaté of the village of Djeliba Koro (Sigiri) in Guinea.[2] Djeli Mamadou Kouyaté is Tamsir Niane's major informant for his invaluable little masterpiece, *Soundjata ou l'épopée mandingue.* This is how Mamadou Kouyaté, an authentic Mandingo griot, introduces himself:

> I am a griot. I am Djeli Mamadou Kouyaté, son of Bintou Kouyaté and of Djeli Kédian Kouyaté, master of the art of speech. Since time immemorial the Kouyatés have been at the service of the Keita princes of Manding . . . The art of speech has no secret for us, without us the names of kings would sink into oblivion; we are the memory of men; by the word, we give life to the actions of our dead kings for the benefit of the present generation . . . My word is pure and stripped of all untruths; it is my father's word; it is my father's father's word.[3]

23

Another great voice of the authentic griot tradition of the Western Sudan is Boubacar Tinguidji, a celebrated Fulani griot (Maabo) from the Republic of Niger. Tinguidji was originally from the village of Tera near the Burkina Faso border. Though he spent many years in Burkina Faso in the compound of Mamadou, the Amirou of Dori, and then in Ouagadougou (the capital city of the Republic of Burkina Faso) and later in Niamey–the capital city of the Republic of Niger where he is now very well known and respected–he still considers as his real home the village in the province of Dargol, between Tillaberi and Niamey, where he settled after leaving Burkina Faso. For as he puts it, this is where he pays his taxes. Even when he is away from the village, the noble family whose "Maabo" he has always been, will pay his taxes for him. Tinguidji learned the art of the hoddu[4] from three maternal uncles and another highly praised teacher, called Galabou, from Kounari.

Christiane Seydou's conclusions after presenting substantial excerpts of her conversations with Tinguidji are very enlightening with regard to the stature of an authentic traditional griot:

> This is how Tinguidji, a Maabo traditionalist, respectful of his art and of himself, speaks of himself. With these remarks he is anxious to distinguish himself from those vulgar and unscrupulous griots whose only purpose is to extort presents and favors and who, in order to reach their goal, will wield praise and insult, dithyrambical panegyric and spiteful diatribe, noble language and the grossest slang with equal ease and daring.[5]

This insistence on the true griot's honesty, trustworthiness and moral distinction appears not only in circumstances such as the above—that is, an interview during which the griot speaks of himself—but even within the creative process itself, that is, in the text that the griot may be reciting. For instance, in the famous Fulani epic *Silamaka et Poullori,* there is an episode in which the old Maabo of Silamaka betrays him to his enemy, Amirou Sa by revealing to the latter the existence of the magic gold ring which protects Silamaka against all his enemies.[6] In all his recorded versions of this epic, Tinguidji insists emphatically on the fact that the old Maabo did not betray his master for material gain, but only because of the deep humiliation he had suffered. In one version the Maabo says:

Yesterday,
He slapped me in the face
Because I had advised him not to beat his wife!
This is why I came to you.
Neither spears nor rifles
Can stop Silamaka and Poullori
But there is a ring
Among the amulets of one of his relatives. Bandado-Ardo;
As long as you are not in possession of the ring,
Whatever you do, he will get the better of you,
And of those who would follow in your steps.
As regards that ring, to obtain it will not
Be easy: neither flattery nor sword would
Be enough.

In another version of this episode by the same Tinguidji, the Maabo says:

Had he not slapped me yesterday,
I would not have come to you, I would not
Have come to another man, I would not have
Followed another man.
But he slapped me, that is why I left the compound.
I would not stay in any compound where they would beat me.
I did not think I would ever have to ask
Myself in my old days whether I was not
A slave![7]

Among the more familiar names of contemporary griots and performers whose names have been popularized across ethnic and national boundaries through records, cassette tapes, radio and television stations, one might cite the Gambian Alhaji Bai Konte, the Senegalese Ablaye Naar Samb and the late Soundjoulou Cissoko, the Malian Alhaji Batourou Sekou Kouyaté. Many of the performances of these popular artists also share the above characteristics, that is, the concern with establishing trust and confidence with one's audience by referring to one's credentials through one's own genealogical line. This is usually done at the beginning of the performance. But further references may also be made later during the performance. For it is indeed from the knowledge and awareness of the griot's ancestry that the serious and initiated listener can establish the authenticity of his training and artistic background.

Anchou Thiam and Haja M'Bana Diop, two Wolof griots from Waalo,[8] also share with these famous griots the same pride and

25

faith in their inherited art, the same sense of discretion and modesty in the practice of their art.

M'Bana Diop and Anchou Thiam originated from two villages just about two kilometres from each other: Thiago and Ndombo, respectively, in the district of Richard-Toll. Haja M'Bana now lives in Richard-Toll, but she travels a great deal within Senegal and has made the Moslem pilgrimage to Mecca twice already.

Anchou also has done a lot of travelling, but he now lives in Thiaroye on the outskirts of Dakar. They both grew up in the country, and remain closely attached to their native villages. They both claim to have learned their art from older relatives: Anchou studied mainly with his father who was a farmer and a practising griot as well, whereas M'Bana learned more from her paternal aunt, Fatou Diop Chaka, and other talented relatives. In an interview, M'Bana emphasized the common practice among traditional Wolof kings and princes of marrying at least one griot wife. She gave the example of Yamar, one of the "Chefs de canton" of Richard-Toll appointed by the French, who married one of her aunts, Yaram N'Deer Diop. M'Bana stated that one of the first songs she learned in her youth was the song with which her aunt Yaram N'Deer welcomed her royal husband Yamar when he returned from the famous battle of Saabu Siri against the Moors. Before chanting this short song, which actually took the shape and form of an impromptu performance, to the accompaniment of a drummer playing a small armpit drum, M'Bana related the circumstances in which the song was composed as well as the actual deeds and actions that constituted the song itself. She confirmed the information that in spite of the strict endogamic nature of relationships within the Wolof caste system Wolof kings and princes have always had at least one griot wife that is why one of her great aunts, Busa M'Baye, was married to King Aram Bacar, and her paternal aunt Yaram N'Deer Diop was married to King Yamar, who fought the Moors at Saabu Siri:

M'Bana: So when King Yamar was preparing for that historic battle of Saabu Siri, it was in my aunt Yaram N'Deer's bedroom that he performed his final preparations, and got ready (for the battle). Yaram N'Deer was begotten by Njambat.[9] Njambat was begotten by Fara Coro. Bubacar Coumba is her father. A relative[10] of her father is Coumba Code Njambat; and also Njaantu Njambat. Njambat Fara

Coro. So the day Yamar was fighting at Saabu Siri, he completed his preparations in her room. Also when he fought at Baray Kaat, he prepared for the battle in her room. He dressed there; put on his amulets. And on his return each time, it was in that room that he undressed and took off his amulets. Yes. For that battle (Barey Kaat) they crossed (the River Senegal) on a Tuesday. They crossed on a Tuesday at the Dagana Well. On that Tuesday at Dagana, they spent the day at Barey Kaat where Yamar distributed the ammunition to his men. Then they left for a place called Asbum. (*Pause*) They distributed the ammunition at Barey Kaat; then they spent the day at (*Pause*) Esfuut where they killed a Moor called Ahmet Fall; they killed Malick Kiis and their slave Wulnaa Siri. The Moorish women started weeping and said "Weeyli! Weeyli!" Yamar said: "Who ever says 'Weeyli! Weeyli!' will die." My aunt sang about him thus.

Makward: Do you know that song?

M'Bana: Yes, I do. When he came back from that battle, he brought back many slaves and lots of cattle, cows, sheep and camels. They crossed (the river) back at the Dagana Well. Thus Yamar came back and he stood where he had dressed before the battle, and undressed. From his clothes, they extracted enough bullets to fill six large dishes. Thus my aunt sang about him:

> Brave Mbabaa!
> Brave Mbabaa! Yaram Joop.
> Fara Penda Aadam Sal.
> That Tuesday you crossed the river at Dagana.
> 5 You spent the day at Ngor Madd.
> You distributed the ammunition
> among your men at Barey-Kaat.
> You left in the afternoon for
>   Asbuum where you spent the night.
> There, you killed Ahmet Faal, you
> 10 killed Maalik Kiis and their slave
>   Wulnaa Siri
> The Moorish women wept and cried
>   "Weeyli! Weeyli!"
> Yamar said: "Who ever says 'Weeyli! Weeyli!'
>   will die."
> Fara Kumba, Mataar Naar.
> Ooh Jaajee!
> 15 Brave Mbabaa.
> He is worth singing about.
> Sara Koumba, Mataar Naar. Woi Jaajee!
> Brave Mbabaa!

Brave Mbabaa, Yaram Joop.
20 He (Yamar) fought against Tarxiis
    at Ngor Madd and burnt Saabu Siri.
This is what he got at Xuuma Jankiri.
Mbaye Joop, the country of Samba Wadd.
The Wind of MaaSamba Xosifor.[11]
They all sang: Brave Mbabaa, he is
    worth singing about.
25 Fara Kumba Mataar Naar,
Ooh Jaajeey!

M'Bana: That was how my paternal aunt sang about king
Yamar.[12]

In this short piece of recording, several modes of verbal,
communication can be easily identified.

(a) First there is the telling of a memorized story—somewhat like
a tale. This was the mode used in the interview to tell the details of
Yamar's campaign against the Moors—his victory, his return home
with the booty, his generosity to his wife. Although these facts and
events are supposedly historical and factual, the mode in which
M'Bana tells them is recognizably a storytelling mode.

M'Bana is undoubtedly a good storyteller—a *leeb kat*. The
accuracy and control of her delivery, the tone and the varied in-
tonations of voice displayed here, are unmistakable.

(b) Then there is the praise-singing mode, the *taag* mode. This
mode is based on a sound knowledge of genealogy combined with a
good memorization of accurate historical facts and events. This
mode has its own characteristic rhythm which M'Bana displays in
the short praise of her aunt, Yaram N'Deer Diop. The rhythm of
this mode is essential both for delivery and for memorization.
M'Bana has a good grasp of this rhythm, but as she would admit
herself, praise-singing *taag* is not her forte. Neither is she a good
oral historian. Her weakness in this area is evidenced by her long
pauses, her hesitation in identifying names of places when she tries
to detail the advance of King Yamar and his army on his way to
Saabu Siri. She is definitely not well versed in genealogies and her
incompetence in this area is clear in her short praise of her aunt here.

While admitting that she is not a true "borom xam xam"—that
is, an oral historian—M'Bana would also add that mere memorization of genealogies is a minor art form among the Wolof. It goes
without saying that the old man, Anchou Thiam, a cousin of hers,
would categorically disagree with her on that score.

(c) There is finally the singing mode which is definitely M'Bana's forte. In this short piece, she displays all the basic qualities required of a good Wolof singer, i.e. correct pitch, a rich clear tone, a capacity to sustain the appropriate notes, a good control of delivery and rhythm. Here, M'Bana does not hesitate over names of places or people, and when she pauses, it is definitely not due to a slip of memory or to a lack of confidence, but is a calculated element of delivery and rhythm. In fact, her memory seems irreproachable here. The words and details over which she would hesitate and stumble in the first two modes, do not seem to present any difficulty in this mode.

Without doubt M'Bana is above all a singer and an excellent one. She is a *woi kat*. It is true that the Wolof substantive *woi* means both song and poem, as L. S. Senghor has indicated on many occasions. Likewise the verb *woi* implies to sing a song as well as to praise *(taag)*. However, when one uses the expression *woi kat* to refer to M'Bana Diop or to the famous griot of La Radio-Télévision Sénégalaise, Ablaye Naar Samb, the distinction is clear.

II

Neither Anchou nor M'Bana is literate. For all practical purposes, they cannot read or write French, Wolof or Arabic. Thus the whole of their repertoire is memorized orally without the help of the written word. Anchou, however, says that he has used the written word in his younger days to memorize some historic details with the help of a reader who would have him repeat the written material as many times as necessary. The script used in these cases to transcribe the Wolof texts was exclusively Arabic (Wolofal). Anchou Thiam was in his mid-sixties and M'Bana Diop in her late forties in 1973. Though neither of them attended the French school, and their Koranic education was minimal, their outlook and their reputation in Senegal were—and still are—not quite identical. M'Bana Diop is definitely a modern artist—and not in any pejorative sense. Although her art still stems from tradition, her material deals more specifically with the actions and events of her time, rather than with those of the past—the latter remaining the forte of a truly traditional performing griot, such as Anchou Thiam.

M'Bana is definitely much more at ease in the urban setting of Dakar and St. Louis than her cousin Anchou. Although Anchou has resided in the Dakar area for several years, and is also much travelled within Senegal and even beyond, he remains very much a peasant and a rural man in his manner and presentation. A cursory look at M'Bana's living-room at Richard-Toll with its air-conditioner, refrigerator and TV set reveals a definitely higher economic status than Anchou's. Lastly, there is M'Bana's prestigious title of Haja, obtained after making the holy pilgrimage to Mecca. By 1973 she had already made the trip twice, while Anchou was still dreaming of making his first.

A brief examination of Haja M'Bana's two songs *Ndyaadyan Ndyaay* and *Sam Samaane* will substantiate the above remarks. First of all, both pieces are songs whose composition is circumstantial; for M'Bana Diop is indeed a singer and a composer of songs, and not a reciter of poems. In *Ndyaadyan Ndyaay*, she does not narrate the career of the legendary first king of the Wolof, as a more traditional griot would do. She only refers to a few very well known legendary or semi-legendary facts about Ndyaadyan Ndyaay, for instance, that Fatumata Sall was his mother; that he spoke at Mengeen Booy; that a woman named Batboor Yaadi Booy made him speak first. According to the legend, he appeared from the river one day and settled what had been constant quarrels among young Wolof men fishing in the river. When the young men returned to their village and related the incident to their elders, everybody agreed that this man was indeed a wise and worthy man to have in one's community. The elders therefore asked the young men to repeat their quarrelsome behaviour the next day on their return from fishing. When the man from the river appeared again to settle the quarrel, he was prevented from returning to the water and was lured to the village. Once in the village, the man remained mute for a number of days and would not communicate with any one. A shrewd woman, Batboor Yaadi Booy, tricked him into addressing her in Wolof and in gesture pretending that she did not know that a round-bottomed cooking pot cannot be stabilized with only two stones. As she repeatedly let the pot full of food spill on the ground out of apparent ignorance, the man from the river could not contain himself, and told her to use three (*net*) stones. The following is a translation of M'Bana's song *Ndyaadyan Ndyaay:*

I

M'Bana: Fatumata Sall is the mother of Ndyaadyan Ndyaay.

Ndyaadyan Ndyaay broke his silence at Mengeen Booy.

Chorus: Fatumata Sall is the mother of Ndyaadyan Ndyaay.
Ndyaadyan Ndyaay spoke first at Mengeen Booy.

II

M'Bana: Senegal is asking me who made Ndyaadyan Ndyaay talk
at Mengeen.
It is Batboor Yaadi Booy who made Ndyaadyan Ndyaay
talk at Mengeen.

Chorus: Fatumata Sall is the mother of Ndyaadyan Ndyaay.
Ndyaadyan Ndaay spoke first at Mengeen Booy.

III

M'Bana: You know that Ndyaadyan Ndyaay left Waalo to take
refuge in Djoloff and left us with Brak Mbarka Mboodji, as our kings.

Chorus: Fatumata Sall is the mother of Ndyaadyan Ndyaay.
Ndyaadyan Ndyaay spoke first at Mengeen Booy.

IV

M'Bana: Yee Haja M'Bana Diop, you composed and sang
Ndyaadyan Ndyaay,
You are a "ndaanan" who seldom goes wrong, Diop, it
is your talent that people seek.

Chorus: Fatumata Sall is the mother of Ndyaadyan Ndyaay.
Ndyaadyan Ndyaay broke his silence at Mengeen Booy.

V

M'Bana: You know that Ndyaadyan Ndyaay left Waalo to take
refuge at Djoloff.
He left us with Brak Mbarka Mboodji as our king.
Fatumata Sall was his mother.
Almaami from Fuuta Lam Tooro brought us Ablaay
Barka.
Ndyaandyan Ndyaay, Saar, you and Jaalo.

Chorus: Fatumata Sall is the mother of Ndyaadyan Ndyaay.
Ndyaadyan Ndyaay broke his silence at Mengeen Booy.

One distinguishing feature of this song is that the chorus often
dwells on the singer's own praises and there are frequent references
to portions of her own genealogy:

Younger sister of Sanu Diop Ndiack at Lewda.
Yirim Kumba Geey, Waali Ndyaay Saar Nduur at Gaaya.
M'Bana Joop, you composed and sang *Ndyaadyan Ndyaay*.
Joop, we seek your art.

She closes her performance with praise for her drummer and co-singer here. She refers to him as a "geer", that is, a member of the Wolof higher "freeborn" or "noble" caste:

> My nobleman, play the drum and sing along with me,
> I will not sing anymore the praises of just any nobleman.
>
> Silxooye Jembe Caam died at Mengeen.
> O! Yaatma Maasan Faal.

M'Bana Diop's "song" or "woi" of Ndyaadyan Ndyaay would be quite different from Anchou Thiam's rendering of the same material which he would also call "woi". The difference would be not only in the content and the wealth of historical details but also and above all, in the form of delivery. M'Bana's "woi" would correspond more to the western popular "song" whereas Anchou's "woi" would be closer to a short "epic" in Western terms. In fact, Anchou would readily refer to his "woi" of *Ndyaandan* as a piece of "cosaan," that is, a historical piece, which M'Bana's is definitely not.

M'Bana's other "song" considered here, *Sam Samaane,* is a deliberately modern composition that tells of the deeds of a modern "hero"—the poet, scholar and former President of Senegal, L. S. Senghor. It is interesting to note in stanza IV the introduction of an authentic hero of Waalo, Muse Saar Fari Joop, followed in stanza V by the first direct reference to L. S. Senghor. The intention is obvious as stanza IV ends with the line: "The heroes of Senegal" and stanza V starts with: "You all know of the year 1960", that is, the year Senegal and a number of other African countries obtained their independence. Here are excerpts (translated) from the song *Sam Samaane:*

IV

M'Bana: Muse Saar Fari Joop
            With his body dotted with wounds.
            There goes a man with courage.
            The King was hit, Dyawdin was hit.
            Musé Fari Joop was hit.
            The injuries were painful.
            So Mboyo, poor Mboyo Maa Caam.
            Yee Sam Samaanee . . . Yaay.
            The heroes of Senegal. Eee!

Chorus: Sam Samaanee . . . Yaay
            Whoever wants to draw water goes to Waalo.

V

M'Bana: You all know of the year 1960.
It is in 1960 that Senghor became our leader.
All nations respect us,
Everybody respects Leopold.
Remember the time of the rice shortage,
And the increase in the price of ground-nuts!
You know that Senghor was then a student abroad.
Sam Samaanee . . . Yaay!
Who wants to draw water goes to Waalo.

Chorus: Sam Samaanee . . . Yaay.
Who wants to draw water goes to Waalo. *(Pause.
Drumming)*

VI

M'Bana: Senghor is our leader.
All nations respect us.
Everybody respects Leopold.
Remember the time of the rice shortage
And the increase in the price of ground-nuts!
You know that at that time Senghor was still a student
abroad.
He obtained degrees and diplomas and the "bac-
calaureat".
These were not enough.
"Agrégé de grammaire,"
You made the demands
And the country got its independence.
Through your intelligence the deltas were developed,
In addition to other projects that you had initiated.
You said to the nation "Work!"
Yee Sam Samaanee . . . Yaay!
The heroes of Senegal. Loo!

Chorus: Sam Samaanee . . . Yaaye
Whoever wants to draw water goes to the Waalo.
(Repeat)

VII

M'Bana: Yaay Ngilaan Baxum Jaay (your son)
Leads the nation admirably.
You wanted independence,
Senghor, you were our ambassador
To Canada; you passed through the United States.
When we were behind, and when we were on the brink
of disaster,
It was you who took the initiative.
You appealed to the people to have patience and to pray.

The course of destiny cannot be stopped.
Thus the marabouts and the people invoked the name of
God.
Senghor, you were our ambassador
To Canada; you passed through the United States.
On your return, ships berthed in Dakar.
Each region received its fair share.
You brought back peace and harmony.
Oh! Leopold, oh! Independence is pleasant!
You are not a man of war.
Not a shot fired, not a sword drawn.

M'Bana refers to this song as "un chant du développement", that is, a song whose major function is to enhance the development of her country and its government. As she put it to me in her introductory comments before singing this song: "The wars that Waalo and Africa on the whole are fighting today, are not fought with spears and rifles, but with ploughs and tractors and with dedicated hard work in the fields." The song is also a "political song" and M'Bana insisted on the fact that she sang it first at an annual convention of the U.P.S. (Union Progressive Sénégalaise), Senghor's party.

It is also significant to note here that there is only one line referring to genealogy throughout the whole song: "Yaay Ngilaan Baaxum Jaay", which refers to Senghor's mother and maternal grand-mother. This is not typical of a traditional Wolof "praise-song." The explanation is two-fold: first, as we have seen earlier, M'Bana is no genealogist or historian; secondly, since Senghor is not a Wolof but a Serer from Sine (Joal), a faraway southern province of Senegal, his genealogy is not readily available to M'Bana, who spent most of her life in the province of Waalo, in northern Senegal. To be able to treat Senghor *appropriately* in terms of his genealogy, she would have had to "research" the latter thoroughly among his people in Joal and Sine. But this concern with historical accuracy and detail is definitely not essential to M'Bana's art and reputation.

III

Anchou's work, as well as his outlook, is definitely more traditional than M'Bana's. Although he lives in Thiaroye now, and goes into Dakar almost every day to visit his "geers"—his "noble" patrons—and attend their weddings, their naming ceremonies and their funerals, he also occasionally runs some of their special personal or family errands. In spite of all these activities in the city, Anchou still remains very much a village griot. He keeps in close touch with the native village of Thiago in Waalo, and carries out all the old traditional functions of the griot for the descendants and relatives of his "geer" who live in the capital city or elsewhere and call upon his services. For instance, he would still worry about finding a suitable young griot boy, usually a relative, who would serve as a "beyleket"[13] for the circumcision rites of the sons of concerned "geers".

The two texts chosen here are *Muse Fari Joop* and *Talata N'Deer*. They are appropriate samples of Anchou's work. *Muse Fari Joop* is a short heroic poem which concentrates on the bravery of a noble warrior of the past, who happens to be an ancestor of the late Lamine Gueye, the well-known Senegalese lawyer and politician. The following are excerpts from the poem:

VII

Muse Fari Joop did not betray the Brak.
Muse Fari Joop fought at Jaalo Waaly.
Jaalo Waaly paid for N'Deer.
They fought at Jaalo Waaly.
They hit Dyawdin.
They hit the Brak.
They hit Muse Saar Fari Joop.
They took Dyawdin to Njaw.
They took the Brak to N'Deer.
They took Muse Fari Joop to N'Darto, the compound of NeeneJoop Maar, to soothe him.
Muse Fari Joop refused to leave.

VIII

Muse Fari Joop did not betray the Brak.
Muse Fari Joop fought at the well of Ndombo.
Jaalo Waaly paid for N'Deer.
They fought at Jaalo Waaly.
They hit Dyawdin.
They hit the Brak.
They hit Muse Saar Fari Joop.
They took Dyawdin to Njaw.
They took the Brak to N'Deer.[14]
They took Muse Fari Joop to N'Dar, to the compound of Neene Joop. Maar to soothe him.
Muse Fari Joop refused to leave.

IX

Muse Fari Joop did not betray the Brak.
Muse Fari Joop fought at the well of Njange.
They hit Dyawdin.
They hit the Brak.
They hit Muse Saar Fari Joop.
They took Dyawdin to Njaw.
They took the Brak to N'Deer.
They took Muse Fari Joop to N'Dar, to the compound of
Nene Joop Maar to soothe him.
Muse Fari Joop would not leave.

X

Muse Fari Joop did not betray the Brak.
Muse Fari Joop fought at Talata N'Deer.

Here Anchou spontaneously interrupts the recitation to describe
the circumstances of Joop's death. Though this is not part of the
poem as such, the delivery remains highly rhythmical and the state
of tension in which Anchou recites is only slightly relaxed:

> It was, indeed, at that place that the last battle was fought. He
> got hit in the eye with a spear. It was a spear that they threw in
> his eye, deep into the eye. He grabbed the spear and broke it
> "xateet". He broke it. Yes, he broke it. When I'm finished
> you can ask me who threw the spear into his eye. You hear
> me? He broke the spear and then went away. He went away
> and they begged him to come back and have the spear taken
> out of his eye. He replied that no one would take it out unless
> he had undergone the traditional ordeal.

After this, they sang:
N'dom Booy Maa Caam.
N'dom Booy Maa Caam.
M'boyo Maa Caam.
M'boyo at N'Dyurbel.
Alasaam Mbubeen did not betray the Brak.
He who considers you a "dam" (witch).
Or he who takes you for a good-for-nothing.

Muse Fari Joop said that he was going to put himself through
an ordeal to prove that he did not cry because of pain, when
the spear hit him in the eye, and that the flag which he was
carrying was not torn. Or did he frown because of pain? Did
he lose courage and abandon his gun? They took a piece of
iron. The fire and charcoal were blown until red hot and then

they put the piece of iron in it until it, too, became glowing red. Muse Fari Joop took this piece of red hot iron and licked it until it became black. Then he stretched out and they gradually pulled out the broken sword from his eye. They sang again:

M'boyo, M'boyo Maa Caam Mboo
M'boyo Maa Caam moo. . .
Noble, you did not betray the Brak
Ndomo, Ndomo, Maa Caam
M'boyo, Maa Caam, the nobleman.
Muse Fari Joop did not betray the Brak.
They gradually pulled out the broken sword from his body.

XI

Muse Fari Joop did not betray the Brak
Jaagiri Awa Dembane
Maa Joop Gandiool
Ranaan Joop Maar Sere
Njante Joop Maar Sere
Mbaas Joop Maar Sere
Maa Joop Gandiool.
Malaado Maane Buur Ndyaay.
Bukaar Ndyaay (father of) Amar Paate.
Amar Paaté (father of) Naatuko.
Buri Ndyurbel Koumba with the three compounds.
Kumba Laobé Joop.
Kumba Laobé Ndyaay.
Kumba Laobé Faal.

In the written form, the text has certain features which distinguish it from the texts of M'Bana Diop's songs. First of all, there is the importance given to the genealogical information. It must be noted here that this genealogical information is not given in one uniform tone. The griot has the freedom to vary this tone and Anchou uses this freedom skillfully and not without restraint. Thus the poem starts with a portion of Muse Saar's genealogy:

Jaajiri Awa Dembaane.
Maa Joop Gandiool.
Ranaan Joop Maar Sere.
Njante Joop Maar Sere.
Mbaas Joop Maar Sere.
Maa Joop Gandiool.
Musé Saar Fari Joop, the hero.
Musé Saar Fari Joop, the warrior.
Musé Saar Fari Joop, the courageous.

Musé Saar Fari Joop did not betray the Brak (the king).

Note the traditional Wolof reference to one's mother's name. Saar is the hero's last name inherited from his father, but his full name would traditionally include his mother's name: Fari Joop. Thus, even though his last name is Saar, he is sometimes referred to as just Muse Fari Joop. The repetition of the name of the mother of three brothers Ranaan Joop, Njante Joop and Mbass Joop creates a special rhythm. This rhythm contrasts with three repetitions of the hero's full name, followed each time by a different qualifier: "the hero," "the warrior," the courageous". The first stanza is followed by eight repetitive stanzas each referring to a famous battle in which our hero distinguished himself. Then at the reference to Talaata N'Deer, the last battle fought by Muse Saar Fari Joop, Anchou interrupts the recitation spontaneously to describe the circumstances of the hero's death. Though this descriptive section is not part of the poem as such, Anchou's delivery remains highly rhythmical and the state of tension into which he progressively works himself as he gets involved in a recitation, is not at all relaxed. Anchou sings the little section: "Mboyo, Mboyo Maa Caam. . .," then he closes stanza X. Stanza XI picks up our hero's genealogy again. The genealogical information given in stanza I is repeated here and expanded further.

Talaata N'Deer is a short epic narrated in prose form interspersed with a sung refrain. Even at a private working session with Anchou alone in a small room in his home in Thiaroye, to record one first version of *Talaata N'Deer,* he insisted on calling his wife from the kitchen where she was busy preparing lunch, to come and sing the refrain. He said the narrative was incomplete without the song. *Talaata N'Deer* relates a heroic episode of Waalo history when N'Deer, then the traditional capital of the kingdom, was attacked by surprise by the Fulani Almany from Futa Toro (Northeastern Senegal). The attack came while Brak Ndyaak Kumba Xuri Yaay had left his capital to visit Saint-Louis (N'Dar). By the time Brak Ndyaak returned home, N'Deer was in ashes. This was indeed a surprise attack, as it took place on a Tuesday (Talaata), and in those days, Tuesday was always observed as a day of truce. However, when Brak Ndyaak returned, he was able to pursue the Almany and his men and defeat them at Jaalo.Waali. The song goes thus:

When Almany went to N'Deer
He did not find the Brak there.
Barka Laobe Booy Ndyaay
Returned to N'Deer that day.
When Almany went to N'Deer
He did not find the Brak.
But Jaalo Waali paid for N'Deer
Until the horses returned by themselves to N'Deer.

This version of *Talaata N'Deer* was taped in the conditions of a true performance of modern urban griots of contemporary Senegambia, that is, in an IFAN recording studio at the University of Dakar in December 1973. For this studio appointment, the old man Anchou brought with him one of his wives to help with the singing, his son, his nephew, a xalam player, his brother the late Malal Thiam, an excellent xalam player, and a niece, Absa Diop, a singer in her own right. Thus, with this group of five griots, all related, we have an authentic griot performance, for although Anchou Thiam likes to consider himself a "borom xam xam", that is, an authentic oral historian of Waalo, he is above all an entertainer, an entertainer whose material is almost exclusively rooted in the past of Senegal. While M'Bana can easily incorporate in her material, elements of contemporary Senegalese social and political history, Anchou remains an oral historian of pre-colonial Senegal and a reciter of ancient poetic and heroic texts. Like his cousin M'Bana, he performs in all three modes of storytelling (*leeb*), of praise-singing (*taag*) and of singing (*woi*); but his forte is praise-singing which must include a strong grasp of genealogy and historical narrative.

IV

The aim of this paper is not to propose definitive conclusions on the art of the Wolof griot nor to make prophetic predictions on the future of this art. At this point in my study of the material I collected in the field, my goal is essentially, to share with friends and colleagues the intense aesthetic pleasure I experienced on meeting two great custodians of an age-old but still captivating artistic tradition: the traditional art of the Wolof griot. It goes without saying that M'Bana Diop and Anchou Thiam represent two different trends in this tradition. M'Bana definitely belongs to a modern Senegal. She is indeed more sophisticated and strikingly adapted to a changing society. Anchou, for his part, also lives in that changing

Edris Makward

society. Without rejecting it totally, or wishing to make an impossible "voyage de retour" (journey into the past), he feels very deeply that, unless Wolof people were all to disappear suddenly and totally from the surface of the earth, the tradition of the "true griot" will remain for ever.

If, for my part, I have not succeeded in convincing you that "the word and art of our true griots, be they modern or more truly traditional, deserve your admiration and respect," the blame should be credited exclusively to my own incompetence as an amateur griot, and not to Anchou Thiam, Haja M'Bana Diop,[14] Ablaye Naar Samb or their like.[15]

NOTES

1. D. T. Naine *Soundjata, ou l'epopee Mandingue, Presence Africaine,* Paris 1960, p. 80. "La parole des griots traditionalistes a droit a autre chose que du mepris."
2. Naine, P. 9
3. Ibid.
4. A traditional Fulani lute.
5. Christiane Seydou, *Silamaka et Poullori* (Récit épique), Peul raconté par Tinguidji édité par Christiane Seydou, Classiques Africains, Armand Colin, Paris 1972. My translation from the French.
6. Seydou, p. 113
7. Ibid.
8. A province in Northern Senegal; corresponds to the old Kingdom of Waalo with its traditional capital at one time on the right bank of the river Senegal, that is, in present day Mauritania (Ndiourbel).
9. Here M'Bana falls spontaneously into the praise mode (*taag*) for a brief genealogy of her aunt Yaram N'Der. Then she reverts to a conversational mode to continue the narration of the circumstances in which that same aunt composed the song to honour her royal husband Yamar's victorious return from war. I noted this intriguing practice in a number of instances among Waalo griots and also among griots from other provinces of Senegambia (Saloum, Sine Cayou, Jolof). The most satisfactory explanation of this practice is the desire to express emphatically one's pride in one's caste. Griots want members of other castes (and particularly the free-born caste) to know and be reminded that *they* too have a history and genealogy.
10. This detail is unusually vague in a genealogical praise song–an indication of M'Bana's incompetence as a praise-singer, that is, a *taag kat.*
11. Names of the brave warrior's horses.
12. First King of Waalo, believed by present day traditional historians to have founded and ruled this Northern Kingdom around the last decade of the 12th

40

century.

13. Traditionally, when sons of "geers" (free-born) are being circumcised, they must be preceded by a griot adolescent who should be operated on first. This tradition is no longer prevalent in the cities of Senegal and Gambia.

14. In transcribing proper names of people and places within the poems and songs, I have used the CLAD system. But in referring to names of contemporary figures, artists and places, I have retained the current accepted spelling introduced in the early days of colonial rule, i.e., Diop, N'diaye, Saar for Joop, Ndyaay and Saar.

15. I wish to acknowledge here my gratitude to all the griots—men and women—of Senegal and Gambia and to Mr. Amadou Diagne and Georges Perrin for their invaluable and enthusiastic help and encouragement during the collecting, transcription and translation of the material used for this paper. *Jere jef waai!*

Kaalụ Igirigiri: an Ọhafịa Igbo Singer of Tales

Chukwumà Àzụonye

Introduction

AMONG the numerous singers of heroic tales in the formerly warlike Igbo community of Ọhafịa in the Cross River area of south-eastern Nigeria, by far the most widely-acclaimed virtuoso in the 1970's was a peasant farmer with a mellow singing voice named Kaalụ Igirigiri.[1] A member of the relatively isolated patriclan of Ọkọn (close to the Cross River itself, in the extreme north-eastern corner of Ọhafịa), Kaalu Igirigiri, who died in 1980, probably in his early sixties, was, like his predecessors and contemporaries, a non-professional but specialist amateur. He was also a highly articulate connoisseur and critic, whose views on the functions and aesthetic principles of the oral epic song, as practised by the Ọhafịa people, seem to be truly representative of the tradition as a whole. This paper is a study of the compositions and performance of this distinguished oral artist.[2] Based on recordings made in the field between 1971 and 1977, the focal interest of the paper is on the distinctive artistic qualities of Kaalụ Igirigiri's compositions seen in the light of the traditional aesthetic principles enunciated in various tape-recorded interviews, not only by the singer himself, but also by his rivals and some other well-known local connoisseurs.[3] The paper also compares the performance of Kaalụ Igirigiri with those of his known predecessors, contemporaries and one identified apprentice, and considers the dynamics of the growth of his art over the period during which the recordings were made.

Kaalụ Igirigiri: the man and his art

Kaalụ Igirigiri did not insist on the facts of his ancestry and personal upbringing as an important background to the understanding of his art. He was not one of those singers in the Ọhafia bardic tradition who claim to be descended from a long line of master-singers; nor did he—like some others—make any pretences to divine or other supernatural inspiration.[4] The only information we have from him about his ancestry is of the kind contained in the following signature in which he invokes his maternal and paternal forbears as a line of eminent diviners:

> This is Kaalụ Igirigiri,
> Son of my great mother Ogbenyealu—
> Woman of the matriclan of Anyanwu Ezhe,[5]
> Woman who was the people's diviner,
> Woman of the patriclan of Ibina in Egbenyi Uka,
> Daughter of Ezhiukwu Ọhọm
> Woman of the Marshy Lands
> (No woman from the Marshy Lands ever goes to live with a
> friend)—
> Great father Kaalụ Ọbasị of Nde Awa Ezhema was her elder
> brother;
> And when Agwunsi Ọbasị died,
> Tooti Ọbasị became her elder brother,
> Kaalụ Ọbasị,
> He that makes sacrifices to Njoku in the middle of the night,
> He was her elder brother,
> And was a high-priest,
> And was a man of the people.

Beyond this kind of sketchy genealogy, Kaalụ Igirigiri said little more in interviews recorded in the field about his personal life, parentage, childhood, etc. Rather, he focused attention on what may be described as his "poetic ancestry", a bond of genetic relationship of a traditional kind with various master-singers through which he emerged as an accomplished singer. Kaalụ Igirigiri refers to the master-singers involved as *nde-mu-m-ni-n'abu* (my fathers-in-song).[6] Among these are three men who are recognized throughout Ọhafia as belonging to the pedigree of the most accomplished singers in the history of the people's oral epic art. These are: Oke Mbe of Asaga, Okonkwo Oke of Akaanụ and Ibiam Nta of Ọkọn. Kaalụ Igirigiri does not go into specific details about the nature of his relationships with these men, but he gives a general account of a process of apprenticeship and training which is

43

decidedly informal and inductive rather than formal and institutionalized as in some bardic traditions elsewhere in West Africa.[7] But inspite of its informality, the training of the singer in the Ohafia Igbo epic tradition is one of the *sine qua non* conditions for general acceptability. Accordingly to Kaalụ Igirigiri:

> If you are a singer and people recognize the fact that your voice is sweet but know that you have not been trained by a person well-versed in the art of historical rememberance (*iku aka*), that is, a person who says what Ohafia people as a whole accept; if you simply lock up yourself in your house singing to please yourself, or even if you go out and sing with others, you will never be credited as singing with the voice of an experienced singer: you will never be able to sing what Ohafia people as a whole will accept. The truth is this: if you are a singer, if your voice is sweet, Ohafia people will tell you, "Go and meet Kaalụ Igirigiri. He will teach you songs. Your voice is sweet." When you come to me, I will tell you all those stories which the old masters told me. If you sing these stories as told, Ohafia people as a whole will accept: women will accept, men will accept, everyone . . . . But if you stay in your house singing to please yourself, without any course of training under a master-singer, your songs can never be sweet; you will never be able to sing properly (Interview, March 1976).[8]

It would appear from the showing of Kaalụ Igirigiri in various performances that the essential legacy which training under a master-singer bestows on the young practitioner is confidence and authority. Through contact with the master, the young practitioner acquires the *mana* by which the community at large was beholden to the master, submitting to the spell of his narrations as if he were an unerring repository of the history and wisdom of the clan. But apart from this more or less external mantle of authority, the apprentice-singer acquires from the master certain essential requirements of the oral epic art. These include the aesthetic principles of composition in the oral performance, the major heroic tales[9] which occur in the repertoire of practically all known singers, and the system of epithet and other formulae which constitute the linguistic core and the mainstay of the structure of the songs.[10]

Unfortunately, we are not in possession of any extant recordings of the compositions of two of Kaalụ Igirigiri's known fathers-in-song (Oke Mbe of Asaga and Ibiam Nta of Ọkọn). However one version of the Epic of Nne Mgbaafọ (see Appendix 2, Tale No. 7) by his third father-in-song (Okonkwo Oke of Akaanu) has survived in a recording made in 1966 for a Radio Nigeria broadcast from Enugu.[11] A comparison of this with versions of the same tale by Kaalụ Igirigiri (see, for example, Tales 1A) reveals a lot about the nature of the development of Kaalụ's art over the years. One general inference we can make from such a comparison is that what the apprentice learns from his master is not the *lexis* (by which I mean the narrative text comprising a certain unique combination of words and other structural features) but the *praxis* of the oral epic art (by which I mean the conventions and traditional style of the genre). Okonkwọ Oke's Nne Mgbaafọ—as will be seen from a comparison of the following extract with the text given in Tales 1 A below—is similar to a large extent to Kaalụ Igirigiri's version in its clarity of diction and structure as well as in the directness of its presentation of the heroine and her actions:

> A certain woman was called Nne Mgbaafọ
> She was of Arọ-Oke-Igbo.[12]
> She was of the matriclan of Okwura-Egbu-Enyi
> That Nne Mgbaafọ, she behaved very much like a man
> Her husband had died at Arọ-Oke-Igbo
> And when Nne Mgbaafọ finished mourning her husband
> When she finished mourning her husband, finished
>   mourning her husband,
> She came out to the Ncheghe Ibom market
> She came out to the Ncheghe Ibom market, bought a
>   matchet and sheathed it,
> And she bought a war cap and put it on
> And she took some money and bought a dane-gun
> Put a sling on it
> Charged the dane-gun, and took her matchet, sharpened
>   and caught it in the air
> And she said she was going to look for a husband. . . .

As has been observed above, the praxis of this piece closely resembles that of Kaalụ Igirigiri's version presented in Tales 1A below, but neither does the lexis nor the vocal presentation as can be perceived on listening to the tape-recordings. There are even more glaring differences in the content of the two versions, especially in the conception of the heroine and her husband's fate. In Okonkwo Oke's versions, Nne Mgbaafọ is presented as a woman who behaved very much like a man. After the death of her first husband, in her native community of Arochukwu, she sets out fully armed and clothed like a male warrior to search for another husband. She searches in a number of localities, but fails to find a suitable husband in any of them. At last, she arrives at Nde-Ana-m-Ele-m-Ulu-Ụma where she meets and marries a man named Uduma. Uduma had not yet *fulfilled* his manhood as required by the heroic ethos of his age by winning a human head in battle. But anxious to fend off the shame of living with such a man whom his age-mates would despise as a dishonourable coward *(onye-ujọ)*,[13] Nne Mgbaafọ cooks a special meal for her husband and urges him to go to a war which had just broken out in Ibibioland.

Uduma goes but is slain in battle. When the news of his death reaches Nne Mgbaafọ, she immediately approaches the people of Ama Achara, the patriclan that took the lead in the battle, and they provide her with escorts to the battle-ground where she discovers the beheaded body of her husband in a heap of slain warriors. She dutifully buries the corpse under a tree and sacrifices a goat on the grave. Three market-weeks after returning from this expedition, Nne Mgbaafo assails and overpowers a young man whom she finds wandering alone at Usukpam. She chops off his head and buries his body in her husband's grave as a fitting sacrifice "to wash his right hand and his left".

Needeless to say, this is not one of the versions of the story of Nne Mgbaafọ by Okonkwo Oke to which Kaalụ Igirigiri was exposed in the course of his training. He no doubt heard many other versions, and there is no reason why these may not have varied in structure and even content like the versions in his current repertoire (see Azuonye 1983). One of the traditional aesthetic principles of the Ọhafia epic song positively encourages and even requires such variations. This feature of the oral performance is as manifest in the song-repertoires of other contemporary singers as in that of Kaalụ Igirigiri. But the variations notwithstanding, variant versions of the same tale by the same singer, irrespective of their place and occasion of performance, do exhibit a certain degree of consistency in their essential details. In Kaalụ Igirigiri's versions of Nne Mgbaafọ, the heroine is consistently represented as a woman of the matriclan of Eleghe Ọfọka, born in the patriclan of Asaga (praise-named 'Nde-Awa-Ezhema-Elechi'), and married to a man called Ndukwe Emeuwa who goes to battle in Ibibioland of his own volition despite the womanish pleas of his wife that he should not go lest he be killed by the inveterate Ibibio enemy. In the battle, Ndukwe is captured and held prisoner but is released and delivered to Nne

Mgbaafọ when she boldly confronts the enemy and demands death or the release of her husband. In the end, Nne Mgbaafọ returns safely home with Ndụkwe Emeuwa.

It seems quite clear from the enormity of the thematic differences between Kaalụ Igirigiri's version and that of his father-in-song, Okonkwọ Oke, that, their similarity of style notwithstanding, the sources are different. In my interviews with him, Kaalụ Igirigiri persistently evaded all attempts to pin down his sources, either because, like Christopher Okigbo in his *Limits* (1962),[14] his versions have been synthesized from so many different sources that it is difficult to pin them down precisely, or because he simply regards his sources as a secret of his art which is not to be given away. But the possibilities are twofold: in a situation in which the singer seems to have listened to many different versions from various fathers-in-song, he may have adopted one father's manner of telling the tale or created his own tale by the conflation of elements taken from the father's tales with those borrowed from other singers.

The most likely single source for Kaalụ Igirigiri's Nne Mgbaafọ is Ogboo Ogwo[15] of Akaanụ, a veteran singer who is acknowledged as their father-in-song by two of Kaalụ's leading contemporaries and rivals, Ọgbaa Kaalụ of Abia and Njọkụ Mmajụ of Uduma Awoke. However, the evidence on which this speculation is based is not very reliable, namely a claim in testimonies recorded by Ọgbaa Kaalụ and Njọkụ Mmajụ that their versions of Nne Mgbaafọ —which are strikingly similar in content to those of Kaalụ Igirigiri —are exactly as received from the master. Ọhafịa singers of tales are prone to exaggerate issues in their testimonies. It is not unlikely that when they say that their versions are exactly as received from their master, they are merely referring to what I have elsewhere (Azuonye 1983) described as the "heroic essence" of the tale. This is the sum of what Bowra (1966:454) calls the "limiting factors" to the freedom of the oral epic performer to vary his narrative, factors which include "the personality of the hero", the overall "emotional effect" of his representation, and "the main point of the narrative" which in the oral performance is usually established by means of an irreducible minimum of particularized and indispensable themes and formulae constant in all versions of the tale irrespective of the singer and the occasion and place of performance (see also section 4 below).

The case for a single source for the tales sung by any singer in

Ọhafịa should not be pressed too far even if we grant the possibility. The incontestable evidence before us shows quite clearly that the training of the Ọhafịa singer is essentially a process of prolonged exposure to a wide variety of rich and alternative epic materials out of which he forms the tales in his repertoire and their versions. This he does by the rejection of some in favour of others, by selective borrowing from masters and contemporaries, and by the conflation of themes, episodes and tale-types.[16] The Ọhafịa singer of tales is not a passive traditor but a creative artist equipped by his training and practice to make a distinctive and original contribution to the living epic tradition. He helps to refine and vitalize the tradition by constant remoulding within a set of well-defined traditional aesthetic principles.

The traditional aesthetic principles of the Ọhafịa Igbo oral epic song, of which Kaalu Igirigiri is one of the leading exponents, cover a wide area. They focus mainly on the necessity for variety and change in the tale-repertoires of individual singers; variety and change in their performance strategies; the value of clarity in the art of composition in the oral performance; the responsibility of every singer to maintain the heroic essence of the tales (i.e. the "truth" and "reality" of the heroic ethos of the community) and their dynamic socio-psychological functions. I have elsewhere discussed these four principles at length, quoting extensively from the recorded testimonies of various singers and local connoisseurs (Azuonye 1979: 349-383 and 1986a); but it may be useful at this stage to outline them briefly.

The first of the four principles may be described as the principle of *functionality*. By this principle, the Ọhafịa people evaluate the songs purely in terms of their manifest effects on culture and society and on the behaviour of individual members of the society. On this level, this principle refers merely to the practical utility of the songs, especially when performed in association with the well-known dramatic war dance of the people and its accompaniment of martial music as part of the integrated heroic musical whole (*iri-aha*) on various ritual and social occasions (see Azuonye 1979: 65-67). On another level, it refers to the documentary and affective roles of the songs: (a) as a record of the lives and careers of heroic ancestors and of various landmarks in the history of the clan, and (b) as a source of enlightenment and edification, in response to which contemporary **generations draw** the inspiration to rise up to the challenges of their own age in the same way as their ancestors are believed to have risen up to the challenges of their own more difficult times, in the heroic age.

The second principle is related to the first. This may be described as the principle of *authenticity*. In order to fulfil effectively the dynamic socio-psychological functions assigned to them by tradition, it is important that the content of the songs should be in conformity with the cherished values and beliefs of the society. Thus, various informants in their testimonies describe what they expect to find in the songs as *ezhiokwu* (truth) or *ife mee eme* (what actually happened, i.e. reality). There is frequent insistence in these testimonies on *ife mee eme mgbe ichin* (what actually happened in the days of the ancestors). However, the expectation of most informants is not so much that the songs should be informed by the literal facts of history, as that they should reaffirm the traditional ethical and moral values of the heroic society and the network of relationships between individuals and their clans, and between clans and clans, in the traditional body politic.

The third principle of the songs may be described as the principle of *clarity*. As will be seen in sections 3 and 4, this is perhaps the most important principle so far as the orality of the songs is concerned. Best expressed by the phrase *imezikwa ka o doo anya nke oma* (making sure that what is said is clearly perceptible), this principle applies to various facets of the form, content, language and vocalization of the songs as realized in the oral performance. It pays particular attention to such indispensable requirements of oral art as audibility and the proper modulation of voice-pitch. Thus Kaalụ Igirigiri, for example, is often rated more highly than his peers because *olu ya di ụtọ* (his voice is sweet) and *Ọ na-akapusa ife anu anu na nti* (he speaks in such a way that what he says is clearly audible).

The last, but by no means the least important of the four principles, may be described as the principle of *creative variation*. In invoking this principle, many informants use the word *mgbanwo* (change or variation) and various images of growth (*ùto*) to stress the need for singers to build up in the course of their artistic careers a large and varied repertoire of tales (including the traditional heroic tales and new tales of their own making) and to effect pleasing and instructive variations in their renderings of each tale on various occasions of performance.

49

In what follows, the distinctive artistic qualities of the songs of Kaalu Igirigiri and their actual performance will be discussed-both in themselves as they really are and by comparison to the songs and performance of other singers-on the basis of these four principles. It is hoped that this discussion will reveal the warmth and strength of his artistic personality, his historical sense, his responsiveness to criticism and his capacity for self-improvement, qualities which are the basis of his fame throughout Ohafia and even beyond, as one of the most outstanding singers of tales in recent times.

Variety and change in Kaalụ Igirigiri's repertoire of tales

One of the recurrent themes in the recorded testimonies of Kaalụ Igirigiri is the variety and change manifest in his personal repertoire of songs:

> I make many changes when I sing my songs. I even make changes in the traditional choric songs (*abu-okwukwe*). But more importantly, I can easily switch from the old heroic songs—the ones inherited from the ancients—to new songs about the events of today. I can sing newly-created songs, those which nobody in Ohafia has ever heard before (Interview, March 1976).

The first part of this testimony refers to the changes in theme and structure which occur in variant versions of the same tale presented on the same or on different occasions while the second refers to the variety and range of genres of heroic song in his repertoire. As can be gleaned from Tales II below, the variety and range of tales in Kaalụ Igirigiri's repertoire is very high indeed: there are 21 out of 34 distinct tales collected so far (an impressive 63 α), which is far in excess of the range of five other singers whose compositions have also been recorded (see Azuonye 1986b). There is also variety in Kaalụ Igirigiri's repertoire. In fact, he is the only one of the six singers whose compositions include at least one tale from all the major thematic categories into which the 34 tales may be grouped. The details are as follows:

2 out of 2 creations myths (Tales II, Nos 1-2);
2 out of 2 migration legends (Tales II, Nos 3-4);
10 out of 20 heroic legends (Tales II, Nos 5-15);
6 out of 8 allegories and fabular tales (Tales II, No. 21). !1).

The statistical evidence given here in support of Kaalụ Igirigiri's very high rating throughout Ọhafịa as the most versatile singer of recent times is no doubt open to question, on the ground that I credit him "with greater variety of repertoire than the other singers because I have spent more time with him" in the field.[17] It is indeed true that I have spent more time with Kaalụ Igirigiri than with the other four of the five singers, whose compositions and performances I personally recorded in the field; but this is precisely because of the richness and variety which I found in his repertoire after the first three recording sessions. No other singer was able to display a similar range after the same number of recording sessions, and none has so far been able to render as many as the 22 tales which I was able to record at one sitting from Kaalụ Igirigiri, in July 1977. It may well be that some of these less versatile singers will in future be able to build up repertoires comparable in range to, or even more impressive than that of Kaalụ Igirigiri; but at the moment, their repertoires are not only quantitatively poorer but also lack the rich thematic variety which Kaalụ Igirigiri's repertoire exhibits.[18]

But whatever may be the range of an individual singer's tale-repertoire, the praxis of the Ọhafịa Igbo oral epic performance allows for dynamic variations in mode and tenor. These satisfy an important facet of the traditional aesthetic principle of creative variation inasmuch as such variations contribute to the overall emotional effect of the tales themselves. As singer C (Egwu Kaalụ of Asaga) says in a testimony:

> In general, I begin my performances by eulogizing my hosts, after which I proceed to tell them about the lives of their ancestors (Interview, March 1976).

This is a general convention which is clearly evident in the performance of Kaalụ Igirigiri. After the initial eulogies, which in the performance of Kaalụ Igirigiri often includes eulogistic signatures of the kind quoted on page 43, as well as the praises of the musicians who supply the instrumental accompaniment and of the leading heroes in the traditional pantheon, Kaalụ Igirigiri would normally proceed to the narratives themselves, interspersing them with traditional battle songs and other sequences of heroic invocation. The resultant interplay of song, invocation and narratiave, gravitating between the singing, the chanting, the reciting and the speaking modes of vocalization, generally tends to resemble an

51

oratorio—drama with music and voices but without scenery and action. While the narratives and the invocations are solo recitatives or chants, the battle songs are lyrical choruses in which the audience joins. The interplay of song, invocation and narratiave in Kaalụ Igirigiri's performance is similar to that found in the performances of all other singers recorded so far, except that of Singer F (Njọkụ Mmajụ of Uduma Awoke) in the narrative parts of which there is an additional element—the chorus-man (Onye-nkwechi). As I have pointed out elsewhere (Azuonye 1979: 89-91), the chorus-man is a kind of co-vocalist who sits beside the main singer repeating a series of words and praises which, though figurative and often witty in themselves, are in no clearly-discernible way related to the meaning of the narrative themselves. No clear explanation has so far been offered, either by the singer or his critics, as to the exact function of the chorus-man in his performances. However, any suggestion that the chorus-man's words may be distracting—as indeed they would sound to an outsider to the Ọhafịa oral culture—is firmly denied. It may well be that the Ọhafịa audiences have developed, through some kind of cultural conditioning, an inner ear which enables them to hear and enjoy the undercurrents of the words of the chorus-man and at the same time to hear and enjoy the main currents of the lead-singer's performance. On the other hand, it may be that the listeners are not really interested in the words at all, but in the polyphony created by the combination of the singing of the chorus-man and that of the lead-singer. In the final analysis, there is one aspect of the chorus-man's performance which even the bemused outsider can enjoy, if he has an ear for the Ọhafịa dialect of Igbo. This is when there is a major pause in the sequence of story-telling—as is often the case—and the voice of the chorus-man surfaces with the witticism and humour to be enjoyed on its own as an item in a mixed programme of verbal artistry.

Whether or not the singer employs the services of a chorus-man, he will normally make use in his performances of four distinct voices[19] recognized by the hearers as one of the chief means of highlighting specific types of themes. Ogbaa Kaalụ of Abia (Singer D) refers to those voices when in a testimony he criticizes one of Kaalụ Igirigiri's known sons-in-song, Echeme Ugwu of Ebem (Singer E), for singing in a monotonously harsh voice *(Olu ya ada ikike:* his voice sounds too monotonously harsh). The principle of creative variation demands among other virtues that the singer's voice should be sufficiently flexible to be able to simulate the varied mood of the tales.

The basic voice is the narrative voice, generally in the reciting mode, and it is this that carries the momentum of the tale. It is the voice of the omniscient narrator speaking of a third person (the hero) without addressing the audience directly. See, for example, the extract from Okonkwo Oke's *Nne Mgbaafo* on page 45 and portions of the texts in Tales 1.

The narrative voice is interspersed by the lyric, the invocative and the oratorical voices. The first of these - the lyric voice - is usually in the singing mode and functions in the narratives as a medium for the representation of the emotional states of various characters. One of Kaalu Igirigiri's rivals, Qgbaa Kaalu of Abia (Singer D), has in one of his usual detractive criticisms of Kaalu accused him of lacking the virtuosity to exploit the affective value of the lyric voice at points of intense emotional distress in his narratives. This virtue Qgbaa Kaalu claims for himself:

> There are many things which we spell out clearly by name which Kaalu Igirigiri does not put into his songs. Thus, he fails to represent things as they really are. He cuts everything up into small unrelated bits. But when we on our part sing, we explain to you quite clearly how everything happened, from the beginning to the end. . . He cuts up everything into small bits. . . There is a person whose story he tells — I mean Amoogu, the person that first fired the gun with which the short-armed-one of Aliike was killed (see Tales II, No. 3). If you are told how this really happened, from its beginning to the end, tears will roll down from your eyes. But he compresses it far too much. The pathetic cry of Amoogu's mother, he did not cry it properly. . . But when we on our part sing it, we put in the lament of that woman when her son failed to return. There is a way in which one can simulate that lament and tears will roll down from your eyes (Interview, March 1976).

This is a response to versions B2 and B3 of the Epic of Amoogu (Tales II, No. 8), not to the version (B1) presented in Tales I below, a version in which the lyric voice is clearly evident in the indented portions of the text (lines 147-157). But even so, the criticism is grossly unfair. In versions B2 and B3 of Amoogu, as well as in three other versions (B4, B5 and B6) of the tale, Kaalu Igirigiri does indeed make effective use of the elegaic form of the lyric voice *(akwa)* to dramatize the grief of Amoogu's mother when the news of his assasination at the hands of jealous comrades-in-arms reaches her.

Apart from the elegaic form of the lyric voice, Kaalụ Igirigiri in his performances also makes effective use of two other forms, the apostrophic form *(mkpọku)* in which an impassioned appeal is addressed to the hero as if he were standing directly before the narrator, and the rhapsodic form *(abu-obi-ụtọ)* in which the successful and overjoyed hero expresses his sense of total well-being and happiness with himself and with the world. An example of the apostrophic form of the lyric voice will be found in lines 93-103 of the version of Amoogu in Tales II. Here, a situation of intense desperation arises and the omniscient narrator "jumps the gun", apostrophizing the yet undiscovered hero to come forward and fulfil his destined messianic role. An example of the rhapsodic form occurs at the end of the version of Nne Mgbaafo in Tales 1.

The third voice of the narratives is the invocative voice. This is the voice of the traditional praise-chanter addressing a second person in an attitude of veneration. Passages in which this occurs are generally in the form of hero-lists with associative epithets, linking the heroes presented with particular ancestors and clans. The version of Amoogu in Tales 1A below contains two variants of this form. The first (lines 1-9) identifies the hero and links him with a number of other illustrious ancestral heroes while the second (lines 38-63) enumerates the leading warriors of the clan in a situation of crisis leading up to the climax of the unfolding drama. The implications of these and similar hero-lists in the representation of heroic reality and in enhancing the emotional impact of the narratives on the hearers will be further discussed.

The fourth voice of the narratives is the oratorical voice of the singer as teacher, moralist, explainer and revealer of secrets. Passages featuring this voice generally appear on the surface to be in the speaking mode, but this is largely due to their conversational tone and the fact that in them, the singer addresses his hearers directly in his own personal voice, rather than in the fictional voices of the other types of passages. Kaalụ Igirigiri makes little use of the oratorical voice in the main body of his narratives; in his compositions, this voice is almost always confined to introductory statements which do not form an integral part of the tale or to con-cluding remarks in which the moral of the tale is drawn. See, for example, lines 194-196 of Amoogu B1 (Tales 1A).

Apart from its role as a device for delineating aspects of the themes of the narratives, the interplay of emotion-toned rhetorical voices in the performance of Kaalụ Igirigiri and other Ọhafịa singers is one of the features of their art which their listeners enjoy for its own sake, much as the interplay of modes is enjoyed for its own sake in the classical Western oratorio. Local connoisseurs in Ọhafịa are not always specific about this in their testimonies, but quite often, when pressed to account for their high-rating of Kaalụ Igirigiri, they refer to the variety of voices which he is capable of assuming with such inimitable virtuosity in his performances.

Let us now proceed to examine the internal patterns of variation which occur in the individual singer's renderings of particular tales on different occasions as exemplified by the performance of Kaalụ Igirigiri. A comparative examination of the available versions of any tale in the repertoire of Kaalụ Igirigiri will show that such variations are not just a matter of language and structure. This is to be expected in view of the fact that there is no single correct version of any tale and thus no memorization of texts in any kind of fixed form. The variations often affect content, sometimes quite drastically. The events which make up a story might be varied, and so too might be the scenes of action, the characters involved and their doings and utterances. To return to the epic of Nne Mgbaafọ, a tale already dealt with briefly, we find the following thematic variations in the five versions available to us (B1, B2, B3, B4, and B5). First, in the two earliest versions (B1 and B2) which are otherwise almost identical, there are a number of significant variations in some of the key details. In B1, the battle is set at a place called Igbe Mmaku (in Igbo territory) while in B2 it is set at a place called Nnong (in Ibibio land). Igbe Mmaku is reintroduced in the later versions — B3, B4 and B5 — not as enemy territory, but as a friendly Igbo territory where the heroine is able to stop and secure armed escorts for her perilous adventures into Nnong Ibibio land. How are we to account for these significant changes in the location of the key event in the tale? Are we to regard them as errors and inconsistencies of the kind to which oral performers all over the world are well-known to be prone, or are we to admit them as evidence of purposive change leading towards greater refinement and authenticity?

It is of course quite possible, as I have suggested elsewhere (Azuonye 1983), that the location of the battle in Igbo territory (Igbe Mmakụ), in version B1, might be an error of performance which the singer has been able to correct in version B2 by relocating the event in a more likely venue, the territory of the traditional enemy of the Ọhafịa, the Ibibio. But what about the reintroduction of Igbe Mmakụ as the heroine's last stopover before arriving at the enemy Ibibio camp, a detail lacking in versions B1 and B2 alike? It is quite possible that this detail may have been borrowed from versions of the Nne Mgbaafọ legend by rival singers. It occurs for instance in one version recorded in 1977 from Njọkụ Mmajụ of Uduma Awoke (Singer F). But there is also the probability that it has been added in response to criticism such as that by Ogbaa Kaalụ of Abịa (Singer D) quoted elsewhere in this paper (page 53 above), and I think that Kaalụ Igirigiri's portrayal of Nne Mgbaafọ gains in realism by this addition: "The picture of the heroine escorted to her destination by four (or eight) armed men is much more credible than the more sensational picture of her marching alone into the enemy territory. This added realism does not run counter to the heroic essence of the Nne Mgbaafọ legend: it merely eliminates extreme sensationalism without obliterating the heroic image of Nne Mgbaafo as a fearless woman who boldly confronts the inveterate Ibibio enemy, demanding death or the restoration of her spouse" (Azuonye 1983).

The first observation that may be made on the value of the thematic changes in variant versions of the songs of Kaalụ Igirigiri, is that they are editorial means of correcting past performance errors and of creating more refined versions towards the satisfaction of the traditional aesthetic principle of authenticity, a principle which demands among other things "truthfulness" and "reality" in the portrayal of the hero. Secondly, thematic variations enable the singer to draw different morals or to pursue different interpretations of the significance of the hero's life on different occasions of performance, especially in response to the demands of the particular occasion, such as the ethnic composition of the audience. Thirdly and most importantly, thematic changes serve the purposes of clarity.

Thematic changes of the kind which make for enhanced clarity in the performance of the Ọhafịa singers involve either the deletion or compression of themes on the one hand, or the addition or expan-

sion of themes on the other. In response to the jibes of some of his
critics, Kaalụ Igirigiri has over the years opted for the pursuit of
clarity through the addition and expansion of his basic themes.
Consequently he has composed less and less short, highly compressed, ballad-like lays of the kind which I recorded in 1971 and
1972 (see Tales I for example). In apparent response to criticism
such as that of Ọgbaa Kaalụ that "he cuts up everything
into small unrelated bits" and that "he does not seem to have the
ability to sing in such a way that it will be quite clear to you . . .
from what he actually puts into the songs" where the beginning and
the end of the tales fall, Kaalụ Igirigiri has in his more recent compositions exhibited a tendency towards elaboration. This is despite
the fact that in 1976, when Ọgbaa Kaalụ's comments were played
back to him, he dismissed them with arrogant self-confidence as the
rantings of a jealous rival. But the new tendency in the style of
Kaalụ Igirigiri offends the sensibilities of singer-critics like Egwu
Kaalụ of Asaga (Singer C) for whom the "essential details" added
to pad out the narratives are "extraneous" to the realistic style of
historical song:

> He (Kaalụ Igirigiri) is a better singer than myself. He is a bet-
> ter singer than myself. But you must understand that what we
> are dealing with is 'history' . The thing about 'history' is that
> in recounting it, you must do so in a straightforward manner.
> The problem with these people (Kaalụ Igirigiri and Echeme
> Ugwu) is that when they sing, they bring in extraneous
> elements which do not contribute to this straightforward
> manner of representing reality (Interview, March 1976).

It is however less in the thematic than in the structural-linguistic
variations in the versions of the Ọhafịa Igbo epic tales that the
pleasure of novelty emanates. Kaalụ Igirigiri's narrative is generally
herocentric [20] in structure, with all actions, situations and locations
organized in such a way as to point directly towards the revelation
of the hero. The hero may be revealed by direct-pointing at the
beginning of the tale (as in the examples presented in Tales I
below) or by climactic foregrounding, when a series of events are
presented in such a way as to build up to a climax at which point the
hero emerges to save the situation. Within these two basic traditional narration schemata,[21] Kaalụ Igirigiri in his performances in-
dulges in variations of different kinds which ensure that, even if he
is called upon to render the same tale two or more times on the

same spot within the same space of time, he will render it differently each time. Thus, in 1972, two versions of Amoogu were recorded
on the same spot (Pastor Maduekwe's compound in Asaga)[22]
within the space of one hour. In these, Kaalụ Igirigiri was able to
exploit variants of the two basic narration schemata: the direct
pointing schema in version B2 and the schema involving climactic
foregrounding in version B3. Similarly, four other versions of the
same tale, recorded before and after these two versions, exhibit
structural variations involving one variant or the other of the two
basic schemata as well as variations on the epithet and other formulae which constitute the mainstay of the language of the songs.

"Logistics", which for Christopher Okigbo "is what poetry
is",[23] is indeed a fitting metaphor to describe the performance
strategy of Kaalụ Igirigiri. In its relation with strategy and tactics in
the arts of war, logistics is the "art of so moving and disposing
troops or ships or aircraft as to impose on the enemy the place and
time and conditions for fighting preferred by oneself".[24] In performances witnessed and recorded in the field, we get the impression
that Kaalụ Igirigiri has mastered the art of moving and disposing
the traditonal materials of his compositions in such a way as to
impose on his audiences responses preferred by himself. The effect
of his mastery can be observed in the emotions of pleasure written
largely on the faces of his listeners, and in their comments. Of
course, few listeners can fail to applaud a singer who can offer so
much variety in any performance from so rich a repertoire as that
commanded by Kaalu Igirigiri. Between 1971 and 1977, his heroic
epic fare grew from 5 tales (recorded in 1971) to 22 tales (recorded
at a single performance in 1977). With such a rich and varied repertoire, Kaalu Igirigiri can indeed go on for a long time in any performance, without repeating himself. Thus, we are told by Ụkaọha
Agwunsi of Ọkọn (one of his musical accompanists):

> Once he has finished singing about any particular hero, he
> will not mention that hero again in the same performance.
> Other tales will then be told, all in a completely different
> voice (Interview, March 1976).

The trouble with other singers, says Ụkaoha Agwunsi, is that they
are either too parochial or narrow in their repertoire of tales. One
such singer is Echeme Ugwu of Ebem (Singer D), a son-in-song of
Kaalụ Igirigiri himself:

> He eulogizes only his kinsmen since he knows nothing about

heroes that lived in all other clans. He is still a mere apprentice (Interview, March 1976).

By contrast, Kaalụ Igirigiri is the matchless virtuoso who can range over the whole of Nigeria. Says Kaalụ Ikpo of Ọkọn:

> He can range over the whole of Nigeria, and when he sings, he will make sure that he calls this person, calls that person and calls that other person. He does not stick to one person (Interview, March 1976).

Kaalụ Ikpo, who is one of Kaalụ Igirigiri's musical accompanists is probably here referring to *Ogụ Mmekọta Naijiria* (The War of Nigerian Unity), a new addition to the Ọhafịa heroic corpus often cited by my informants in the field as evidence of Kaalụ's originality (See Azuonye 1986). Here are the opening lines of this verse chronicle:

> That time when Nigeria was one
> When Nigeria was one
> We had our armed forces
> We had them together
> We did not have them separately
> That was when Ọkpara was in power
> That was when Zik was in power
> That was when Awolowo was in power
> And a host of others
> In the course of their governance, all of them,
> Zik said to them:
> "Why is it that I do not wield sovereign power?
> My present post is so very low!
> Was I not the one that brought nationhood from England
> and gave to you
> Before you knew what it meant?"
> In the course of time
> He invited the armed forces
> And resigned that post of his to them
> They (the armed forces) summoned the Sardauna
> Of Sokoto
> "Will you not also resign your post?"
> But he said that he would not
> That his father was a ruler, his mother was a ruler
> And so they killed him . . . .

In a fairly long list of villains and heroes that follows, other Northern Nigerian leaders display the same kind of bigotry and are killed while all southern (mainly Igbo) leaders, including the late Professor Kaalụ Ezera of Ebem Ọhafia, prove to be more judicious and are spared. Tendentious and often chauvinistic in stating the Igbo case in the Nigerian civil war, as well as Ọhafia's local pride as one of the few areas of Igbo land not devastated by the war, Kaalụ Igirigiri's *Ọgụ Mmekọta Naijiria* is essentially an artistic transmutation of the mode of the oral epic song into a journalistic medium for the expression of ethnic sentiments in the separatist politics of the day.

Clarity and essence in the tales of Kaalụ Igirigiri

In spite of the variations clearly manifest in different versions of his tales as rendered on the same or different occasions, Kaalu Igirigiri insists in an interview that there is no difference between one version and another:

> I don't sing my songs at Okon in a way different from that in which I sing them at Ebem. The thing I sing at Okon is what I sing at Asaga. It is what I sing at Ebem . . . That is why Ọhafịa people all agree that I am the best of all their singers (Interview, March 1976).

In a similar vein, Egwu Kaalụ of Asaga (Singer C) declares:

> Nothing extraneous is added to the songs (i.e. in different performances). By that I mean that it is exactly what I sang in 1972 that I will sing today (1977). (Interview, July 1977).

There is always in the mind of singers of tales and their listeners, in practically all epic traditions, the impression of something that remains stable in spite of all thematic and structural changes, something that transcends the lexis of the oral performance. This accounts for assertions such as the above, or Kaalụ Igirigiri's retort *Ọ kwahu ife olu ọhụ* (it is exactly the same thing) when I drew his attention in the field to some serious inconsistencies and even outright contradictions in variant versions of one of his tales. The attempt to understand the nature of this stable element has been, over the years, one of the major concerns of scholarship in the field of oral performance (see, for example, Bowra 1966: 454; Finnegan 1977: 76-83; Innes 1973 and 1974: 30; Lord 1968: 26-30; Nagler 1974: 199; and Okpewho 1979: 160). I have in a recent study (Azuonye 1983) described this stable element as manifested in the Ọhafịa Igbo oral epics as the "heroic essence" of each tale:

> In every performance, the *heroic essence* is conveyed by a unique selection and combination of an optimum range of for-

mulae and themes from the traditional repertoire which best define the hero of the tale. Once this optimum selection of formulae and themes is present in any version of a tale, the audience will be satisfied that there has been no deviation from the legend and that the tale they have heard that day is the same one which they may have heard on several occasions in the past, irrespective of who the singer may be, of any changes in language or structure, and of the presence or absence of various elaborative or incidental themes and motifs in the version (Azuonye 1983: 335-336).

A comparison of seven versions of Nne Mgbaafọ by four different singers (four of which are by Kaalụ Igirigiri) revealed a total of 54 different themes in all the versions taken together. But only 2 of those were found to be common to all the seven versions. These themes:

> constitute the optimum selection of particularized themes needed to present the heroic essence of the legend of Nne Mgbaafọ . . . so long as this optimum selection of essential themes is present in any version of the epic . . . it is bound to register the same impression on the minds of the listeners . . . (Azuonye 1983: 336).

Despite the detractive criticism of his rivals, Kaalụ Igirigiri has shown himself in his recorded compositions to be the master of the logistics of presenting the heroic essence of his tales with the utmost clarity. He does so not only by strict adherence to the irreducible minimum of essential and particularized themes which best define the hero, but also quite often by concentrating on certain major themes such as the trial of heroes in *Amoogu Bi* (Tales IA: lines 38-120). This stylized scene in which a long list of established heroes try and fail in turn to produce the potent weapon needed to destroy their great adversary —the Aliike dwarf—is the focal interest of all of Kaalụ Igirigiri's versions of the Amoogu legend because it embodies the heroic essence of the tale, revealing the hero as the unknown warrior who at a desperate moment saves the face of his people by accomplishing a task which no one else could accomplish. The theme, developed by the technique of climactic hero-enumeration (incorporating the praises of the heroes themselves and of their clans) is one of the features of style inherited by the Ọhafịa oral epic songs from the ritual invocations which, with the traditional battle songs of the heroic age, constitute their principal precursors (see Azuonye 1979: Chapter 2). Kaalụ

61

Igirigiri is one of the contemporary singers of tales in Qhafịa who have recognized and effectively exploited the possibilities of developing similar themes for other compositions by the technique of climatic hero-enumeration (see, for example, *Ogu Mmekọta Naijiria,* on page 61).

By their strict adherence to the heroic essence, Kaalụ Igirigiri's compositions—be they compressed or elaborate—represent models of that clarity of form which Ọgbaa Kaalụ of Abia (Singer D) and Egwu Kaalụ of Asaga (Singer C) have both described by the same phrase, *ikowakwahu zhia isi ruo ali* (clearly explaining everything from the beginning to the end). They also reflect what Chinweizu, Jemie and Madubuike (1980: 247) have described as the efficiency of "structure and logistics" which is so highly "valued in orature, for it takes one through the climax without tedious or unnecessary diversions." This clarity of narrative form which is evident in the texts presented below in Tales I is matched in the internal dynamics of the narratives by a clarity of structure arising mainly from stylistic repetition and parallelism.[25]

There are probably three main types of repetition in the compositions of Kaalụ Igirigiri—formulaic, lyrical and mimetic. Formulaic repetition is the kind of repetition which focuses attention on the hero or the subject matter of the tale at the beginning of the tale (e.g. lines 2-3 of Amoogu Bl: Tales 1A) or which in the course of the narration restates a recurrent theme, e.g., in cases of climactic hero-enumeration *(Amoogù BI:* 36-120), the lines which focus on the problem before the heroes are enumerated. Lyrical repetition is of the kind found in song-passages of the tales (see Tales I) which in the course of the narrative is used to convey an emotional state. For example, when Nne Mgbaafọ arrives at the enemy Ibibio camp and demands to see her husband, the flabbergasted enemy brings Ndukwe Emeuwa out of prison and questions him. The insistent and excited tone of this questioning is reflected in the repetition of the line: Tales IA, lines 34-35. Finally, mimetic repetition dramatically re-echoes the intensity or duration of an action, as in lines 166-122 of *Amoogu BI* (Tales IA) or in the climactic hero-lists.

Parallelism—semantic or structural—adds variety and even complexity to the basic roles of repetition through the serial or paradigmatic patterning of lines using identical or completely different syntactic forms to express the same meanings, or lines

possessing the same or identical grammatical or phonological structures but expressing different meanings. Structural parallelism is
extensive in the narratives and its grammatical forms are self-
evident, especially in the noun-adjective collocations with which
the various hero-lists are replete. Much more closely bound up with
the singer's obsession with clarity of expression are the equally
numerous cases of semantic parallelism. There are cases of (a)
synonymous parallelism, involving the identity of meaning between
parallel lines, (b) antithetical parallelism based on contrast and
balance, (c) complementary parallelism based on complementa-
tion, and (d) synthetic or cumulative parallelism, based on the
enlargement of an idea by the presentation of additional, varied or
related elements.

Kaalụ Igirigiri is most efficient in the use of synonymous parallelism for thematic clarity. In the example available in his recorded
compositions, he creates variety, emphasis and rhetorical balance
by means of significant changes in the second parallel line. He is
fond of anastrophic patterns, such as the following, created by the
rephrasing of the second parallel line:

Di ya wu ezhi di   Her husband was a good husband
O wu ezhi di ya lu o   It was a good husband she was married to
    (*Nne Mgbaafọ B1:* The heroine speaking to enemy Ibibio
    about her husband)

By the omission of verbs, pronouns, nouns or whole phrases, as in
Nne Mgbaafọ B1 (lines 8-9), he commonly prunes the second of
two parallel lines, making the theme terse and emphatic. He may
create the same effect through a change in grammatical mood, as in
the change from the optative to the imperative mood in the following lines from *Nne Mgbaafọ B2* (lines 42-44):

He said, "You have bound my feet with ropes,
May you unbind me that I may go and see if she is indeed
    my wife,
Unbind me that I may go and see if she is indeed my wife!"

Writing on what they describe as "the spare, uncluttered
language of our epic, folktales, and court chronicles" and the way
in which "their control of their matter displays an almost ruthless
exclusion of convoluted, jargon-laden chaff", Chinweizu, Jemie
and Madubuike (1980: 246-247) have outlined features of language

which hold good for what my informants in Ọhafịa demand that
the language of their oral epic songs should be:

> Orature, being auditory, places high value on lucidity, normal
> syntax and precise and apt imagery. Language or image that
> is not vivid, precise, or compels the listener to puzzle it out,
> interrupts his attention, and makes him lose parts of the tell-
> ing.[26]

Egwu Kaalụ of Asaga (Singer C) speaks in much the same vein
when in the following testimony he deplores "the excessive use of
proverbs" *(itukarị ilu)* describing it as *ife ọduọ* (something extraneous), the consequence of which may be the production of "a
different type of poetry" *(abu ọduọ)* from that intended by the
bard:

> If a person repeatedly employs proverbs, it can only be said
> that he is creating another kind of poetry, because if you want
> to sing a song in a straightforward manner about the actual
> deeds of a particular person—if you really want to articulate
> the facts clearly, from the beginning to the end—you don't
> need to put extraneous things into it (Interview, March 1976).

Because of his ruthless avoidance of decorative phraseology, including a strict control on even the use of heroic epithets outside the
invocative portions of his songs, the few instances of the use of proverbs or tropes by Kaalụ Igirigiri come through with striking
poignancy. See, for example, *Amoògu BI* (Tales IA) in which
the main theme of the tale—the difficulty of killing the Aliike
dwarf—is introduced metaphorically with reference to the difficulty of catching a wild cow wandering about in the forest (lines
10-13).

Naturally, in the oral performance, a great deal of attention is
paid by the hearers to the quality of the singer's voice. An inaudible
or raucuos voice is as bad as an illegible script. Not surprisingly,
many attempts by critics and appreciators alike to rank one singer
against the other, include comments on the quality of the singer's
voice. A barman at Ebem describes Kaalụ Igirigiri's voice as
"sounding *gam gam* like a bell" and maintains in his testimony
that Kaalụ's voice is the best kind of voice for the singing of oral
epic songs. It is not as flat as that of his son-in-song, which Ogbaa
Kaalụ of Abịa (Singer D) has described as sounding "monotonously harsh" and which another informant compares to "the chirping
of crickets". Kaalụ Igirigiri's voice, of which he is justly proud and

boastful, is a clear, mellow tenor which has won him such professional praise-names as *Olu nkwa* (musical voice), *Olu ogele* (gong-
like voice,) *Okooko turu nkwa yiri olu* (parrot that built a musical
instrument and wears it in his throat), *Okookǒ nkam nka* (parrot,
the talkative artist), *Oji olu ekwu nnu* (he that buys salt with his
voice) and many others. Although the metaphor, *Okooko* (parrot),
might apply to other singers with Kaalu Igirigiri's type of voice and
indeed to any proficient bard in the oral tradition, it seems specially
approriate to Kaalu's voice, a voice so richly flexible that it is able
to intone with ease the various voices of the tales—lyric, invocative,
oratorical and narrative—in their proper modulations. But apart
from its sonority, beauty and flexibility, Kaalu Igirigiri's voice
possesses the most highly valued quality expected of the voice of an
oral artist, namely audibility and clarity. Thus, in ranking him
above his rivals, Kaalu Igirigiri's musical accompanists—Ukaoha
Agwunsi and Kaalu Ikpo, of Okon—stress the fact that "he speaks
in such a way that what he says is clearly audible" (*O na-akapusa
ife anu anu a nti*).

Kaalu Igirigiri and the functions of the oral epic song in Ohafia

Kaalu Igirigiri is not only a gifted oral artist, but a committed
traditionalist deeply concerned with the continuity of the dynamic
socio-pyschological functions of the oral epic song in Ohafia.
While recognizing the complete differentiation of the songs as a
poetic genre, he has nonetheless remained attached to the traditional conception of them as an integral part of the larger complex
of heroic music (*iri-aha*) which includes the well-known dramatic
war dance of the Ohafia people. For him, therefore, the songs—as
part of this larger complex — are first and foremost a dynamic
vehicle for the communication of the myths behind the heroic
rituals of the society, above all, for stressing vital relationships between contemporary achievements in education, commerce, politics
and other walks of life with the achievements, battles and head-
hunting raids of the ancestral heroes of old. Kaalu Igirigiri's position is succinctly summed up as follows in the words of his rival,
Ogbaa Kaalu of Abia (Singer D):

> Today, head-hunting is out of fashion. But if you grow rich
> or become highly educated, especially if you go to the white
> man's land and return with your car and immense knowledge,
> we would naturally come and perform for you . . . for things

of this kind are the only form of head-hunting that exists in our present-day culture (Interview, March 1976).

Under the pressure of rapid social change, the songs are increasingly becoming a popular form of entertainment, farther and farther divorced from their traditional soil and performed for small and large audiences within and outside Ọhafịa, on radio and television.[27] The consequence of this, in the performance of many a modernist singer, is the gradual transformation of the heroic tradition through the assimilation of alien influences. We find, for example, the biblical creation myth (including the creation of Woman from Man's rib) infused into Njọkụ Mmajụ's version of *Ife Meenu Chineke Kwere Ana-Egbu Anu,* "Why God Ordained the Hunting of Wild Animals" (Kaalụ Igirigiri's Tale No. 1).Purist that he is, Kaalụ Igirigiri is opposed to this kind of assimilation which he regards as contamination. His version of the tale is thus confined to the authentic and indigenous lineaments of the original myth in which a folk variant of the evolutionist doctrine of the survival of the fittest is justified not by invoking the principles of natural selection but those of divine ordinance. Even his chronicle of the events of the Nigerian Civil War (Tale No. 21) culminates, as we have earlier observed, in a chauvinistic assertion of the myth of Ọhafịa's uniqueness in Igbo culture and history. For Kaalụ Igirigiri this kind of assertion, directed at constantly reminding the Ohafia people themselves of their common origins and of the grandeur of their past and the greatness of their ancestors, is the inalienable function of the oral epic singer:

> Take Ọhafịa as a whole, I can tell you all about our origins —about the place from which we migrated to this land. None of my rivals knows anything about these things. No one else in Ọhafịa but myself knows anything about these things. This compound of ours, I can tell you all about its founding father. About other people's compounds, I can tell you all about their founding fathers. When I go to Amaekpu, I can tell them all about their founding fathers. None of my rivals knows anything about these things. As you will know, Amaekpu is not my hometown, but I know everything that prevails there. Asaga, I know everything about their founding fathers, and I know everything that prevails there, everything conceivable that prevails there. That is what we call *iku-aka* —knowledge of the ancestors: knowledge of the ancestors of Asaga, knowledge of the ancestors of Akaanụ, knowledge of the ancestors of Uduma . . . My rivals know nothing of such

things (Interview, March 1976).

Kaalụ Igirigiri displays his knowledge of the ancestors through climactic hero-lists of the kind to which attention has been drawn earlier in this paper. In his hero-enumerations, he always manages to create the illusion of *mkpọzu* (complete invocation), i.e. of having called everybody, simply by listing the heroes of the most important patriclans in Ọhafịa and those of the particular patriclan in which he happens to be performing. He may even add a few extra credit lines to the heroes of the host patriclan, especially if the version of the tale in the making happens to involve a hero born in that clan. Less competent singers would spend several minutes trying to list all the heroes in all Ọhafịa patriclans and end up missing important points of the narrative without realizing the illusion of *mkpozu*.

Needless to say, the audience is hardly ever aware of the trick by which Kaalụ Igirigiri is able to create the illusion of *mkpọzu* in his hero-lists. For most of his hearers, Kaalụ is the repository of the truth of "what actually happened in the heroic past" (*Ife mee eme mgbe ichin*), and even his wildest fancies are often accepted as 'reality'. In one of my interviewing sessions in 1976, for instance, some appreciators who had earlier interpreted the *Nne Ache Ugo* fable (Tales No. 16) as a parable *(ilu)* quickly abandoned their interpretation on hearing Kaalu Igirigiri's assertion that the heroine actually lived at Elu, Ohafia's traditional citadel:

> Nne Acho Ugo. . . . behaved very much like what we call *nkita-iyi* (River-dog). *Nkita-iyi* lives in water. It isn't human. It isn't fish, this *nkita-iyi*. It isn't beast, this *nkita-iyi*. It isn't a type of fish. It isn't a beast. It has the tail of a mudskipper. It has a beard—mammalian hair. It lives in water and also lives on land. When it gives birth, this *nkita-iyi,* she can beget a beast of the forest. Quite often when fishes see its tail, they gather round it thinking it is one of their kind. But it eats fish . . . it isn't fish and isn't beast . . . so Nne Achọ Ugo was . . . . She was human as well as bird.

The excited credulity with which the local audience accepted as truth this bizarre description of what is essentially one of the fabulous beasts of universal legend, demonstrates the mesmeric power of Kaalụ Igirigiri's hold over his audience. The Ọhafịa Igbo singer of tales exemplified by Kaalụ Igirigiri is essentially a kind of *magus* in the cultural situation in which history, *akụkọ-ali* (stories of the land)[28], touches on aspects of the people's existence as a corporate group. He not only "awakens the spirit" of the young and "inspires in them that old bravery", he also enlightens them about their past traditions of self-sacrificing heroism "which bind all Ọhafịa people together", which mark them out from other Igbo people", and which call for the continued pursuit for excellence in contemporary endeavour for the glory of the community at large.[29]

TALES I

NNE MGBAAFỌ BI (1971)

Mgbaafọ!
Woman of Nde-Awa-Ezhiema-Elechi!
Her husband went to war —
He went to the war of Igbe Mmakụ;
5   And so her husband went to the war of Igbe Mmakụ.
Three market weeks passed, but her husband did not return—
Her husband did not return.
Mgbaafọ followed her husband, went searching for her husband, came to the Igbe Mmakụ warfront.
10   Ndụkwe Emeuwa was her husband's name.
His name was Ndụkwe Emeuwa, that husband of hers.
She went *mbelege mbelege* and came to Isiugwu.
The people asked Mgbaafọ, "Where are you coming from?"
She said she was searching for her husband —
15   Her husband was a good husband.
It was a good husband she was married to.
If she did not find her husband, she would rather sleep wherever her husband may be sleeping.
She went past their *ogo*.
She went *mbelege mbelege* and came to Atang.
20   The people asked Mgbaafọ "Where are you coming from?"
She said she was searching for her good husband, Ndụkwe:
He had gone to the war of Igbe Mmakụ and had not returned;
Only if she found her husband there would she ever return;
If she did not find her husband, she would rather sleep,
25   And she would dare whoever killed her husband to kill her too.
She went *mbelege mbelege* and at last arrived at the Igbe[30]
Mmaku people, they questioned her, "What are you called.
Igbe Mmakụ people, they questioned her, "What are you called?"
She said that she was called Mgbaafọ.
"And your husband, what is he called?"
30   She said that he was called Ndụkwe Emeuwa.
That place where they put away Ndụkwe Emeuwa,
Where they hid away Ndụkwe Emeuwa,
They went and called Ndụkwe:
"Who are you married to?
35   Who are you married to?

68

What is your wife called?''
He said that she was called Mgbaafǫ.
"And you, what are you called?''
He said that he was called Ndukwe.
40 "Your wife has come searching for you,
Come out now and go meet your wife.''
Those people, our good friends,
The Igbe Mmaku people said that that woman should not
be killed.
"She is truly full of valour!
45 She has come searching for her husband all the way from their *ogo*.
She has come searching for her husband all the way from their *ogo*.[31]
Let her not be killed!''
And so they took her husband and gave to Mgbaafǫ.
Mgbaafǫ took her husband and brought him safely back
to Nde-Awa-Ezema-Elechi.
50 Nwata nwaami achǫwa di ya [32]
Yaa di!
Nwata nwaami achǫwa di ya
Ya iya!
Mgbaafǫ, ǫ chǫwa di ya
Ya di!
Nwata nwaami achǫwa di ya
Ya iya!
. . . .
Mgbaafǫ, ǫ chǫwa di ya
Ya aha di!
55 Ǫ chǫwa di ya
ya aha di!
Ǫ chǫwa di ya
Ya aha di! . . . . .

TALES IA

AMOÒGU BI (1971)

Odududu ndufu![33]

Wardrum, without whose leadership there is fear on the way!
Wardrum, without whose leadership there is fear on the way!
Great spirit, Uduma Ǫlugutu.
Great spirit, Ǫkali husband of my great mother,
Aru!
Great spirit that dwells in the water at Nde-a-Awa-Ezhiema-Elechi!
Great spirit Umezurike of Ebiri-Ezhi-Akuma!
Great spirit Agwu Ǫbasi of Ekidi Nde Ǫfǫali!
Great spirit Kaalu Ikpo of Ugwu-Naka-Oke-Igbemini!
10 We have dragged a cow by the rope and tethered it at
Nde-Awa-Ezhiema-Elechi,
The cow will no longer stray into the forest.

Who will go and catch the cow that has strayed into the forest?
Who will go and catch the cow that has strayed into the forest?
Okoro, medicine-man of Ezhi Abaaba, was the one that brought the charm-
    breaker.
15   (......).
Ohafia people, they were set to go to war:
They were set to go to 'Liike, they were going to fight all the way at 'Liike.
A short-armed dwarf prevented the defeat of 'Liike,
A short-armed dwarf prevented the defeat of 'Liike.
20   The short-armed dwarf that prevented the defeat of 'Liike,
His proper name was 'Miiko.
On the first day of the encounter, the short-armed one came and stood before
    a trench,
And when Ohafia warriors charged to chase them (the 'Liike) back,
He routed them and packed their chopped-up parts in long-baskets.
25   It went on until one night,
Ohafia war chiefs gathered together at Ebiri Ezhi Akuma:
"What shall we do to kill the short-armed dwarf of 'Liike?"
They went and summoned Okoro Mkpi.
He lived at Ibinaji of Egbenyi Uka.
30   He was a medicine-man of Ezhi Ababa.
They asked Okoro Mkpi:
"What shall we do to conquer 'Liike?
The short-armed dwarf prevents the defeat of 'Liike!"
He told them to get into a nest of soldier-ants:
35   "There is a nest of soldier-ants on the way.
Go and place this charm on the way.
Who among you can sit in the nest of soldier-ants and charge guns, so the
    short-armed dwarf of 'Liike can be killed—Twelve guns in all!"

My great father Akwu of Abia Eteete agreed.
He said he would sit in the nest of soldier-ants and charge the guns, so the
    short-armed dwarf might be killed.
40   My great father Iro Agbo of Okpo Ntighiri.....
He said he would sit in the nest of soldier-ants and charge the guns, so the
    short-armed dwarf of 'Liike might be killed.
My great father Iro Agbo Ntighiri.....
My great father Awa Afaka of Udegbe Ezhi Anunu,
He said he would sit in the nest of soldier-ants and charge the guns, so the
    short-armed dwarf of 'Liike might be killed.
45   My great father Mbu Ologho of Ibinaji Egbenyi Uka,
Said he would sit in the nest of soldier-ants and charge the guns, so the short-
    armed dwarf of 'Liike might be killed.
My great father Igbun Awa!
My great father Igbun Awa,
Who is of Nde-Ezhiema Elechi,
50   He said he would sit in the nest of soldier-ants and charge the guns, so the
    short-armed dwarf of 'Liike might be killed.

70

My great father Mkpawe son of Imaga Odo,

He was a person of Ugwu Naka Oke Igbe-mini,

He agreed and said he would sit in the nest of soldier-ants and charge the guns, so the short-armed dwarf of 'Liike might be killed.

Oke Ikwan Ịyam Ọtụtụ of Ebiri,

55 Man of Ebiri Ezhi Akụma,

He said he would sit in the nest of soldier-ants and charge the guns, so the short-armed dwarf of 'Liike might be killed.

My great father, Iro Agbọ Okpe Ntighiri,

Said he would sit in the nest of soldier-ants and charge the guns, so the short-armed dwarf of 'Liike might be killed.

Kamalụ, son of Ngwo, who was of Agaladọ Odo Ukiiwe,

60 Man of Agaladọ Odo Ukiiwe—

People-that-run-in-herds-like-sheep—

He said he would sit in the nest of soldier-ants and charge the guns, so the short-armed dwarf of 'Liike might be killed.

And so they set out for war, on an *Eke* day which was a farming day.

When they reached the outskirts of 'Liike,

65 They gave the guns to Mbu Ọlọghọ,

Man of Ibinaji of Egbenyi Ụka

He got into the nest of soldier-ants.

The soldiers-ants bit him a little, but the guns he could not charge.

He trembled off.

70 They went and called Akwụ, man of Abịa Eteete.

Two guns were given to him, but the guns he could not charge.

He also trembled off.

Guns were given to Kamalụ Ngwo, son of Agaladọ Odo Ukiiwe.

He tried and tried to charge the guns, but the guns he could not charge.

75 Stung by the soldier-ants, he also trembled off.

The guns he could not charge.

They then gave them to Nkụma Obiagụ, man of Ekidi Nde Ọfọalị.

He also trembled off, the guns he could not charge.

Mkpawe Ịmaga Odo, man of Ugwu Naka Igbemini was then given,

80 "You go and charge the guns,"

But the guns he could not charge.

He also trembled off.

They then went and gave them to Nkata Ogbuanụ, Nkata Ogbuanụ,

Man of Igbe Mmakụ,

85 Son of great mother (. . .) of Ndiibe Ọkwara,

Wizard of guns for whom the gun is a plaything.

He also trembled off,

The guns he could not charge.

Ọhafịa warriors, our-little-blameless-ones,

90 Everyone of them,

The guns they could not charge.

And so they said: "Let us go home.

Let us go home, we cannot charge the guns.

Let us go home,

71

95   Let us go home!''
        Amoogu o, Amoogu o, je!
        Amoogu o, son of great mother Ori Ukpo.
        Son of great mother Orieji Ukpo,
        Son of great mother Orieji Ukpo.
100   He is a man of Amuma,
        He is a man of the Etum-Olumba age-set,
        He is a man of Irema Okpurukpu,
        He is a man of of Okpu-Uma-Ofu-Agbala! . . . .
        He asked to be given the guns.
105   "We should all go home if I try and fail!
        Ohafia warriors, give me the guns!''
        But they questioned him: "Of what patriclan are you?''
        And he said that he was a native of Amuma.
        "Let the guns be given to him.''
110   And so the warriors of Ohafia Uduma Ezhiema, they took the guns and gave
                to Amoogu son of Ologho Ikpo.
        He was a man of Okpu-Uma-Ofu-Abala.
        He took two guns and entered.
        (. . . .)
        And so two guns were given to Amoogu.
115   He charged this one, and charged that one.
        The ants stung his laps in their hundreds.
        The ants stung his laps in their hundreds.
        And so he got into the nest of soldier-ants and charged this one, charged that
                one.
        Great father Awa Afaka took one gun from him.
120   Mbu Ologho took one gun from him.
        And they went and killed Mkpisi Ebulebu, the short-armed dwarf of 'Liike.
        The evil genius in the nest of soldier-ants.
        They hacked him mercilessly and packed his body in a basket,
        And so they killed great father Omiko.
125   After all these,
        Ohafia warriors, all without exception,
        They swooped upon those Ishiagu people, makers-of-pots-and-what-not,
        And they unleashed a massacre upon them,
        And they burnt down their houses,
130   All without exception.
        When they returned to their camp —
        When at last they returned to their camp,
        Great father Mbu Ologho asked: "Who was it that charged the guns?''
        Amoogu said: "I am the one that charged the guns
135   With which we went and killed the 'Liike general.''
        They said that they would give him a nice little present.
        And they conspired among themselves:
        "Let us kill Amoogu.
        We should kill Amoogu.
140   If we do not kill him, he shall become the leading hero of Ohafia.''

And so they lured Amoogu to a solitary corner and killed him,
And they gave his chopped-off head to Amụma warriors,
And they took it home
And hung it in their *òbu*. [34]
145 His mother, great mother Ori Ukpo ——
My great mother Ori Ukpo wept:
      Amoogu, son of Ọlọghọ Ikpo,
      Were you killed with a matchet or a gun?
      Be it with a matchet or a gun,
150   O my son, *jo!*
      O my son, *je!*
      Were you killed with a matchet or a gun?
      O my son, *iyeje!*
      Iyeee-je!
155   O Amoogu, *iyeje!*
      Amoogu, O come to me, *iye!*
      Iyeejee-i!
His mother, Amoogu
She dwelt beside a silk-cotton tree,
160 She dwelt beside a silk-cotton tree.
      The mother of Amoogu, son of Ọlọghọ Ikpo, dwelt beside a silk-cotton tree.
      Kites came from that silk-cotton tree and preyed upon her chickens,
      Hawks came from that silk-cotton tree and preyed upon her chickens.
      She said, "O, if my son were alive,
165   He would have shot these kites away ——
      He was a wizard-of-guns-for-whom-the-gun-was-a-plaything."
His age-mates were at watch and heard this.
They summoned everybody in Amụma, all without exception, men of Irema
      Ọkpụrụkpụ.
They gave two cases of wine,
170 And said to them, "We plead with you, let this silk-cotton tree be felled
      That the chickens of my great mother Ori Ukpo may thrive.
      That man we killed is the cause of her great grief.
      He was of our age-set,
      He was of our age-set.
175 Irema Ọkpụrụkpụ all agreed.
      They began felling the silk-cotton tree,
      They began felling the silk-cotton tree, all of them without exception.
      They went on felling the tree and continued on the second day.
      When it got to the third day, they drank palmwine to their fill.
180 And as the tree began to fall, they said they would hold it up with their hands,
            but they were shaken by the wine.
      Shaken by the wine, all without exception,
      Shaken by the wine.
      (. . . .)
185 As they tried to hold up that silk-cotton tree with their hands, the silk-cotton
            tree killed four hundred of them.

73

And so four hundred men got lost in their clan.
They went to a diviner.
My great mother Aja Ekeke thus divined
And told them: "Whatever it was that made you people agree to kill
    Amoogu,
190   It was the spirit of Amoogu that pushed that silk-cotton tree to crush you
    people."
That is why Amuma is still so thinly populated.
It is the wrath of the spirit of Amoogu, son of Ọlọghọ Ikpo.

TALES II

KAALU IGIRIGIRI'S REPERTOIRE OF TALES, COLLECTED *1971-77

A. Creation Myths

1. *Ife Meenu Ana-egbu Anu.* Myth of the origin of hunting. Two versions: B1 (1971) and B2 (1977).
2. *Ife Meenu Iwa na-egbu Ewu.* Myth concerning the reason why goats die when they eat cassava. Two versions: B1 (1976) and B2 (1977).

B. Migration Legends

3. *Ibe Ọhafịa bịa.* Legend of the migration of the founding fathers of Ọhafịa from Benin through Ịdọn (on the Niger) and Ibeku (near Ụmụahia) to their present homeland. Two versions: B1 (1976) and B2 (1977).
4. *Èbùlu Ìjeọ̀mà.* Legend of the foundation of Arọ-Ndi-Izuogụ by an Arọ trader, Ebulu Ijeọma. Two versions: B1 (1976) and B2 (1977).

C. Heroic Legends

5. *Elìbe Àjà.* Legend of the fearless Ọhafịa hunter who kills a leopardess harrying Aro country and later dies in an attempt to kill a bush-hog that was ravaging farms at Amụrụ. Four versions: B1 (1972), B2-B3 (1976) and B4 (1977). B3 does not contain the episode in which the hero's death is reported.
6. *Ìnyàn Ọ̀lùgù.* Legend of a brave woman who kills four men during a raid on palm trees in the enemy territory. She gives their chopped off heads to her cowardly husband to take home as his own accolade of prowess in single combat as required by the heroic code of the day. Five versions: B1 (1971), B2 (1972), B3-B4 (1976) and B5 (1977).
7. *Nne M̀gbaàfọ̀.* Legend of the valiant and loving wife who goes into enemy Ibibio territory to search for her lost husband. See Appendix 1A above. Five versions: B1 (1971), B2 (1972), B3-B4 (1976) and B5 (1977).
8. *Amoògu.* Legend of a little known warrior whose power of endurance enables the Ọhafịa to overcome their great adversary, the short-armed dwarf of Aliike. See Appendix IA above. Six versions: B1 (1971), B2-B3 (1972), B4-B5 (1976) and B5 (1977).
9. *Ọ̀gbaka Okorìè.* Legend of a famous Ọhafịa dancer of the *Ekpe* dance killed

after his knees had been shattered with a gun by jealous rivals in a neighbour-ing clan. Four versions: B1 (1971), B2 (1972), B3 (1976) and B4 (1977).

10. *Egbele.* Legend of a thrice-bereaved mother whose joyful song (on the vic-torious return of her lastborn whom she had tried in vain to shield from the wars) is believed to be the origin of the Ọhafịa war songs. Four versions: B1 (1972), B2-B3 (1976) and B4 (1977).

11. *Ijeọma Ebulu.* Legend of a prosperous Ọhafịa merchant killed and robbed of his wealth by his greedy wife and her relatives. One version: B1 (1977).

12. *Egbè Nri Adịghị.* Legend of Ìnyima Kaalụ, a famous hunter whose newborn baby is killed by an unloaded gun which fires itself. Two versions: B1 (1976) and B2 (1977).

13. *Kaalụ Ezè Nwa Mgbo.* Legend of a great wrestler cursed by the gods with in-fertility until the day his back touched the ground in a wrestling contest. One version: B1 (1977).

14. *Ụcha Àruòdò.* Legend of a woman who conceives an only child (a girl) in her old age and has a hard time fending for her. Three versions: B1 (1971), B2 (1972) and B3 (1977). No version was recorded in 1976, but then the heroine's name was assigned to the mother of the hero of tale No. 10.

15. *Ịhọgbọ.* Legend of an acrobatic dancer able to dance the *Òkerenkwà* heroic dance while climbing up a tree. Two versions: (1976) and B2 (1977).

D. *Allegorical and Fabular Tales*

16. *Nne Acho Ugo.* Fable óf five birds who boast among themselves what great things they would do for their mother, on the day of her death, to give her a befitting burial. But when their mother dies, none of them shows up. Four versions: B1 (1972), B2-B3 (1976) and B4 (1977).

17. *Agwù Akpù.* Fable of the spirit doctor who is said to have introduced the use of the lizard as a sacrificial animal. One version: B1 (1977).

18. *Àkpala.* Aetiological animal fable purporting to account for the origin of the dancing habits of the sunbird (*àkpala*). One version: B1 (1977).

19. *Ṅkelu.* Aetiological animal fable purporting to account for the origin of the bluebird's *nkelu* habit of shaking its head while sipping water from the stream. One version: B1 (1977).

20. *Nkakwu.* Aetiological animal fable purporting to account for the origin of the bush mouse's *(nwakwu)* awful smell. One version: B1 (1977).

E. *Chronicle of Contemporary Events*

21. *Ogu Mmekota Nàịjirià.* Kaalụ Igirigiri's original account of "the war of Nigerian Unity", from the *coup d'etat* of January 15, 1966 to the end of the Biafran War of Secession in January 1970. Three versions: B1-B4 (1976) and B5 (1977)

NOTES

1. Kaalụ Igirigiri is one of the six singers of tales whose compositions and performances form the basis of my study of the Ọhafia Igbo oral epic tradition in my doctoral thesis (Azuonye 1979). The others are Okonkwọ Oke of Alaanụ, Egwu Kaalụ of Asaga, Ọgbaa Kaalụ of Abịa, Echeme Ugwu of Ebem, and Njọkụ Mmajụ of Uduma Awoke. In referring to variant versions of the same tales by these singers, I use the following alphabet codes: "A" for Okonkwo Oke (d. 1966), whose recordings I obtained through an Ọhafịa indigene in London, "B" for Kaalu Igirigiri (d. 1980) and "C", "D", "E" and "F" respectively for the others, in the chronological order in which I first met them. For the variant versions of the same tales by each singer, the relevant alphabet code is coupled with numeral codes (e.g. B1, B2, B3, etc) as in Tales II and in the main body of the paper. Throughout the paper, I use the term "oral epic song" as defined in Wilgus 1959, Bodker 1965 and Lord 1968, i.e. oral narrative verse which is heroic in matter and manner but of brief compass.

2. This is a modified version of the paper presented at the Sixth Ibadan Annual African Literature Conference on the Oral Performance in Africa (University of Ibadan, July 27 - August 1, 1981). I am grateful to many participants at the conference, especially Professor Isidore Okpewho, Dr Kofi Agovi and Chief Oludare Olujubu, whose comments and criticism both inside and outside the conference hall have guided me in my revision.

3. For further details see Azuonye 1979 (Chapter 9) and my more recent paper (Azuonye 1986a).

4. e.g. Singer D. See Azuonye 1979: 102-4.

5. Although Ọhafịa is a double-descent society, matrilineal relations are much more highly stressed than patrilineal ones: "Not only is the Ọhafịa matrilineage the main property-owning and inheriting group, it is also the only exogamous group; the patrilineage is non-exogamous and not the main property-owning or property-inheriting group" (Nsugbe 1974: 121). This and other psychological factors discussed in Nsugbe may be the basis of the stronger attachment displayed here by Kaalu Igirigiri to his matriclan than to his patriclan.

6. Lit. "Those who gave birth to me in singing".

7. e.g. the Mandinka bardic tradition (see Innes, 1974: 2-7).

8. This and other testimonies from the Ọhafịa singers and their critics and appreciators are given in free English translation. The original Igbo will appear parallel to the English translations in an Appendix to my forthcoming collection, *The Song of Kaalụ Igirigiri: Compositions of an Ọhafịa Igbo Singer of Tales.*

9. Among these are tales Nos. 1, 3, 6, 7, 8, 10 in Tales II.

10. For a detailed discussion of the traditional and other formulae in the songs, see Azuonye 1979 (Chapter 6) and 1986b.

11. I am grateful to Mr. and Mrs. Ukpai Emele for making this recording available to me from their private collection in London (1976).

12. *Aro-Oke-Igbo (Aro,* supreme Igbo) is the patronymic praise-name of the people of Aro Chukwu, south of Ọhafịa.

13. See Azuonye 1979: 32-34, for a detailed description of the humiliations suffered by the *ujo* as opposed to the honours heaped on the *ufiem* (honourable warriors) in the Ohafịa heroic society.

14. On the composition of this sequence, Okigbo says in an interview, "my *Limits*. . . was influenced by everybody and everything. . . . It is surprising how many lines of the *Limits* I am not sure are mine and yet do not know whose lines they were originally" ("Transition Conference Questionnaire"). *Transition*, 11 (July - August 1962): p. 2.

15. No recording of the performances of Ogboo Ogwo appears to have survived, except perhaps in the archives of Radio Nigeria (Enugu).

16. Cp. the process of "selective borrowing" in the Mandinka heroic tradition: Innes 1973: 118.

17. The question was first raised at the conference by Chief Oludare Olajubu and again by Professor Isidore Okpewho (the quote is from Okpewho, in one of his editorial letters dated October 17, 1981, in connection with the present volume).

18. The details are as follows: Singer A, 6α (2 out of 34 tales); Singer C, 9α (3 tales); Singer D 12α (4 tales), (in spite of his boast in several interviews about the richness and variety of his repertoire); Singer E. 21a (7 tales) and Singer F, 33a (11 tales).

19. The "voices" here are co-terminous with the "passages" discussed in Azuonye 1979 (Chapter 2) and are comparable to the "modes" of performance discussed in Innes (1974) and Johnson (1980) with reference to the Mandinka epic.

20. See Kunene 1971 and Azuonye 1979: 293.

21. These narration schemata are described in detail in Azuonye 1979: 291-297.

22. The retired Presbyterian pastor O. Ukiiwe Maduekwe in whose house I recorded most of the songs of Kaalu Igirigiri listed in Appendix II.

23. See Christoper Okigbo's *Labyrinths* (London: Heinemann, 1971:) 3.

24. *The Concise Oxford Dictionary,* 5th edition, (Oxford· Claredon Press, 1975).

25. See Azuonye 1979: 242-271 for a detailed discussion of various forms of stylistic repetition and parallelism in the songs.

26. I cannot however agree with the troika that "these qualities which are made mandatory in the auditory medium, should be insisted upon in the written" (Chinweizu, Jemie and Madubuike, 1980: 247).

27. Both singers E and F have produced some long playing records.

28. See Azuonye 1979. pp. 110-115

29. *Ibid:* 351-355

30. The ideophone *mbelege mbelege* (which is of frequent occurrence in the performance of Kaalu Igirigiri) has no specific lexical value. Its meaning depends on the context in which it occurs. In this particular context, it may be properly taken to imply "steadily and fearlessly on"

31. *Ogo* means "village square", but it is also used (as in the present context) metonymically to refer to the village or clan for whose members it serves as a central meeting-place.

32. This song repeats the phrase "A young woman is searching for her husband", with the heroine's name (Mgbaafo) being occasionally used in place of "a young woman" in a couple of lines. The refrain is a lyrical interjection expressive of joyful emotion.

33. *Odududu ndufu* is one of the many untranslatable epithets in the songs. Rendered literally, it says "He that leads (*Odu*) leading (*du*) leading (*du*) leading astray (ndufu)". But it really describes an inimitable war leader who can lead his men to dangerous places from which he can easily return unharmed while others, less valiant, get lost. No translation can effectively convey these and other connotations of the epithet. There is for instance a *du-du* sound in the two parts of the epithet which appears to foreshadow phonaesthetically the performance to the war drum (*ikoro*) in the couplet that follows. It is indeed unfortunate that the epithets on which so much of the emotional effect of the songs on their intended local audiences depend cannot easily be translated. In this sense, translations are essentially useless except as an aid to the non-speaker of the language (or dialect) who merely wants to follow the main outline of the tales. See Innes' contribution to this volume for a more detailed discussion of the problem of the untranslatable formula in another West African heroic tradition.

34. An *Obu* is a type of hall of local heroes found in each Ohafia village. It usually features wooden images of the leading ancestral heroes of the locality and battle trophies (including the skulls of slain enemies).

REFERENCES

AZUONYE, Chukwuma, 1979. "The Narrative War Songs of the Ohafia Igbo: A Critical Analysis of their Characteristics Features in Relation to their Social Functions. " Unplished PH.D'thesis, University of London.

AZUONYE, Chukwuma, 1983, "Stability and change in the performance of Ohafia Igbo Singers of Tales;" *Research in African Literatures,* (Austin Texa) Vol. 14, No. 3: pp. 332-380.

AZUONYE, Chukwuma, 1986a. "Principles of the Igbo Oral Epic: A Study in Oral Literary Criticism." Paper Presented at the 2nd International Seminar on Igbo Oral Literature, University of Nigeria, Nsukka, August 12-15. Forthcoming in Obiechina and Azuonye, Chapter 35.

AZUONYE, Chukwuma, 1986b. "The Oral Formulaic Character of Igbo Narrative Poetry." Ibid. Forthcoming in Obiechina and Azuonye, Chapter 8 under the title, "The Traditional Epithet.in the Igbo Epic Song".

AZUONYE, Chukwuma, 1986c."The Recording, Transcription and Preservation of Igbo Oral Performance: Problems and Methodology."

Forthcoming in Obiechina and Azuonye, Chapter 44, under the title, "The Collection and Transcription of Igbo Oral Literature: Problems and Methodology"

AZUONYE, Chukwuma, 1986d. "Ọgụ Mmekọta Naijiria: An Account of the Nigeria Crisis and Civil War by an Ọhafịa Igbo Bard." *Uwa Ndi Igbo*, No. 2 (December)

BOWRA, C. M. 1966. *Heroic Poetry*. London and New York: Macmillian and St. Martin's.

BODKER, Laurits. 1965 "Folk Literature (Germanic)". *International Dictionary of Regional European Ethnology and Folklore* Vol. II Copenhagen:

CHINWEIZU, JEMIE Onwuchekwa and IHECHUKWU Madubuike, 1980. *Towards the Decolonization of African Literature* Vol. 1, Enugu: Fourth Dimension Publishers.

FINNEGAN, Ruth 1977. *Oral Poetry: Its Nature, Significance and Social Context*. Cambridge: Cambridge University Press.

INNES, Gordon. 1973. "Stability and Change in Griots' Narrations" *African Language Studies*, 14.

INNES, Gordon. 1974. *Sunjata, Three Mandinka Versions*. London: School of Oriental and African Studies.

JOHNSON, John William , "Yes, Virginia, There is an Epic in Africa" *Research in African Literatures*, Vol II (3): 1980.

KUNENE, Daniel. 1971. *Heroic Poetry of the Basotho*. Oxford: Claredon Press.

LORD, Albert, 1966. *The Singer of Tales*. New York: Athenaeum Press.

NAGLER, M.N. 1974. *Spontaneity and Tradition: A Study of the Oral Art of Homer*. Berkely and Los Angeles: University of Califonia Press.

NSUGBE, Philip. *Ọhafịa: A Matrilineal Ibo People*. Oxford: Claredon Press.

OBIECHINA, Emmanuel and Chukwuma AZUONYE (eds.), 1986. Forthcoming *A Critical Source-Book for Igbo Literature, Vol. I: Oral Literature*. Society for Promoting Igbo Language and Culture in association with University Press Ltd, Nigeria.

OKPEWHO, Isidore, 1979. *The Epic in Africa: Toward a Poetics of the Oral Performance*. New York: Columbia University Press.

WILGUS, D. K. 1959. *Angle-American Folklore Scholarship Since 1898*. New Brunswick: Rutgers University Press.

The Performance of *Gule Wamkulu*—An Introduction

Enoch S. Timpunza Mvula

WRITING about the *gule wamkulu* performance in Nkhotakota district, a government district officer, Rangeley, wrote that "although the term *gule* dance is used, these *gule* are really mimes or small plays".[1] He described the masks and animal structures without presenting the form and content of the performance in which the masqueraders are actors. Moreover, his description shows that he looked at the parts only, and not the whole dramatic performance. About twenty years later, Schoffeleers worked on the religious aspects of *gule wamkulu* as performed in the Lower Shire. He stated that *gule wamkulu* performance should be seen as a mystery play as well as ritual drama, in which masks and animal structures represent ancestral spirits and animals of the forest temporarily come from the bush to the village to associate with human beings.[2]

The concern here is, however, not to show whether *gule wamkulu* performance is a form of ritual drama or not, but to discuss the functions, structure and content of *gule wamkulu* performance as an aesthetic art form in which music, dance and drama are totally integrated to constitute one indivisible dramatic performance. Since *gule wamkulu* performance sometimes covers a period of six days, we will discuss the events of one day, such as the performance on the final day of thanksgiving.

Initially *gule wamkulu* was performed in conjunction with girls' initiation into womanhood,[3] and their incorporation into the adult society. The public dance could be attended only by women and other initiated girls and not men. Later on, *gule wamkulu* changed in scope and objective, so that today it plays a major role in both female and male initiation ceremonies. Other occasions of *gule wamkulu* performance include funeral ceremonies of a chief or any

80

other important member of the community; commemorative rites for the dead *(mpalo);* festive occasions such as independence and republic anniversary celebrations and political rallies.[4] In the performance, artistic talents are put into visible and audible form through songs and dramatic sketches, which are performed to entertain as well as to ridicule and satirize the behaviour of some members of the community.

The organization of *gule wamkulu* for public performance involves three groups, namely: the executive committee, the dancers and the audience-participants.

The executive committee comprises the village-headman who is *mwinimzinda* (patron), *chiwinda* or *wakunjira, tsabwalo* and tsang'oma.[5] The village-headman, as honorary owner of the *gule wamkulu* society, is vested with the powers of deciding when and where performances should take place. He also settles any disputes which arise during performances. *Chiwinda* or *wakunjira,* who is equivalent to a prime minister, is usually the patron's nephew, the likely heir according to the Chewa system of inheritance. *Wakunjira* has the duty to protect his dancer and the performance arena from bewitchment which may result from competition between actors, jealousy of either *enimizinda* or audience, or may just be the result of mere ill-feeling. He is further charged with the responsibility of maintaining the smooth running of the *gule wamkulu* performance by seeing to it that all the necessary preparations for the performance are ready at the *dambwe, liunde* and *bwalo* as well.[6] *Tsabwalo* is responsible for the dancing arena. He looks after the cleaning and clearing of the *bwalo* before the performance. If there is need for fencing the *bwalo,* he is also responsible for doing this. Furthermore, he liaises with *Chiwinda* as to where the *liunde* should be in relation to the *bwalo* and the *dambwe.* *Tsang'oma's* duties include collecting *ng'oma* (drums)—such as *mbalule* (ndewele), *mpanje, mbandambanda, gunda* and *mtiwiso*—for the performance; knowing the condition of each drum; and ensuring that the drummers receive the prizes due to them.

In a strictly conservative *gule wamkulu* society, all the main actors are male, although some of them dress themselves like women to depict the behaviour of women. However, in modified *gule wamkulu* societies, the performances include both women and men participants playing major roles. The performers wear masks

81

to conceal their identity and to imitate certain persons and animals. In their masks the actors are known as *virombo*—animals of the forest. These masqueraders are not supposed to expose their faces or any other means of identity in public. The identity of each actor is kept top secret. The actors are regarded as spirits of dead ancestors who have come back in the form of *gule wamkulu* to dwell temporarily among the living.

Each masquerader is given the name of the character or personality he signifies. They are usually divided into masks and animal structures in terms of their physical appearance. They may further be divided into groups according to the various dramatic roles they perform.

The first category is that in which man imitates animal. In this group, most of the animals represented are those which persist in the folklore of the Chewa communities. For example, in Chewa folklore, *Kalulu* the hare is the outrageous trickster hero, the counterpart of the fox in Indo-European folklore. Hence in *gule wamkulu* performance he is agile, cunning, small and four-legged. He is the curtain raiser so that he dispels any magical spells which might have been put on the arena. *Njobvu* the elephant is an imitation of the wild elephant which is enormously strong and is king of the animals of the jungle. As such, *Njobvu* appears only on special occasions as a symbol of power and authority. For instance, he will perform at the funeral ceremony of either *chiwinda* or *mwinimzinda*. He dances on the last day of *gule wamkulu* performance, and only during the daytime. Moreover, he leaves the dancing arena only after *mwinimzinda* has given him a cow. Other masqueraders which imitate the behaviour of animals are *mkango* (lion), *nkhwere* (baboon), *ng'ombe* (cow), and *nguluwe* (bush pig).

The second category of masqueraders comprises those which depict certain traits and characteristics of some individuals in the society. Such masquerades are, for example, *Kavinsabwe* (the lousy one), *Chadzunda* (the deaf man), *Mbiyazodooka* (broken pot), *Namalocha* (the woman who plaits her hair to beautify herself), *Chabwerakumanda* (the one who arose from the dead), and *Natola* (the one who picks up or steals anything left lying about in the village).

The audience-participants fall under the illusion that the actors are spirits of the ancestors which must be feared and revered. Thus the performers in this category freely sing and dramatize sketches

82

about the corrupt village chief and court counsellor: foolish husbands who are hen-pecked by their possessive wives; lazy or impotent husbands; the stupid and selfish chief who does not protect the interests of his people; the untidy and quarrelsome wife; the uncle who wants to bewitch his nephew; the bad father-in-law or mother-in-law; the good for nothing son-in-law. *Kamchaa* acts and sings songs which depict the behaviour of sexually loose women. While dancing in the arena, she leaves the arena and walks towards the audience to court a man. Then she moves to another group to pick a quarrel with the women. Thereafter, she comes back to the *bwalo* to continue dancing seductively to provoke the men. *Kavinsabwe* is an example of a masquerader who is supposed to teach the community cleanliness and personal hygiene routines. He wears dirty dress rags full of lice. He enters the *bwalo* while scratching his body and killing lice. *Kambulitso* characterizes the problems of women whose husbands are too lazy to work hard in the maize fields to realize bumper harvests. The masquerader looks very untidy, haggard and hungry, and does not dance but mimes by wandering from one place to another in the arena as if looking for some maize to roast or to fry.

In the third group are masqueraders who ridicule and satirize the habits, beliefs and behaviour of ethnic and professional groups such as early missionaries and Europeans. For example, there is *Simoni Petulo,* who is named after the apostle Simon Peter. There are also masqueraders depicting Joseph and the Virgin Mary known as *Yosefe* and *Maria.* In addition to these are *Mzungu,* the whiteman driving a car (*galimoto*). These characters are clothed in western dress. *Mjoni* is yet another actor who satirizes human vices and follies. He portrays behaviour similar to that of whites bossing labourers in the Rand mines of Johannesburg, thus the nickname *Mjoni.* Wearing a white-faced plastic mask, dressed in sack-cloth with a hood and a whip in his hand, *Mjoni* is harsh, cruel, churlish, brutal, crusty, rude and rough.[7]

As the various characters have different roles to play in the dance, music and drama, their actions contribute to the overall function of the performance. *Gule wamkulu* performance has a number of functions some of which are educational, psychological, social and aesthetic.

Educationally, the performance is instructive because the masqueraders are concerned with how to live and how to act in the society. The masks do not mean just what they are called and what actions they perform. Continued use of these characters in *gule wamkulu* has given them such prominence and individualism that they have become symbols of particular human behaviour whose parallels are obvious to the audience-participants. As a result, the performance is a medium through which, in a subtle and complex way, ideas of opposition to the normal world or of the distortion of accepted human and social values are expressed. The characters represent traits and personalities which people both recognize and fear, the vices they abhor, the follies they condemn, and the virtues they esteem.[8] At the same time, the animal structures are employed to record the society's environment and their experience of the fauna.

Psychologically, the performance is an outlet for the shadow part of the ego, the aspects of personality which the performers have been taught by the society to sublimate. They can sing about their darkest or suppressed desires and act them out while claiming that the protest or words are not theirs, but those of the characters in the performance.

A son-in-law, residing uxorilocally, may release his tension by indulging in obscene songs directed at attacking his father-in-law, who is the source of his emotional tensions. In normal circumstances, such behaviour by a son-in-law to his father-in-law would earn him a heavy fine, or even divorce. But the *gule wamkulu* performance offers a structural and socially legitimate means for the expression of such tensions, without resulting in disrupted social relationships within the family. This means of expression has sometimes proved very useful to some sons-in-law because their fathers-in-law have reduced their demands on them as *akamwini* (sons-in-law).

Furthermore, *gule wamkulu* performance gives licence to the performers and the audience-participants to behave outside the norm. Men can behave like children while children can behave like adults, and men can behave like women. Women may joke anyhow with men other than their husbands without blame. Such a relaxed and jocular atmosphere permits the actors and the audience-participants to gratify their egos and libidos which would have been suppressed under normal circumstances.

Apart from the above functions, *gule wamkulu* performance provides an opportunity for meeting old friends and making new acquaintances. Usually some friendships which have developed from *gule wamkulu* performance sessions have led to marriage. However, the performance is also a medium through which the actors display their various skills in singing, dancing and mimicking. In addition to that, the imaginative mind of various mask and animal structure craftsmen is presented to the audience for appreciation.

The time for holding *gule wamkulu* performances is determined by the agricultural cycle as well as national agricultural policies. Because one of the major objectives of the national agricultural development programme is for the country to be self-sufficient in food, the people are advised to hold performances in the dry season. At village level, the preference is also for the dry season because of a number of factors. As there is little or no work to be done in the fields, village life becomes monotonous and boring. Thus, *gule wamkulu* performances entertain the people as they relax after their hard agricultural work. Furthermore, the people have enough maize, some of which can be used to brew beer for the performance. The materials—for example, maize-cob leaves and dry grass—essential for the construction of masks and animal structures are available in abundance during the dry season. In addition, after the sale of their agricultural produce, the people have enough money to sponsor performances or to give as prizes to the performers of *gule wamkulu*.

Whenever there is to be a performance, the executive committee fixes the date for it. There is usually a period of four weeks before the performance day. This allows ample time for the composition of new songs which will contain current events and issues that are sources of gossip in the village and the revision of old songs to accommodate new dancing patterns and phrases that have become fashionable. Materials needed by the village artists for constructing masks and animal structures also have to be collected within this period. Drums have to be either tuned or made. Women have to collect firewood, to make maize malt and brew beer, which normally takes four days before it is ready for drinking. In addition to this, the women require time to decorate their houses before guests come to the performance. Guest performers also have sufficient time to make the necessary preparations.

As soon as the day for *gule wamkulu* performance has been announced, people excitedly begin to make preparations for the day.

85

At the *dambwe,* craftsmen are very busy making masks and animal structures. Since the construction and decoration of these masks and animal structures require materials such as the leaves of maize cobs, ashes, chicken feathers, rags, sack, fibre and banana leaves, this provides an opportunity for dramatic sketches performed by *Ajere* (masqueraders) who run about the village collecting materials.

While collecting materials in the villages, the *Ajere* entertain the public. They conceal their identity by wearing head-gear and a long beard made of the leaves of maize cobs. Round the middle of the body, the waist, the elbows and knees are fastened maize cob leaves, so that the entire body of the person is hidden. The masqueraders carry an axe in the hand. In most cases there are more than one, roaming about the village imitating elephant hunters. Their song is:

Yapita muno nyama ya alenje	The hunters' prey has passed here.
Nyama ya alenje yapita	The hunters' prey has gone
Yapita muno nyama ya alenje	The hunters' prey has passed here.
Ha, nyama, nyama, nyama!	Ah! we have got it now!
Bwenzi langa ha!	Ah! my good friend;
Ha, nyama, nyama, nyama!	Ah! buy my meat; buy my meat!

As the above song is sung, the *Ajere* act, in pantomime, the stalking, approach and hamstringing of an elephant and the selling of its meat.[9] They then carry the materials they have found to the *dambwe* for use.

On the other hand, the *akang 'wing 'wi,* one of the masqueraders who does not sing but just hums, escorts women to the forest to collect firewood for brewing beer. Apart from giving the women escort, the masquerader gives them the feel of the forthcoming performance. The *akang 'wing 'wi* plays the role of a lecherous man who is nevertheless conscious of the social norms of the society. Normally, two or even three of them find the women busy fetching firewood in the forest. They hum to announce their arrival. Then they try to court the women. The women shout at them to scare them away. At the *akang wing 'wi* withdrawal, the women provoke them by singing:

Eee eyaye chilombo msala!	Oh, what a lecherous animal!
Eee eyaye chilombo msala!	Oh, what a lecherous animal!
Bwera, bwera!	Do come, do come!
Bwera!	Do come!
Bwera, bwera!	Do come, do come!
Bwera!	Do come!
Nanga umadzachita	What did you want then,
Apo ubwerera, aye?	Since you are running away?
Eee eyaye chilombo msala!	Oh, what a lecherous animal!

On hearing the song, the akang 'wing 'wi go towards the women, and the women wriggle their hips and buttocks to tease them but they withdraw again without taking advantage of the women's provocation and challenge. This drama goes on and on until the women have had enough entertainment and company.

The *akang 'wing 'wi* and *Ajere* as heralds of the performance continue with their small plays within the main play which has not been put on yet. However, song composers and men well versed in dancing and drumming patterns also busy themselves. The songs composed might deal with any subject which excites the emotions and calls for a release in musical words. Nevertheless, they usually deal with the more intimate aspects of family life — affections and hatreds, and all the incidents which the people encounter in their daily experience.

They may talk about the wife who does not look after her husband's interest, the impotent husband, and the bad chief. After such songs have been composed and the composers have agreed on the dancing patterns, they now present the song for audition at the *dambwe*. The others may criticize a sentence here and a word there so that the song becomes acceptable for public consumption. After the audition, the composers teach the others the song and the dancing style that goes along with it. They decide on who should be singing the solo while the others take up the chorus.

The drummers introduce their drumming patterns; those specialized in hand-clapping also teach the others the appropriate hand-clapping patterns. Old songs are rehearsed so that everything is well polished and mastered for the performance.

There is more preparation to be done even on the day before the performance. *Tsabwalo* works on the *bwalo* and ensures that all is well. The *bwalo* is cleared, and positions are set for the actors, audience-participants, drummers, children, women and the elders of the village. On the other hand, *tsang'oma* ensures that all the essential drums are well tuned for the occasion, and that the drummers are in good spirits.

As it grows dark, guests from other areas come with their animal structures ready for the following day. Bonfires sparkle and glow in the village as the people warm themselves, praying that it should soon be daybreak. Then all of a sudden as a prelude, *Kwinimbira Kusacha, Nkhandwe* (jackal), and *Mkango* (lion), prowl in the corners of the village. The jackal barks, the lion with its hoarse voice makes terrible roars like *Konden Diara;*[10] and *Kwinimbira Kusacha*—a band of unmasked men covered with blankets, representing the passage of the spirit of ancestors like a cyclone through the village—sing:

Pilimbira, Pilimbira	Pilimbira, pilimbira
Pilimbira, kusachaye, yeyeye aye.	Pilimbira, let it not be dawn.
Pilimbira, pilimbira	Pilimbira, pilimbira
Pilimbira, kusachaye, yeyeye aye.	Pilimbira, let it not be dawn.
Madzi akadazala, madzi akadzala	When the pool is full
Mkaolokera poti yee?	How will you cross the pool?
Madzi akadzala mkaolokera	When the pool is full
Pa chala yee, eyaye ayee	Toes will be used to cross the pool.

The jackal, the lion and *pilimbira* fill the village with their mysterious barking, roaring and singing, respectively.

This stirs the people's anxiety and makes them more expectant, especially when the spirits pray that the night should be long. These harbingers of the performance prowl in the corners of the village, alternating for nearly the whole night. On the day of the performance the *bwalo* is set, ready for the dramatic experience. The *bwalo* is usually an open space which has a natural setting of grass, trees and houses as its background. Sometimes it is enclosed with a grass fence which limits the acting space. The actors and the audience-participants are on the same level, and this gives an opportunity for the actors to mix easily with the audience-participants as part of the performance. However, even without a physical fence, the audience-participants, actors, drummers, and elders are positioned and grouped in a way which determines the acting area, as illustrated below:

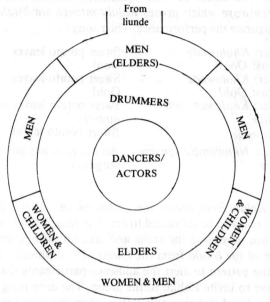

The elders, who are the living store-house of *gule wamkulu* performance customs, practices and belief systems, are positioned at the entrance of the *bwalo* from the *liunde*. They prompt the actors and inspect their costume before they appear to the audience. After them the drummers are lined up facing the audience. The area for the actors is right after the drummers. The audience-participants form a horse-shoe figure facing the drummers and the elders.

The audience-participants are composed of women, girls and boys. To complete the circle from each side of the horse-shoe between the elders and the women, are the men, who group themselves according to their social status in the *gule wamkulu* society.

Before the performance begins, the people chat with each other, looking forward to some great entertainment. They laugh, scream, shout, make body movements, sing, and so on. At the *liunde,* the performers eagerly wait for the performance to begin so that they may demonstrate their expertise, release their tensions, and experience a mental state different from that of their daily life.[11]

At the signal of *chiwinda,* who is the master of ceremonies, the performance opens with drumming and clapping. A procession of the elders of the village with their song becomes part of the opening formula. The elders in their every-day costumes solemnly sing *thungo/chiwoye* which invites *Kalulu mtengo wa bwalo* to come and inaugurate the performance. Their song is:

Leader: *Kholowade*	Sweet potato leaves
Chorus: *Ooh!*	Ooh!
Leader: *Kholowade*	Sweet potato leaves
Chorus: *Ooh!*	Ooh!
Leader: *Kholowade ndi mtambe*	Sweet potato leaves and *mtambe*
Kholowade	Sweet potato leaves
Chorus: *Nkhalamba yanyera mapira*	An old man has passed sorghum

Before *Kalulu* inaugurates the performance, all the performers must get ready to be requested to act. The song is sung two or three times, then they leave the arena and take up their positions at the entrance of the *bwalo* from the *liunde*. The drummers change the drumming pattern to alert the audience-participants that they will soon have to invite Kalulu to the arena. The drumming is accompanied by hand-clapping and rattles, then the song for Kalulu to perform his art fills the air:

Leader: *Kalulu mtengo wabwalo*	Kalulu, medicine of the arena
Bwandende, bwandende	Dispeller of evil spirits
Bwandende, bwandende	Dispeller of evil spirits
Chorus: *Kalulu mtengo wabwalo*	Kalulu, medicine of the arena

Kalulu, as agile as ever, enters the *bwalo* and dances swiftly for a short time. It does so just to get rid of any spells which might have been on the *bwalo* after *chiwinda* had visited it. Since his responsibility is to confirm that the *bwalo* is safe for others to come and perform, there is no need for him to dance up to the climax. As *Kalulu* leaves the floor, *chiwoko,* a huge and dignified animal structure which might be seventy-eight feet long and fifteen feet high, with as many as ten humps, slowly enters the *bwalo*. Boys ululate, run round the *bwalo* shaking rattles close to the ground and up in the air, while the audience-participants are busy clapping hands and singing the song for *chiwoko* to dance:

Leader: *Chimkokodeee!*	*Chimkoko, chimkoko*
Mwini wake bwalo aye!	The proprietor of the *bwalo*

Chorus: *Bwalo walanda*   He has reigned over the *bwalo*

The animal structure dances about the *bwalo* while the audience-participants make comments as to how marvellously or badly it is acting. Some of them make body movements to imitate it, and others keep on taking up the chorus and hand-clapping. The structure gives way to *visudzo* or *akapoli,* plaited *virombo.* These masqueraders are among those who perform more dramatic and humorous sketches because they sing songs about the events and issues that have been discussed and joked about by some people in the village. Because members of the audience know each other and are aware of the events which have been the source of much gossip in the village, and because the players know the audience, the sketches are meaningful and humorous to the actors and the audience. The *akapoli* sings songs of hate, love, hope, despair, joy and so on. As soon as the *akapoli* enter the *bwalo,* the audience's tension and excitement build up because they are anxious to listen to what current issues he is going to sing about. He hums a tune to the drummers, the lead drummer signals the tune, and the rest of the drummers join in the accompaniment. The women start clapping their hands in harmony with the drums, and *Kapoli* bursts out with his song:

Tengani mitala ndiomboke	Go and marry a second wife
Ndiomboke, ndiomboke iya;	I be liberated; I be liberated.
Ndiomboke, ndiomboke iya.	I be liberated; I be liberated.
Amuna wanji odya ngati nguluwe,	What a husband as greedy as a wild-pig
Mwandisinjitsa m'manja muwawa?	You make me pound maize when my palms hurt
Tengani mitala ndiomboke	Go and marry a second wife, I be free.
Ndiomboke, ndiomboke iya.	I be free, I be free.

Kapoli begins to dance by paddling with the left leg, then the right one. The dancing builds up slowly and warms up to the required climax. The drummers play the drums with their palms, but one sees from their head and body movements and facial expressions that they are part of the song and the performance too. The audience-participants wear beaming faces; and they imitate the continuous elastic and plastic body movements of the *Kapoli,* as they take up the chorus and clap their hands.

Some of them talk to each other, indicating that the song refers to so and so who is among the crowd. They point at him and laugh as the performance goes on. The *Kapoli* acts the role of the woman complaining in the song. He moves towards the audience-participants, bends slightly towards them, claps his hands and puts them behind his back as the women jubilantly join him in singing the song melodiously. He shakes his head as the woman's gesture of making a plea to her husband to let her be free. He dances with a lot of elasticity and plasticity, and a cloud of dust rises up. The dancing, clapping of hands, singing, drumming, rising dust and acting, mix harmoniously to reach the climax of the situation.

People who have been impressed with the performance fish out money from their pockets, enter the acting area, and give coins to the *Kapoli*. The performance by *Kapoli* has its aesthetics and meaning for a number of reasons. The audience already knows the song as it might have been sung before to depict a similar situation. The rhythmic clapping of the hands; the rhythmic body movements which correspond to the drumming; the melodious singing; the language; the facial expressions to show sadness and joy; the costume of the actors: all these blend to contribute to the beauty and the semantic content of the song and the performance. In the song, the basic message is that the wife would like her husband to marry a second wife because she is tired of cooking for him, since he is "as greedy as a wild pig". But the audience knows that the song says more than the language would mean in day to day conversation. At a deeper level, they understand that the woman's husband is so lecherous that his wife does not rest at all, even when she is unwell. Figuratively the husband is compared to a greedy wild pig.

The chorus of the song enables the audience to participate actively in the performance. At the same time, there is repetition of some lines which contributes to the rhythm and substance of the song and the performance.

After such a dramatic sketch, the *Kapoli* introduces another sketch. This time it might be one which depicts a woman who quarrels with her husband because he comes home late from beer parties. Thus the song:

Leader: *Chimbiri, chimbiri;*   Rumour, rumour;
        Chimbiri, chimbiri;   Rumour, rumour;
        Chimbiri, chawanda;   Rumour has spread.
Chorus: *Chingawande;*

Ena atukwana akazi	Some husbands insult wives
Pochoka ku, mowa,	When they are drunk;
Ine ntukwana khoswe	I rebuke the rat
wanga	
Wandyera lichero.	That gnawed my winnowing basket
Chimbiri chawanda.	Rumour has spread.

The audience-participants intensify their clapping of hands and singing of the chorus as *Kapoli* displays his art. He responds to the rhythm of the song, the language of the drums, and the clapping of the hands. Under emotion the dancer performs as if his body is elastic and supple. He moves his hands, legs, head, body, shoulders and neck in unison with the magical powers of the drum, ululating, music and hand-clapping as the performance reaches its peak. Among the audience-participants, the atmosphere is also emotional and jubilant. As they sing the song, they address each other so that there are smaller dramatic sketches. When the song talks about husbands who insult wives, the women project their voices to the men. When the part that talks about women comes, the men address the women. But at the same time, women address each other as some men address each other too when the appropriate reference is being sung. The *Kapoli*, as well as the audience-participants, temporarily lives in a world of ecstasy. Then the master of ceremonies, *Chiwinda,* announces, *Kwawo gule, kwawo,* (Let the dancer retire). The performer returns to the *liunde* for *nyolonyo* to enter the *bwalo*.

The drumming for *Kapoli* fades and, as *nyolonyo* enters the *bwalo*, there is a new drumming pattern to suit the new sketch which is about to start. The pair of *nyolonyo* enters the *bwalo* in the spirit of competition. They would like to perform better than the *Kapoli* which has just left the *bwalo*. They walk towards the drummers, hum a tune, listen to the language of the drums and certify that that's the rhythmic pattern they would like to dance to. If the drums are played out of tune, the *nyolonyo* just shake their heads as a gesture of disapproval. On the other hand, the audience-participants clap hands as an accompaniment to the drums. Then the *nyolonyo* start their sketch with the song:

Leader:	*Yoyo, yoyo!*	Please, please
	Yoyo, yoyo!	Please, please
Chorus:	*Icho chilombo*	That's an animal.
	Yoyo, yoyo	Please, please

93

Chorus: *Icho chirombo*   That's an animal.
Leader: *Amuna anga*   My husband
       Gulani wailesi   Buy me a radio
       Ndziyimbaye;   To listen to
       Ndiyese mwana   Instead of a child
       Mukachoka   While you're away.

The song depicts a woman who is childless and whose husband is going away to work. She implores him that since she is childless, he should purchase a radio to keep her company. The *nyolonyo* sing the song solemnly and sorrowfully to portray the sad mood of the woman in the picture. They sit down facing each other so that the audience sees the family situation. One of them acts as if imploring the husband to buy the radio so that she is not left desolate. They stand up and start to dance. The beginning is slow but the pace builds up to the climax in accord with the drums and the way the audience-participants respond to the performance. The dancers dance competitively so that dust rises up as the drummers sweat, and the men and women laugh at each other. The men blame the women, saying they are the ones who are barren and that's why they can't have a child in the family. The women counter that they have proved their fertility somewhere, somehow, and so on and so forth. The performance of the *nyolonyo* hypnotizes the audience so that they also act the situation which the *nyolonyo* are singing. Those who have been greatly impressed pour praises on *nyolonyo* and give prizes. If someone is impressed by one of the drummers, he too gives money to the drummer. After the *nyolonyo* have acted for some time, the *chiwinda* requests them to leave the *bwalo* for the *liunde* so that other masqueraders such as *Sajeni/Makanja, Chadzunda, Namalocha* and *Kavinsabwe* may perform too.

When *Namalocha* enters the *bwalo*, the character is dressed like a woman and performs a sketch which depicts a woman who complains that her husband does not buy her enough clothes. She is dressed poorly so that the message is driven home even by just looking at the costume. The song she sings is:

Leader: *Adandigulira kopere-*   He bought a small piece of
       wera   cloth
       Kosatha usiwa toto.   That does not cover me
                       enough

Chorus: *Kuopa ntchito*   He dislikes working
Leader: *Adandigulira kopere-*   He bought a small piece of
       wera   cloth

	Kosatha usiwa toto.	That does not cover me enough
Chorus:	*Kuopa ntchito.*	He dislikes working.
Leader:	*Ulekeranji usapita, kwa Namkumba*[12]	Why don't you go to Namkumba
	Ukaone kubvala kwa mitundu-mitundu:	To see how people dress?
	Kubvala kwa mitundu mitundu:	There are fashions:
	Pitikoti mkati,	A petticoat inside,
	Andiloko n'malaya,	A top and a skirt.
	Andigulira koperewera toto.	He bought a small piece of cloth
	Kosatha usiwa toto,	That does not cover me enough.
	Kuopa ntchito abambowa.	This man dislikes working.

After the masquerader has sung the last part of the song, the audience takes it up as chorus. They also clap hands as the drummers display their drumming skill. The dancer acts as he dances, so that the picture of the woman in the song is vividly conveyed.

The audience, especially the women, hold their *zirundu* and complain that they are not long enough to cover their knees because their husbands are too lazy to work to and find money to buy them enough cloth. They also use gestures to show the various types of clothes which women in other villages such as Namkumba wear. To make the song more meaningful, the performers mention the names of villages which the audience knows. After all the masqueraders have performed, the finale is when *Mbiyazodooka* (beer pot with holes) enters the *bwalo* carrying on his head a leaking broken pot in which there are stinking things that attract flies. One hand supports the pot while the other holds a leafy twig for driving away flies. *Mbiyazodooka* has a major role to play in *gule wamkulu* performances because he gives a final picture of the performance. In addition to that, because the masks and animal structures are symbolically spirits which have come from the grave-yard to live temporarily with men, it is their time to return to the graveyard, their abode. The stinking pot is the symbol of a corpse which must be buried in the grave. Thus the song:

Leader:	*Mbiyazodooka*	Mbiyazodooka
	Tiye kwanu,	Do go back home,
Chorus:	*Kwanu n'kumanda,*	Your home is the grave-yard

Leader: *Mbiyazodooka,*   *Mbiyazodooka*
     Tiye kwanu   Do go back home
     Kwanu n'kumanda Your home is the grave-yard.
     Mbiyazodooka   *Mbiyazodooka.*
     Bwerera
     Tiye kwanu;   Do go back home
     Kwanu n'kumanda Your home is the grave-yard,
     Mbiyazodooka.   *Mbiyazodooka.*

On hearing the song the audience-participants know that the *gule wamkulu* performance will soon end as *Mbiyazodooka* has come to invite the spirits. The drummers increase their drumming and the clapping of the hands becomes heavier as this is the last stage of the performance. This also means that the life which the audience and the performers temporarily led is going to end; they will enter the daily world which has social norms, taboos, practices and customs.

The performace is closed with the master of ceremony's announcement: *Kwawo, kwawo gule!* (Let the *gule* retire). *Mbiyazodooka* leaves the *bwalo* and that marks the end of the performance which is a composition of spontaneous, planned and improvised sketches. These sketches might occasionally be linked by a common theme, but they are mostly dramatic units on a variety of themes within a single integrated dramatic performance.

The foregoing discussion has shown that *gule wamkulu* performance is an art form in which social crises of daily life are dramatized in a blend of music, dance, language, movement and rhythm. The meaning of the words and sketches depends upon how artistically they are conveyed by the performer; how well the audience-participants are acquainted with the events or issues referred to; and the significance of the gestures made by the performers. Furthermore, the discussion has shown that *gule wamkulu* performance relies on group co-operation. There has to be good coordination between song composers, drummers, dancers, and those who make the masks and animal structures. The dancers are central to the performance but the audience is an integral part of the performance too.

We have also seen that *gule wamkulu* performance is functional in that the performers and the audience-participants find means of expressing their suppressed desires which can legitimately be released in the world of *gule wamkulu* performance. Moreover, the performance is good entertainment and an occasion for meeting old friends and making new ones.

The performance has its messages as well as its aesthetics which can be learned through the songs, the language of the drums, the clapping of hands; the characterization and the elastic and plastic body movements of the actors; the participation of the audience and their imitation of the masqueraders; and the ululating, the rattles and songs which accompany these dramatic aspects.

NOTES

1. W. H. J. Rangeley, "Nzau in Nkhota-Kota District" *The Nyasaland Journal* 2, No. 2 (1949) pp. 35-49

2. M. J. Schoffeleers, "Social and Symbolic Aspects of Spirit Worship among the Mang'anja" D. Phil. thesis, Univ. of Oxford, 1968.

3. W.V. Brelsford, "African Dances of Northern Rhodesia" *Rhodes-Livingstone Museum* No. 2 (Livingstone, 1948), p. 3.

4. "Gule Wamkulu" *STAR*, April 1976, p. 9.

5. The executive committee also incorporates *namkungwi* (chief instructress) when the performance is for the initiation ceremony of girls.

6. *Dambwe* is a place where the *gule wamkulu* members meet for rehearsals and the construction of masks and animal structures. The most preferred place for a *dambwe* is a grave-yard because it is naturally thick with bush and trees. Thus, the structures and masks can easily be hidden from non-members. The *liunde* is a dressing-room near the *bwalo*. There the masqueraders polish up the costumes and put them on for the performance. The *bwalo* is the performance area which is an open-air space in the village.

7. The masquerader is an invention based on the people's experiences in the mines of South African when working there as migrant labourers. The masks are bought in Johannesburg and are incorporated into the locally made masks.

8. A.M. Dale, and E.W. Smith, *The Ila-speaking People of Northern Rhodesia* (London: Macmillan 1920), Vol. 2, p. 21.

9. Rangeley, pp. 20-21.

10. See Camera Laye, *The African Child* (London: Collins, 1969), pp. 82-85.

11. W.V. Brelsford, p. 3.

12. The performers mentioned Namkumba, an area which was closest to the place of the singers of this song when I was doing my research.

Part Two

From Performance to Print

Formulae in Mandinka Epic:
The Problem of Translation

Gordon Innes

THIS paper is concerned with the Mandinka oral epics which are performed in Gambia by professional bards and which celebrate the careers of heroic figures in Mandinka history. The bards' repertoire falls into two parts: first is the Sunjata epic, which celebrates the career of Sunjata Keita, reputed founder of the Mali Empire in the 13th century; second are epics concerned with the careers of warriors who established local hegemonies along the Gambia valley in the latter part of the 19th century. There appear to be no accounts relating to events in the six hundred years which separate Sunjata from the 19th century figures, but it seems reasonable to suppose that there has been a continuous epic tradition over several centuries but that with the passage of time, heroes disappear over the horizon of memory, with the single exception of Sunjata.

The Sunjata epic differs from accounts of the 19th century heroes not only in respect of time—it is much older—but also in respect of geographical distribution—it is much more widespread. The Sunjata epic is the common property of all the Manding people, dispersed over an enormous area of West Africa, and there are grounds for thinking that the Sunjata epic has been a factor in maintaining the cultural homogeneity of the Manding people. Bards are generally great travellers and it is common for a Gambian bard to have plied his craft in Senegal, Mali, Guinea.

The Sunjata epic occupies a unique place in the corpus of Mandinka oral literature; it is by far the most highly valued item of oral literature which the Mandinka possess. Though it is similar to other epics dealing with the careers of great warriors, it is sharply distinguished from them by the very special place which Sunjata occupies in the hearts of the Mandinka and of all Manding people. He is a hero of such tremendous stature as to be a different kind from other Manding heroes: he is much more than just a great warrior, more even than the man who established the Mali Empire; Sunjata is also a cultural hero–it was he who established the network of social relationships found in Mandinka society, and who established the norms of social behaviour. For the Mandinka, as for the Manding generally, it is Sunjata who gave them their glorious past and their soical institutions, and they have therefore a stronger emotional set toward the Sunjata epic than they have toward other items of their oral literature. It is some aspects of this emotional set that I wish to touch upon briefly here.

First, however, I would like to say just a word on the form of the Sunjata epic; but to do this is not as straightforward as it might appear. Though I have talked about the Sunjata epic, it is not at all clear just what this means. What is the Sunjata epic? There is in fact no entity to which I can point and say 'This is the Sunjata epic'. As with oral literature generally, there is no Sunjata epic in the sense of a particular piece of literature which may be repeated in substantially the same form. One bard's account of Sunjata's life may differ markedly from that of another bard both in form and in content; we may speak of all such accounts as versions of the Sunjata epic, but there is no authoritative version, no one version to which one can point and say, 'This is the Sunjata epic.' Perhaps the Sunjata epic is ultimately just the knowledge of the story, of many literary motifs and formulae stored up somewhere inside the bards' heads, together with a technique for giving this knowledge verbal expression; a valid performance of the Sunjata epic is a performance which is accepted as such by listeners who are themselves well-versed in the Sunjata epic.

To enable him to give the Sunjata epic verbal expression, a bard has at his disposal three styles or modes, of vocalization, which I call the speech mode, the recitation mode, and the song mode. Of these, the speech mode is closest to ordinary speech, the song mode is self-explanatory, the recitation mode may be said very roughly to be somewhere intermediate between the other two. In the versions of the Sunjata epic which I have collected, the great bulk of each one is in the speech mode; this is the mode in which the story is told. The song mode, rather naturally, is used for songs; it was the custom for a hero to have a song or songs composed in his honour, usually referring to some highlight in his career. The hero's song appears to have been an important part of the hero's equipment, and, like his praises, it both exalted and identified him. The recitation mode usually occurs with praises and also with fixed phrases of a somewhat philosophical kind, such as those expressing the thought that we know the past and the present, but not the future, or that no man can escape death when his time has come.

Though there is a correlation between certain modes of vocalization and certain kinds of content, this is not a one-to-one correlation, except in the case of songs, which are always in the song mode. But praises, for example, though usually in the recitation mode, are commonly found in the speech mode. The mix of the modes in any particular performance is a matter for the bard himself to decide.

I have sketched very briefly some of the main features of Mandinka epic; it remains to say a word about the other term in the title of this paper, viz. formulae. The term 'formulae' in relation to oral epic inevitably brings to mind Lord's *Singer of Tales,* and it is important to make clear here that I am not using the term 'formula' as defined by Lord. I use it to refer to a fixed form of words which are used in particular circumstances, in the sense in which we speak of greeting formulae such as 'How do you do?' in ordinary conversation and of opening and closing formulae in tales. Mandinka oral epic is a free-phrase genre with short fixed-phrase passages scattered throughout it; it is to certain of those fixed-phrase passages, here called 'formulae', that I direct attention.

The language of Mandinka oral epic is essentially everyday Gambian Mandinka, except for some formulae and for a few obsolete words; but the latter do not appear to be used with the deliberate aim of achieving any poetic or literary effect: they are simply words which have fallen out of use because the objects which they denote, such as certain kinds of weapons, are no longer in use. In English we tend to associate poetry about a heroic age with a special 'elevated' variety of English, but in Mandinka there is no special 'elevated' language. The careers of Sunjata and of the more recent heroes are described in the sort of language that a man might use to recount some personal experience. There is also in Mandinka an extreme paucity of two other features which listeners acquainted with heroic poetry in European literatures might expect—imagery and description. Both are almost non-existent; there is virtually no description of any kind—we are told nothing of the appearance of the heroes, of how they were clad or armed, no description of their horses, their buildings, their food or any other aspect of the world in which they moved. By chance, I happened to have read Hatto's translations of the Song of Nibelung while I was working on some Mandinka texts, and the contrast was most striking. The German poet, you will recall, is constantly telling us of the outstanding beauty of the women, of the richness of their gowns, of the magnificence of the warriors' arms, of the vast quantities of gold. There is nothing of this in the Mandinka narratives. The almost total absence of description is of course a feature of all Mandinka oral literature. This austere style in which the narration is pared to the bone, in which the sequence of events is recorded in the briefest and starkest terms, might be thought liable to produce a rather bleak effect; it is scarcely a style which one would expect to arouse much of an emotional response in the listener, and yet a narration by a Mandinka bard can be a deeply moving experience for a Mandinka audience. This seems a somewhat paradoxical situation—whence arises the affective power of the narrative? The emotional aspect of oral epic forced itself upon my attention in the course of my translation of several texts; put rather crudely, the translation could be expected to have little emotional impact on an English reader, and yet those texts, in the original Mandinka, obviously had a powerful emotional impact on the Mandinka listeners.

A bard's performance is a complex artistic creation and it would be difficult to determine what factors in the total performance combine to produce the audience reaction, but it seems to me that there are at least four aspects of a bard's performance which we would need to consider relevant here. These are the content, the language, the modes of vocalization, and the musical accompaniment. Here I confine myself to a brief look at only one of these, namely the language, but before leaving the others, perhaps I could just say a word about them. The content is of course such as to stir most Mandinka listeners; not only are the narratives about great warriors, they are about great *Mandinka* warriors, indeed about men with whom many members of any audience may well claim kinship. Many a member of an audience may well be able to identify rather closely with the hero, to feel himself and his family share some of the hero's glory, to feel himself grow in stature as he hears of the hero's exploits. The musical aspect of a bard's performance is of the greatest importance, and it is not because of any lack of awareness of the importance of the musical component that I leave it out of account here, but merely because I have no competence in this field. I need hardly mention the obvious fact that words can be given an enormously enhanced emotional impact by being set to music. We are all familiar with the frenzied reactions of many teenagers at pop concerts, where lyrics of the greatest triviality are put over so successfully by means of a particular vocal style, accompanied by ear-splitting music.

Turning now to the linguistic aspect of a bard's performance, I have already mentioned that the language is essentially everyday Mandinka and that the style is straightforward, with almost no imagery or description. This may sound rather unexciting, but what, in my view, saves it from dullness and gives it liveliness and also imbues it with a certain heroic aura is (a) direct speech, and (b) formulae, mainly praises and songs. Direct speech brings the narrative alive, gives it much greater immediacy and impact, and a skilled bard can exploit to great effect the dramatic potential of dialogue, which commonly makes up half or more of the whole narration. Mandinka historical narratives are not mere chronicles of events; they are accounts—always favourable accounts—of the career of a particular hero. The focus of interest is the hero. The interest of a Mandinka audience is in the personality of the hero, in the relationships between the hero and his supporters, his rivals, his opponents. And this is just what direct speech brings out; for direct speech, from its very nature, occurs in the context of an interpersonal relationship. Direct speech in the narratives occurs most commonly in situations of conflict, where the hero is in disagreement with colleagues or where he confronts an enemy. The bard's account of the hero's career is episodic; he vividly re-creates by means of dialogue certain crucial incidents, and he links these together to form a coherent account. We are told nothing directly about the personality of the hero; we can only infer what manner of man he was from what he says and does in a variety of situations.

The second linguistic device which I wish to discuss briefly is the use of formulae, and this brings me to the main topic of this paper. The great bulk of an oral epic is delivered in the speech mode and in free-form, that is, the bard gives the account in his own words. Interspersed throughout this free-form narrative, however, are certain formulae, notably the songs associated with the hero, and, more commonly, the hero's praises. As is common in Africa, the words of each line of the hero's praises are fixed, but there is some flexibility in the ordering of the lines relative to each other. As well as occurring from time to time throughout a performance, formulae occur at the beginning, usually in heavy concentration. This is the part of a bard's narrative which I call the prelude, and it consists usually of praises of the hero of the forthcoming performance or of associated heroes, perhaps with the hero's song, and perhaps with a few general observation on life, and perhaps with an allusion to the bard's patrons. Usually the whole of the prelude consists of formulae strung together and uttered in the recitation or song mode. The purpose of the prelude seems to be to provide a transition from the everyday world in which the listeners are situated to the heroic world into which they are to be transported by the bard. The prelude creates the appropriate atmosphere for the forthcoming narrative; it arouses in the audience the appropriate emotional set toward the epic.

The formulae with the greatest emotional impact on the audience are the praises of the heroes. As is common throughout Africa, a Mandinka hero's praises are in terms of (a) his ancestry, and (b) his personal achievements or characteristic. In some cases, a hero's praises are entirely in terms of his forebears, though this is not common. For example, in a recording of the Sunjata epic by one of Gambia's finest bards, the praises of one of Sunjata's generals consists of four lines made up entirely of personal names. We must assume that these are the names of great ancestors of the general in question, though as far as I have been able to discover, nothing is known about them. A list of personal names might not seem very exciting, especially when the listener knows nothing about the bearers of these names, yet such lists do have an emotional impact for a Mandinka audience. A member of the Kamara family, for example, could hardly fail to feel a stirring of family pride as he listens to the names:

> Foobali Dumbe Kamara,
> Makhang Koto Kamara,
> Jukuma Makhang Kamara, Baliya Kamara,
> Makhang Nyaame Kamara.[1]

This string of names comprises the praises of a Kamara who rallied to Sunjata's call to arms against Sumanguru.

Praise names based on some outstanding event in the hero's career are also often obscure. Such names commonly allude rather obliquely to an incident, and in the process of time the particular incident becomes forgotten and the meaning of the praise name becomes obscure. A further factor leading to obscurity is that the Sunjata epic presumably originated far to the east of Gambia, in a variety of the Manding language different from that of present-day Gambian Mandinka. Though the free-form parts of the epic are told in Mandinka, there are not uncommonly in the formulae certain words and phrases which are not Gambian Mandinka and which the bards invariably explain as the language spoken to the east. Sometimes bards can explain praises which are unintelligible to their listeners, but often when a bard is asked to explain a praise name, he will reply simply that it is a praise name. I believe that in these cases the bard is not deliberately withholding information, but is simply stating a fact. He had learnt such phrases as part of his stock in trade and his listeners likewise had been familiar with them from infancy, and the precise meaning of them was not something that anyone was concerned with. Though such phrases would appear to have no meaning, they are nevertheless of great importance for the narratives in which they occur. By and large, the meaning of praise names is not of great importance: praise names have little cognitive function, but they have an extremely important affective function. It is the praise names above all else which elevate the epic far above a mere recital of events. It is the repetition of the praise names which stirs the blood and makes the listener swell with pride.

From an examination of the occurrence of praise names in some of the texts which I have collected it is clear that one important use of praise is to mark points in the narrative which describe outstanding events in the hero's career which reflect his heroic stature. The bard seems to be using formulae and the recitation mode to elevate the performance at such climactic points beyond the resources of ordinary language. In this usage, praises are almost like an exclamation of admiration and wonder following the description of some outstanding incident in the hero's career.

I have recently been translating several oral epics and I have become increasingly aware that although it is possible to translate the narrative part—the account of events—reasonably satisfactorily, I am failing to convey to the English reader the emotive force of the formulae. Annotation can go some way towards helping the reader to understand why certain formulae have powerful emotional overtones for a Mandinka listener, but it cannot enable the reader to share the Mandinka listener's response. It would of course be unrealistic to expect of any translation that it should evoke in a foreign reader the same response as that of a reader belonging to the culture—especially is this true in the case of epic, with its strong historical and cultural resonances. I would certainly not expect non-Scots to share my emotional response to place names such as Glencoe, Culloden, Bannockburn, or to praise-names such as Cock o' the North or the Wolf of Badenoch.

As far as the linguistic aspect of oral epic is concerned, it is the formulae and especially the praise names (including genealogies) which give the epic its heroic aura and which have such powerful emotional force; for the reader of an English translation, however, the emotion most likely to be stirred by these formulae is boredom or irritation. In my own translation work I have often felt that in trying to discover the meaning of an obscure praise name I was concentrating on the aspect of the praise name which is of least importance for the Mandinka listener. As far some of the obscurer praise names are concerned, I am inclined to doubt if much—indeed, anything—is to be gained from translating them. If I take a Mandinka praise name whose literal meaning is largely irrelevant but which has acquired profound emotional significance for Mandinka listeners and I turn this into some sort of English, it seems to me that I have confined myself to what is perhaps the least important aspect of the Mandinka phrase and have left out of account what it is that really matters, namely the emotional impact of the phrase. I can illustrate the sort of thing I have in mind with the line *Nyankumolu khaba la*[2] which occurs as part of Sunjata's praises and which recurs frequently in a performance of the Sunjata epic recorded for me by Banna Kanute, one of Gambia's leading bards. For the great majority of Mandinka listeners, the meaning of this phrase is obscure; it has lexical and phonological features which distinguish it from Gambian Mandinka, so it has a rather mysterious and exotic flavour. The bard explained to me that the phrase refers to an incident in Sunjata's life when he was left in extreme poverty after the death of his father; he had nothing to give to the bards whom he had inherited from his father, so he went off and seized a cat and brought it back slung over his shoulder to give to them. I have translated the phrase as 'Cats on the shoulder', but even with the explanation, the English phrase is flat and sounds far from heroic, conveying absolutely nothing of the emotional force of the Mandinka phrase. I think that it is open to doubt whether anything of importance is gained by translating *Nyankumolu khaba la,* and whether it might not be better to leave it untranslated, with a footnote giving the translation and the bard's explanation. At least that would avoid the risk of bathos, but it would do nothing to convey to the reader the affective value of the Mandinka phrase, except perhaps its obscurity.

I do not believe that any translation, however felicitous, of Mandinka praise names can convey their emotive power and the heroic aura which they give to the epic, since they are generally allusive, obscure and genealogical. The question which I should like to put to the reader is whether we should try to convey to English readers something of the heroic aura by our translation of the epic as a whole, bearing in mind that the great bulk of it is in everyday Gambian Mandinka. John Johnson seems to be attempting to do this in his recent translation of the Sunjata epic from Mali;[3] he relies for poetic effect on such stylistic devices as inversion (e.g. 'it will next Friday be'), past tense with 'did' (e.g. 'and to us they did give it') and a liberal sprinkling of the text with o'er, where'er ne'er, 'gainst, twill (*sic*), 'tis. Though Johnson's translation generally reads well, it strikes as not altogether successful; the stylistic devices which he exploits for poetic purposes irritate after a while.

Also to be considered here is the strategy adopted by Niane in his highly successful translation.[4] Though cast in the form of a performance by an old bard, Niane's text seems to be a literary recreation of the Sunjata epic, based on Niane's profound knowledge of the epic tradition, rather than the translation of one particular text. Such a procedure would be deplored by folklorists, who demand the text as it issued from the lips of the performer. On the other hand, Niane's book has been extremely successful and is probably better known, especially among non-specialists, than any other version of the Sunjata epic. His translation has a dignified and slightly elevated tone which distinguishes it from everyday speech, without straining for literary effect. It seems to me to succeed in the difficult aim of conveying to the reader something of the feeling of a bard's performance. In a similar way, Birago Diop's literary recreation of Wolof tales[5] succeeds admirably in catching the tone of a story-telling session.

This paper arises from my work on translating Mandinka epic

and in particular from my realization that the resultant English texts, aiming at a close and faithful translation of the Mandinka, convey little, if anything, of the emotional overtones of the original. A translation which is as close as practicable to the original, with copious notes, is no doubt appropriate for publications aimed at a mainly academic readership, and aimed also, if sometimes unconsciously, at establishing African oral literature as a field of serious academic study. That this second aim has been achieved cannot be doubted. Our aim must now surely be to secure for the best in the oral literature of Africa its rightful place in world literature, and the appropriate strategy for achieving this aim seems to me less clear. I suggest that this is a question which deserves further consideration.

NOTES

1. See Gordon Innes (ed.), *Sunjata: Three Mandinka Versions* (London: School of Oriental and African Studies, 1974), p. 64 (lines 530-33).
2. See *Sunjata,* p. 149 (line 119), and passim.
3. John W. Johnson et al. (eds.) *The Epic of Sun-Jata According to Magan Sisoko* (Bloomington: Folklore Publications Group, Indiana University, 1979).
4. D. T. Niane *Sundiata: An Epic of Old Mali,* trans. G. D. Pickett (London: Longmans Green, 1965).
5. Birago Diop, *The Tales of Amadou Koumba* (London: Oxford University Press, 1965).

Towards a Faithful Record: On Transcribing and Translating the Oral Narrative Performance

Isidore Okpewho

IT SEEMS ONLY FAIR that, as greater interest is taken by scholars in the aesthetic and other qualities of oral literature, there is an equally increasing obligation on editors of oral literary texts to represent them with due propriety. This propriety implies that, since part of the business of the oral literary scholar seems to be to establish the peculiar poetics of this genre of literature (understandably, as against that of written literature), a considerable amount of care should be given to highlighting some of the things that add up to its uniqueness. Perhaps it should be stressed that, as editors of oral texts, we have undertaken a by no means easy responsiblility of reconciling two media of cultural expression, and that we owe at least to the culture from which we have taken something, the duty not to violate our charge, but to accord it as much of its integrity as the host culture will allow. For the oral culture *does* have some integrity, and even those who, like Ruth Finnegan, question the validity of a demarcation between oral and literate poetics[1] do concede that the circumstances of the delivery of oral literature deserve careful attention. Perhaps the best we can do at this stage is to represent as much of these circumstances as possible in the hope that they can tell us how seriously we should pursue the quest for a separate oral poetics.

Before we go into some of the general statements that may be made about the transcription of the text into the original African language, let us first make some general observations about the translation of the text into a language like English in which (fortunately or unfortunately) the text claims wider readership. Within the last few decades we have seen the publication of texts of

African oral narratives in translations that reveal various shades of loyalty to the original material both in linguistic and contextural terms. A brief review of some of the works will show how much care needs to be taken if we must do justice to whatever virtues we may recognize in the oral art.

On Translation

In terms of language, we will recall that most earlier collectors/editors of African oral narratives or folktales had·far less interest in the fine details of the form than in the outlook revealed by their texts. As comparative ethnologists - concerned, that is, with how the world of the "primitive" compared with that of "civilized" man— they put almost total emphasis on units of thought and culture to the exclusion of the aesthetic substratum of the text. There is perhaps no greater articulation of their programme than in the statement which Lévi-Strauss made in the mid-fifties from his observation of Amerindian mythology: "Myth is the part of language where the formula *traduttore, tradittore* reaches its lowest truth value. From that point of view . . . . the mythical value of the myth is preserved even through the worst translation. Whatever our ignorance of the language and the culture of the people where it originated, a myth is still felt as a myth by any reader anywhere in the world. Its substance does not lie in its style, its original music, or its syntax, but in the *story* which it tells."[2] If it is the message and not the medium that counts, then all that is needed is a purely functional translation—sometimes even in summary fashion—which gives us a working distillate of the message. We need only turn to collections of African folktales such as by Robert Rattray from the Ashanti or Henri Junod from the Thonga for representative samples of the functional translation.

A greater concern, however, for the quality of the indigenous expression and culture invites a certain amount of care in translation, and here it will be interesting to observe a variety of techniques among more recent editors. At one extreme we have an editor like Daniel Biebuyck who, in his two collected translations so far of oral epics from the Banyanga of Zaire,[3] has chosen to be so close to the original as to be somewhat tasteless, only volunteering in his overloaded footnotes to explain what he thinks the original is trying to say. Hardly could Dryden, who identified "metaphrase, or turning an author word by word, line by line, from one language to another"[4] as the first of three stages of translation, have conceived of that level of tastelessness whereby Biebuyck has "Where is it close?" for the Nyanga original, meaning "where are you going?" *(Hero and Chief, p. 269).*

At the other extreme, however, we have those who are so enthused by what they judge to be the poetic quality of African heroic narratives, that they are inclined to dress them in the diction of classic European poetry. For all the usefulness of John William Johnson's recent edition of the Sunjata epic, one must beware of the overzealousness into which Johnson frequently falls with phrases like "the one whose knife into it fits", "it will next Friday be", "and to us they did give it", etc.[5] Such mannered translations can only arouse, in the mind of an intelligent reader, uneasy echoes of a dated style and a sense of disalignment rather than of fitness. However long these stories of Sunjata have been around, they appeal to contemporary audiences largely because they are recreated in a language that is understood by them and even with references to incidents and locales that are part of the present-day environment.

In between these two extremes we have various degrees of caution. I must confess that, despite my ignorance of the various Manding dialects from which they have worked, the translations of *Kambili* by Charles Bird and *Sunjata* by Gordon Innes[6] strike me as two of the most level-headed I have read so far. I leave it, of course, to native Manding and other experts to say how well these men understand the language(s) which they have turned into English. But I applaud their efforts because as "outsiders", they have donned the cloak of humility rather than of presumption in their dealings with a foreign language. If they have indeed adhered to the programme that they each announced in their introductions, they have stayed safely within the borders of an enterprise that recognizes, on the one hand, that these epics are narrated primarily in the everyday language of the people and, on the other, that "all translations are at best only impressionistic approximates of the original" (Kambili, p. iii).

We must not, however, completely rule out the potential, if not indeed the advisability, of some measure of licence in translation; or what Dryden in the same essay calls a 'paraphrase." Gordon Innes is perhaps right in saying of his versions that it would be "a falsification of the tone of the texts to translate them into high-flown English" in the belief that epic narratives are charaterized by an "elevated style" (Sunjata, p. 15). Although one does not miss the forcefulness of the story in any of his three versions of *Sunjata,* there is little evidence of a borrowed or affected poetic afflatus. But we can hardly escape the fact that even a translation is, like an original creation, the product of a specific sensibility, sometimes working under the influence of a larger environment of expression. In his essay titled "Seven Agamemnons", Reuben Brower uses translations of Aeschylus' classic across three centuries to demonstrate how a translation invariably reflects the age or poetic culture in which it is made;[7] it will be interesting to compare Daniel Kunene's recent translation of Thomas Mofolo's *Chaka* with F. H. Dutton's (Oxford, 1931) translation as a reflection of both man and culture. It will become clear that each version invariably reflects the translator's understanding of what the "appeal" of the original is, whether to himself or to the culture for which the work is intended.

In my translations of heroic narratives I have myself collected—a sample of which is appended below—I have not hesitated to feel (perhaps against Innes) that there is a poetic aura, indeed a touch of elevation, surrounding these tales which are clearly marked by a certain sense of remove from contemporary reality. It is true that the stories are told in an everyday diction which will be easily understood by the indigenes and neighbours of Ubulu-Uno (Bendel State, Nigeria). But I observed and recorded the performances myself and recall the level of excitement and inspiration surrounding them. I must confess that, as I turn into English (a language which I understand very well) I have allowed myself a few liberties in representing what I consider to be the appeal of the texts. Though I present basically literal versions, I have stopped every now and then to decide, between any number of alternatives, what phrase would do most justice to the poetic circumstances of the performance, and to the skill and seriousness which the bard brought to the job. Clearly, without taking undue liberties, the translator of an oral narrative performance must see himself as the kind of creative middleman whom Horst Frenz once aptly identified in the following injunction: "It is clear that a translator must bring sympathy and understanding to the work he is to translate. He must be the original author's most intimate, most exact, in short, his best reader. But he must do more than read. He must attempt to see what the author saw, to hear what he heard, to dig into his own life in order to experience anew what the author experienced . . . The translator must be creative."[8] If Frenz can say this for the translator of the cold print of a text, how much truer, then, are his recommendations for the translator who actually witnessed and recorded the performance and can thus easily recall the context.

Context and the oral poetics

But it is not enough to recall or subsume the context in our transcriptions and translations; we should, ideally, record them. I say "ideally" because I am aware what an expensive affair a full documentation of context can be, and we cannot blame publishers for their reluctance in publishing many a worthwhile text of the oral performance. The case for faithful documentation needs to be constantly made in the prospect that, in the not too distant future, some mode of production will be discovered that satisfies the expectations of both publishers and consumers. In this connection, we should give some recognition to a scholar who has long articulated this need.

Dennis Tedlock has in various publications recognized the dimensions of an "oral poetics" and the need for a proper documentation of the oral performance.[9] Having worked mainly in the area of Zuni oral narratives (explored before him by scholars like Ruth Benedict), he came to the conclusion that one of the main reasons why the earlier scholars had such a defective understanding of the culture of the so-called "primitive" was that they had such an imperfect record of his speech behaviour. They gave rather perfunctory translations of the tales which they collected, in the belief that content or message was more important in these matters than style. The tales were also invariably rendered in prose, and here Tedlock has objected strongly that, given the emotionally charged atmosphere of the narration of a tale and the poetic possibilities of the counterpoint of moods within the narrator, it would be wrong to represent the results in the rather grey, cheerless, unelevated landscape of prose; for "prose (as we now understand it) has no existence outside the written page." Accordingly, Tedlock has often transcribed his oral narrative texts into verse lines which respect the appropriate breaks that he has identified in his recording, even when—and this is the essential point—the narration was not accompanied by instrumental music.

There is another interesting observation that Tedlock has made. Since the story is not simply told but *re-enacted* with due resources of vocal modulation, histrionic movements, and so on, the result is not simply poetry but *dramatic* poetry. One other factor that reinforces the element of the dramatic is the active participation of the audience both in terms of an emotional dialogue (i.e. an interplay of intentionalities) and of overt gestures like occasional questions or other kinds of interjections. Tedlock has been so obsessed with this element of the *dialogue* or interplay that, in an issue of the journal *Alcheringa: Ethnopoetics* edited by him and some colleagues at Boston University, he published a rather revealing poem entitled "Dialogue":

> — I could tell you a story.
> It's the story told to all boys when they are initiated.
> Do you want me to tell it? —
> — If you want to tell it go ahead.—
> — Don't say that.
> Say *you want me* to tell the story.[10]

There is, Tedlock seems to be saying, much more than a monologue to the narration of a tale in an oral performance. He has accordingly warned: "If anthropologists, folklorists, linguists, and oral historians/are interested in the full meaning/of the spoken word/then they must stop treating oral narratives/as if they were reading prose/when in fact they are listening to dramatic poetry."[11]

In this statement Tedlock clearly implies that a proper record of the speech behaviour of a people will give us a better understanding than hitherto of their way of life. In a lecture delivered at the University of New Mexico, he carried his message home to the discipline which has been most avowedly concerned with the "way of life". Titled "The Analogical Tradition and the Emergence of a Dialogical Anthropology",[12] the paper urges the anthropologist to turn away somewhat from the established method of treating his subjects with an impersonal distance in the form of an "objective" exegesis which is simply an "after-statement" *(ana-logos),* and instead give due consideration to publishing in full the discussions between the field scholar and informant. Such a practice will provide a reliable inter-subjective portrait of two people speaking across *(dia-logos)* to each other on equal terms and make anthropology a truly inter-cultural enterprise rather than what it has hiherto been - a superior comment by "us" on "them". Some of the arguments of that paper may sound unduly romantic or overzealous, but we cannot fail to recognize in Tedlock's oral narrative scholarship so far, the concern of a man whose studied experience in the field has made of him the kind of sympathetic and creative translator that Horst Frenz has recommended.

Tedlock's concern with presenting on the printed page a proper picture of what goes on in the oral narrative performance is, to a certain degree, a product of the revolution in behaviour research —championed in the sixties by members of the "ethnography of speaking" school like Dell Hymes—which advocates a proper and detailed documentation of the social and other contexts of speech.[13] This revolution has clearly brought about a great deal of new and worthwhile insights into folklore research, as evidenced by publications in the seventies. In a separate paper,[14] I have examined, as closely as I could, some of the important aesthetic as well as sociocultural questions raised by one of the books published in this period—J.P. Clark's *The Ozidi Saga*[15]—which has done more than any other edition of African oral literature before it to give us a good picture of the oral performance in context. Now, I am not sure how much Clark has been influenced by the thinking of the "ethnography of speaking" school. But I feel certain that as an acknowledged poet-playwright he is as sensitive as anyone could ever be to the dialogical imperative which Dennis Tedlock has recognized in the oral narrative performance and so is immensely qualified to give us a representative edition of such an event. It took Clark about a decade and a half — between the actual initiation of research (1963) and final publication (1977) — to overcome the tremor of intent and live down the professional struggles which such an enormous project inevitably generated. The result is a work which has set a considerable standard in African folklore editing, emphasizing as never before the relevance of, among other things, contextual circumstances (e.g. audience interjections) to the text of the oral narrative performance.

Any editor of the oral narrative text today should, I believe, consult the contributions of both Tedlock and Clark. There is no doubt. that the results are liable to be more expensive than with the normal methods of transcription: it is well known that the delay in publishing *The Ozidi Saga* had partly to do with the reluctance of one of the publishers to take on, unaided, this stupendous manuscript. In the rest of this paper I intend to offer some brief observations on how I have so far handled the problem of transcription of oral narrative texts—performed by Mr Charles "Boy" Simayi of Ubulu-Uno, Bendel State of Nigeria—which are fortunately not as long as the material Clark had to cope with.

Speech forms

Ubulu-Uno is in the Aniocha local government area of Bendel State, and the language spoken here is a dialect of Igbo. Apart from very occasional mention in the official reports of Northcote Thomas[16] and such rare sources, Ubulu-Uno as a community has not enjoyed much ethnographic attention. Its dialect is, to my knowledge, undocumented and will therefore present some difficulties to anyone transcribing its folklore. Though there is now a well-accepted orthography for the Igbo language,[17] its practical usefulness is minimal as far as the transcription of the tales I have collected from Mr Simayi are concerned. I say so not only because the Ubulu-Uno dialect is far removed from the central Igbo employed in working out the Onwu orthography, but because the tales were told in basically colloquial forms and I believe that the colloquiality of the narration should be preserved against the claims of grammatical forms recognized in standard orthographies which linguists and educators are, understandably, anxious to establish on a firm footing. In colloquial speech there are frequent elisions, contractions and other forms of abbreviation; so it would be a misrepresentation of the raw vitality of Mr Simayi's performance to spell out his lines into all their constituent syllables just so as to make them intelligible in terms agreeable with the recommendations of the Onwu orthography. Let me give an example with a line from one of the tales which I collected from him on the night of October 12, 1980, a tale in which a young man wins a girl from her father by a combination of cunning and bravado:

N'im' ik'ọọbia asaa nụ; nke nụ jek'aanu nwata nị
(Among those seven young men, the one that was to marry this young *girl).*

A full grammatical transcription of the Igbo line (following the Onwu orthography) would read something like this:

N'ime ikolo obia asaa nu, nke nu jeko ga-anu nwata ni
But it would be a gross distortion of the facility of the colloquial

diction, in which the story was told throughout, to attempt to be so pedantically formal in the transcription. It would be like transcribing "I will" or "going to" for a singer who invariably used "I'll" or "gonna". Perhaps we should advise our zealous linguists and educators early enough, that oral narrative texts of this kind are hardly the place to press the rules of orthography.[18]

Prosody

This is probably the most nagging issue in oral narrative scholarship, especially in respect of African oral narrative performances which are marked by a far greater looseness of textual structure than seems to be the case in other cultures. Considering that, in many cases, the tale is performed against a regulated musical background, are we thereby obliged to transcribe the text in "verse" lines rather than in prose? or, considering that the story is told mainly in ordinary, everyday speech, should we rather do the transcription in prose sequences?

As we have seen above, Tedlock (guided basically by considerations of the emotive charge of the narration) has resolved the issue for himself by transcribing in independent lines, corresponding with the respective breath stops observed by the narrator even in stories unaccompanied by music. In their editions of African heroic narratives accompanied by instrumental music, both Bird *(Kambbili)* and Innes *(Sunjata,)* adopt as the basis of their transcriptions the fundamental rhythmic structure; every line of text thus represents all that is said within the scope of the corresponding rhythmic line. However, both Bird and Innes basically agree about the prosodic looseness of the narration and the absence of any strict correspondence between rhythm and content. I find myself in agreement with Tedlock on the one hand. On the other hand, the present state of my musical knowledge does not permit me to attempt a detailed analysis of the relationship between rhythmic line and content line in the performance of Mr Simayi. He was regularly backed by two men who struck bottles at varying but complementary pitches and paces and so provided a regulated percussion. The pace of the overall percussion in turn depended on the tempo which the bard chose at the start of the story (sometimes by humming a guide tune). Although Mr Simayi told his stories in everyday diction, and although there was general irregularity between the statements which he pronounced in successive breath sequences, I was sufficiently impressed by the emotive charge of each performance to treat the narration itself às a form of unconstrained *song*. I have therefore transcribed the narrative texts in "verse" lines.[19]

The point about the emotive charge is borne out by the proverbs with which Mr Simayi besprinkles every story. Again, let me cite a line from that same story about the young man who wins a girl from her father. To underscore the mistake made by the girl's father in allowing her to escort the young man and his friend after one of their visits, the bard uses the following proverb:

Mkpikpa wa ji kp'esu yi elu mmoo.

(The stick used in getting rid of a millipede joins him in damnation).

The word "esu" (millipede) is normally unaccented in ordinary speech; indeed in a normal conversational situation where such a proverb is used, the word would very likely remain unaccented. But there is an intensely performative value to its usage here, marked by a high emotive charge in the narration of the tale which precipitates the accentual changes on the word.

Such a line may thus be seen as a chant; because in terms of vocalization it enjoys a certain elevation over the ordinary narrative line, some editors have come to treat it differently. Bird puts all his "praise-proverb" lines in italics, while Innes indents such chants a few notches deeper than the lines transcribed in the ordinary narrative mode. However, while in these Mandinka cases the chants often extend to considerable lengths (over a hundred lines in one of Bird's cases), my narrator hardly exceeds one or two lines. I sometimes get the impression that for the Mandinka bards the chants are little more than interludial devices and that the link between the various constituent ideas in a whole segment of lines is tenuous. But such is the wit of Mr. Simayi that he will simply employ a single saw to drive home a point in true proverb fashion. In many cases these proverbs are woven into statements made in the ordinary speech mode: that is, they are only part of what is said in one "breath group" and do not constitute an independent "verse" line. Despite the level of poetic elevation in these proverbs, therefore, I have not transcribed them any differently from the ordinary speech lines.

I am however in agreement with Bird and Innes in giving a deep indentation to the sung passages, especially because at such points there is a clear break in rhythm; the musical groups are invariably cued to change from the rhythm of the narration into one suited to the tune about to be sung. Mr Simayi does not often play an instrument himself while he narrates; but sometimes when he changes from narrating to singing the songs tied to a tale, he picks up his thumb piano and, in time with the other instrumentalists, strikes his chords to the tune. There is often a change of vocal key as well as of rhythmic tempo, and a more formal or conscious vocal modulation here than in the case of the proverbs; it is this extra poetic elevation in the performance that justifies the deep indentation given to the text of the song.

Transcribing the text of the song within an oral narrative could, however, present some logistical problems to the editor, particularly because some songs run to lengths that may be simply unacceptable to the publisher. As I have observed elsewhere,[20] music plays an inestimable role in the oral narrative performance; and some bards sometimes have a tendency to indulge the musical feeling which the song interludes within the tale tends to enhance. In transcription we may feel like exercising a little economy, but this in itself may not quite do justice to the full text of the singing. If for instance, neither the "call" by the bard nor the "response" by the chorus changes throughout the singing, it may be sufficient to transcribe only a few lines of this exchange and indicate how many times the exchange happens. If the bard varies his call but the response is stable, then it may be well to transcribe every line of call and have at the end of it, in parenthesis: (Repeat chorus).

But what do we do if, after a long stretch of unvaried call and response, one member of the group suddenly throws in (maintaining both the tempo and sometimes the logic of the song) a random salute to a member of the audience or an observation of an event happening at that particular moment of singing? For instance, in one of the songs accompanying his story about a contest for chieftaincy in the nearby town of Ogwashi-Uku, Mr Simayi had occasion to observe that his first percussionist is dozing off. Observe the changes in the following song:

Bard: Mm, let's go to the palace. Oh—
Chorus: Let's go to the palace
Bard: Nwadobe, my son   ⎫
Chorus: Let's go to the palace ⎬ seven times

Bard:	Just look at you!
Chorus:	Let's go to the palace
Bard:	Let's go to the palace
Chorus:	Let's go to the palace
Bard:	You're sleeping off!
Chorus:	Let's go to the palace
Bard:	Let's go to the palace
Chorus:	Let's go to the palace
Bard:	Let's go to the palace
Chorus:	Let's go to the palace
Bard:	Music man, save your pay
Chorus:	Let's go to the palace
Bard:	Save your pay
Chorus:	Let's go to the palace
Bard:	Mm
Chorus:	Let's go to the palace!

At the end of the last line the bard tells the percussionist (Mr Okondu Enyi), whose striking of the bottle had noticeably slackened, "You're sleeping off, didn't I tell you?"—then, adding a proverb—"A child cannot wait out the pumpkin". Mr Enyi replies, "You've scored one!" It would appear from this that there is a subtle competition between bard and accompanist in stamina for the craftsmanship of song! The entire audience laughed heartily at this banter, and the narration continued. What editor would want to omit such an incident from his transcription, with all the rich information it gives us about the creative atmosphere of good-humoured confrontation between bard and accompanist? But we can well imagine what problem the editor (or publisher) faces if this happens to be only an infinitesimal part of a very long and otherwise unvaried call and response.

Tonal levels

One of the virtues of Dennis Tedlock's plea-that we represent the oral narrative performance as dramatic poetry-is that we may thereby hear the voices and see the faces with minimal effort, though the actual event be now a matter of history. There is very little in the surviving classics of European oral narrative peotry that recalls the virile tone of the narrator's voice; perhaps the closest we get to the face of the bard is the clamorous "Hwaet!" that starts off *Beowulf*. Though some editors of African oral narratives tell us in their introduction how effective the voice is in carrying the performance, the actual texts leave no trace of this effectiveness.

Tedlock and his colleagues[21] have shown how a proper differentiation of tonal levels in the printed text can help to convey something of the dramatic variation of moods in the narrator's delivery. In contemporary fiction, the only way we can tell at what pitch of voice a character makes a statement is by the author expressly describing this to us after, or sometimes before, the statement, for example:

"Get out!" he ordered quietly but firmly.

But Tedlock and his colleagues have proposed some useful typographical devices whereby the various tonal levels used in story-telling can be distinguished. For words said in a high tone they propose boldface type; for word said in a low tone they propose italic type; and for ordinary speech levels they propose the normal roman. I accept everything except the boldface type, partly because it may be difficult to tell boldface from normal type if the printer does not apply the ink properly and the intended effect will be lost.[22] In place of boldface I am therefore applying capital type. It is not a really new device. LeRoi Jones (Baraka) once used it quite effectively as a cardinal element of his aesthetic of the "scream" in the sixties;[23] though the oral narrator is not ruled in his art by the frustrated anger which informed Black American poetry of that period, I think there is at the bottom of both usages the sense of the alert.

This point leads me to disagree with Jeff Titon's injunction that these notational distinctions are "meant as an aid for performance, not analysis."[24] There would be no point using these typographical and other adjustments of our texts if they did not lead to useful literary analyses and (hopefully) larger cultural judgments. Let me illustrate what I mean with a few general observations from my texts, some of which will, I think, become clear from the story appended to this paper. I have noticed that when my narrator speaks in a high voice, it is either because he wishes to indicate a new turn in the development of the story, which helps us to understand something of the organization of the oral narrative; or because he wishes to underscore the heroism of a character by endowing his statements with a due touch of menace, which helps us to understand something of the narrator's conception or development of character; or because he wishes to emphasize the significance of a particular event or act in the story. It may even have something to do with the personality of the narrator. Mr Simayi, from our various general discussions, has struck me as a man with considerable personal pride and self-assuredness. He once told me that he had trained his children and made something of them and that modern civilization therefore held no surprises for him! A man of such inclinations is therefore unwilling to be superseded or preempted; thus every once in a while, whether during the narration of a tale or in the course of our general discussions (at which other members of the group participated), he raised his voice whenever he felt an interpolator was, as it were, trying to get the better of him. By putting such high-toned words or statements in bold print or capitals (which eliminates the need for further "stage directions"), we will certainly be aiding analysis from various perspectives.

A similar value could be seen in italicization. In a number of cases, for instance, Mr Simayi makes his characters say something like *"Ọ si n'ọ di nma"* (He said it was all right) in a low tone when he wishes to indicate the patience or quiet discretion with which they accept a situation they are faced with. If I may refer again to that story about the contest for a chieftaincy title, Mr Simayi uses the low tone to underscore the element of favouritism and intrigue by which one of the rivals is finally cheated of the title: at one point when the Obi (King of Oguwashi-Uku), who awards the title, speaks to the candidate whose victory he has helped to engineer, he does so in a conspiratorial whisper. Surely the italicization of such a statement is not simply a fanciful device: it invites us to explore the dramatic or other significance of the statement in the scheme of the story.

Conclusion

In the final analysis, the discipline of oral literature owes its viability, to the seriousness and understanding which we bring to our treatment of the texts that we collect from our performers. In the matter of language we should, by a discrete combination of loyalty to the forms and sounds of the original language and a certain tastefulness in handling turns of phrase, aim to do justice to the vitality of the culture which we are trying to translate. There is an equal need to do justice to the context of creation which makes more than a little difference to the results of the oral performance. In the case of narratives, for instance, a due recognition of the dialogue of intentionalities between artist and audience will help us to appreciate the oral narrative event more as dramatic poetry than as the prosaic monologue more fittingly descriptive of contemporary fiction. But of all the steps which we have to take to preserve a proper record of the oral text, perhaps none is as demanding as the need to make the proper distinctions to the levels of intonation in the artist's delivery, especially in the oral narrative performance. Within the scope of his dramatic act, the oral narrator has sufficient resources for coping with some of the responsibilities of representation which contemporary fiction seems to have assumed. For instance, where the novelist would go into verbal descriptions of the manner in which characters make their statements, the storyteller would accomplish the job by sensitive vocal modulation. A proper transcription should be able to account for the peculiar techniques adopted by the oral tradition in coping with such problems of representation. In these various ways, oral literary scholars could help to build the right foundations for a proper understanding of the oral culture.

NOTES

1. Ruth Finnegan, "How Oral is Oral Literature?" *Bulletin of school of Oriental and African Studies,* 37 (1974); *Oral Poetry* (Cambridge: Cambridge University Press 1977).
2. Claude Lévi-Strauss, *Structural Anthropology* (London: Allen Lane, 1968), p. 210.
3. Daniel Biebuyck and Kahombo C. Mateene (eds.), *The Mwindo Epic from the Banyanga* (Berkeley: University of California Press, 1969) Daniel Biebuyck (ed.), *Hero and Chief* (Berkeley: University of California Press, 1978).
4. John Dryden, Preface to *Translations from Ovid's Epistles,* 1680.
5. See John William Johnson (ed.), *The Epic of Sun-Jata According to Magan Sisoko* (Bloomington: Folklore Publications Group, Indiana University, 1979).
6. Charles Bird et al, *The Songs of Seydou Camera: Volume I, Kambili* (Bloomington: African Studies Center, Indiana University, 1974); Gordon Innes, *Sunjata: Three Mandinka Versions* (London: School of Oriental and African Studies, 1974).
7. Reuben A. Brower (ed.), *On Translation* (Cambridge, Mass: Harvard University Press, 1959), pp. 173-95.
8. Horst Frenz, "The Art of Translation", in *Comparative Literature: Method*

and Perspective, (Carbondale: Southern Illinois University Press, 1971 edn.), pp. 119-20.

9. See Dennis Tedlock, "On the Translation of Style in Oral Narrative", *Journal of American Folklore,* 84 (1971), pp. 114-33; "Learning to Listen: Oral History as Poetry", in *Envelopes of Sound,* ed. Ronald J. Grele (Chicago: Precedent Publishing, 1975), pp. 106-25; "Toward an Oral Poetics", *New Literary History,* 8, (1977), pp. 507-19; *Finding the Center: Narrative Poetry of the Zuni Indians* (Lincoln: University of Nebraska Press, 1978).

10. Dennis Tedlock, "Dialogue" Alchering *Ethnopoetics,* 2 (1976), p. 128.

11. "Learning to Listen", p. 123. The slashes stand for the line breaks that Tedlock has characteristically observed.

12. *Journal of Anthropological Research,* 35 (1979), pp. 387-400.

13. Sample studies: Dell Hymes, "The Ethnography of Speaking", in *Anthropology and Human Behaviour,* ed . T. Gladwin and W.C. Sturtevant (Washington, D.C.: Anthropological Society of Washington, 1962); *Foundations in Sociolinguistics: An Ethnographic Approach* (Philadelphia: University of Pennsylvania Press, 1974); E. Ojo Arewa and Alan Dundes, "Proverbs and the Ethnography of Speaking Folklore", *American Anthropologist,* 66 (6), pt. 2 (1964); Richard Bauman and Joel Sherzer (eds.), *Explorations in the Ethnography of Speaking* (New York: Cambridge University Press 1974).

14. Okpewho, "The Oral Performer and His Audience: A Case Study of *The Ozidi Saga".* See below.

15. Ibadan: Ibadan University Press and Oxford University Press, 1977.

16. See Northcote Thomas, *Anthropological Report on Ibo-Speaking Peoples of Nigeria,* Vol. 4. (New York: Negro University Press, 1969 (1914).

17. See sample material in M.M. Green and G.E. Igwe, *A Descriptive Grammar of Igbo* (London: Oxford University Press, 1963), pp. 9-10.

18. For J.P. Clark's battles with the professional linguists over the Ijo orthography, see *The Ozidi Saga, pp. xvii-xix.*

19. For the record, I should perhaps recall a conversation that Clark, Dr Chukwuma Azuonye and myself had in October 1979 at this university. Azuonye had asked Clark if he ever considered transcribing *The Ozidi Saga* in verse lines; Clark emphatically shook his head and said no, pointing out that his narrator used plain, everyday language.

20. Okpewho, *The Epic in Africa* (New York: Columbia University Press, 1979), pp. 57-66.

21. See, for example, Jeff Titon's transcription of (the Black American blues singer) Son House's narratives, in "Son House: Two Narratives", *Alcheringa: Ethnopoetics,* 2 (1976), pp. 2-9.

22. For the same technical reason I have not adopted the Tedlock group's recommendation of gaps within the line to represent fractional pauses. I have, instead, perferred to use dots within the line to represent not only fractional pauses but the occasional stumble or search for *le mot juste.* If the pause is substantial (say two seconds), then of course the line is broken.

23. See LeRoi Jones, *Black Magic Poetry 1961-1967* (Indianapolis: Bobbs-Merrill, 1969).

24. Jeff Titon, "Son House: Two Narratives", p. 2.

STORY

The following tale was recorded at about 10 p.m. on October 12, 1980, at Ubulu-Uno in the Aniocha Local Government Area of Bendel State, Nigeria. The bard, Mr Charles "Boy" Simayi, was accompanied by three men. Two of them struck empty bottles at different but complementary pitches and tempos while the bard occasionally played a small thumb piano made of metal strips strung to a hollow semi-circular calabash. The third accompanist simply gave occasional promptings. With me in the general audience were three friends, some four members of the bard's household (where the recording took place), and some of the bard's neighbours. On the whole there were about twenty people at the scene of the performance. The following story lasted 18 minutes.

MEEME ODOGWU (or THE RESCUE)

Bard: My tale captures Onukwu . . . of Ogwashi, Onukwu Agbada.
      (*coughs*) The nobility of Ogwashi were all assembled:
      IN AN AGE WHEN MEN SPOKE WITH THE POINT OF THE
          MATCHET.
      When whoever showed no daring would not join in such drinking
          as we have laid out here on the table.
      Onukwu Agbada was an olinzele (i.e. privy councillor).   5
      The entire nobility of Ogwashi was assembled to the brim.
      ONUKWU'S WIFE—
      Long ago, women would trade in cocoyams towards Agbor, towards
          Abba, towards . . . Ado Nta, in cocoyams fetched from the
          farm.
      Onukwu's wife came to where she would . . . buy cocoyams.
      Odogwu of Abba came   10
      Told her he would marry her. What!
      She said to him, "Don't you know my husband Onukwu Agbada?
      How would it be told,
      That I went to the cocoyam market and did not return,
      With Odogwu claiming me for his wife? You have defiled me.   15
      If you don't give me articles for purification I will not return."

First per-
cussionist: It's a matter for the matchet.

Bard: Odogwu pushed her into . . . his yard
         (*Laughter*)
      Saying, "You have neared me. When the goat nears the yam he eats
         it."

HA! What á shame! Odogwu looked out for his wife . . . I mean,
Onukwu Agbada looked out for his wife but she never return-
ed.   20
Those who went to the market told him, her fellow-women told him
that . . . Odogwu of Abba had taken his wife.

First per-
cussionist: Abomination.
Bard: *Onukwu said, "Oh, really."*
Laughed softly,
Said, "All right.   25
Three seasons are normally allowed for (the return of) one who
has . . . gone to afo market
If things don't go well this afo, the next afo a delegation will be sent.
She will return."
HE LOOKED ALL OUT, but she never returned.
Too soon for words, Odogwu laid hands on his (new) wife.
A notice was served on him.   30
He came to the house of their king
And paid his respects
Where he had taken his title.
ON THE APPOINTED DAY
The king (of Ogwashi) was performing his rites.   35
The entire nobility had to assemble.
Everyone that came brought along yams, brought along palmwine.
His kinsmen accompanied him to the palace, to swell his pride
At the rites of the king.
                           (Interruptions)
THEY HAD ASSEMBLED TO THE BRIM,   40
Bringing their rifles with them.
WHEN THEY HAD drunk their wine for some time just as we are
doing now,
MEEME ODOGWU rose up, rifle in hand
And gave a goodly blast, gidim!
What! Onukwu said to him, "What, how dare you fire your gun
over us?"   45
He replied, "Damn you, damn you, and off with your neck!"
                           (Laughter)

First per-
cussionist: Poor wretch!
Bard: "Telling me . . . before the nobility of Ogwashi,
Where I am giving the king a gun salute, you are telling me about
particles falling over you,
When your wife has been away trading cocoyams for three long
years and has not returned."
                           (Laughter)

First per-
cussionist: How the man has suffered!   50
Spectator I : There's trouble afoot!

128

Spectator 2: **In whose reign was this happening?**

Bard: EHM . . . Told him, "I will tell you I am greater than you.
We are all olinzele, but I am greater than you."

**First per-
cussionist:** An answer is as good as a warning! 55

Bard: TOLD THEM "Watch me while I . . . Your Highness, with what
will you perform your rites?
The human being you will slaughter, have you procured him?
(*First percussionist to second, "Keep striking!"*)
The bull you will slaughter, have you got it?
Well, the nobility of Ogwashi are assembled.
Hey, you cuckold Onukwu, whose wife is away trading cocoyams, 60
See what steps you will take
So we can procure the articles
For the rites of the king.
I am off to Abba to fetch your wife home for you."
LOADED HIS RIFLE, and told him, "If your wife does not come
home with me today, 65
Onukwu, you may have me bound."
Fired the rifle, gbulam, right at Onukwu's feet.
(*Exclamations*)
That was the second blast.
Loaded his rifle again, picked up his matchet,
Strapped his dagger to his arm, fitted on his amulet, stormed out. 70
(*Side comments*)
CAME OUT, SNAPPING.
Okeeme Gbude lived at Mkpolenyi,
On the road to Abba.
SNAPPED OUT TO OKEEME, SAYING , "I'M ON MY WAY!
What are you doing sitting in your farm, when the nobility of
Ogwashi are all assembled? 75
Er . . . Onukwu's wife has been away trading cocoyams for three
long years. I am off to fetch her home. Look out on the way
And listen."
WHAT!
Okeeme said to him,
"So there are still men left among that nobility of Ogwashi? 80
The reason I don't come (to council) any more is that you have all
gone asleep."
(*Exclamation and laughter*)

**First per-
cussionist:** WHAT A MAN! WHAT A TIGER!

Bard: "WELL, WILL YOU LET ME COME ALONG WITH YOU, to
bring home the woman?"

Spectator: Man surpasses man!

Bard: Our man picked up his matchet, that had never known cutting and
was consecrated to the shrine, and followed him. 85

129

First per-cussionist:	Beauty is one thing, bravery another!
Bard:	THEY WALKED ON—the chick cries after its mother—right up to Abba.

His friend Eboka
Was Iyase of Abba.
You know that these strongmen, comrades in robbery, know one
    another.   90
He went to his friend's house
And told him —

First per-cussionist: At the farm, that was.

Bard: AND TOLD HIM, "The king is performing his rites, and we have
    nothing for sacrifice.
The king could not buy a bull, nor could he buy a goat.   95
We have come looking for articles for him to do the rites, for the
    nobility of Ogwashi are all assembled."
(Eboka) said, "Really?
Odogwu has summoned a meeting today,
And we are on our way there."
He said, "Odogwu of Abba? So he is at home?" He said,
    "Yes."   100
"All right.
Er . . . this goat-pen, who owns it?" "It's mine," he said,
"That's where the goats eat the palm fronds."
He said to him, "Go snap off some palm fronds.
Show me one head of palm.   105
Snap off some palm fronds," he said .
He grabbed one head of palm fronds, cut it up briskly,
Piled the fronds in a heap,
And sat by somewhere. Behold goats,
In a stampede! He grabbed seven goats   110
Bound them with a rope, and wound it round his waist.

First per-cussionist: WITH EVERYONE LOOKING!

Bard: Er . . . (*chuckles*) looked fearsomely
And said, "Are you still going to this meeting?" He said he was
    going.
HE SAID, "I ASK YOU to tell Odogwu to release Onukwu's wife
    from his keeping.   115
And to bring in addition a cow, one cow, which I will take home
    along with the woman,
Onukwu's wife."
Eboka went to the meeting.
On entering he said . . . to the nobility of Abba,
"There is trouble afoot.   120
Odogwu, Ogwashi has sent word

130

	And the emissary is at my house this moment,	
	Asking you to let go the wife of . . .	
Prompter:	Onukwu.	
Bard:	"Let go Onukwu's wife."	125
	Odogwu shook, looking aghast.	
	He addressed the kingmakers,	
	Eboka did,	
	That man's friend,	
	Addressed them and said, "Do you see what's afoot?	130
	Er . . . Odogwu, let go the man's wife	
	And provide him articles for cleansing his home.	
	I have no hand in this and cannot pass on the articles myself."	
First per-		
cussionist:	BEHOLD TROUBLE!	
Bard:	FOR IT'S LYING THAT CAUSES WAR!	135
	(*Laughter*)	

Er . . .

(*Someone knocks at the door. Bard says, "Yes?" Young boy
enters and sits. Bard motions him and says, "Be careful"*)
SHORTLY AFTER, BEHOLD OUR FRIEND rushed out, driving
the goats into the goat-pen.
TOLD THEM (i.e. the council), "CHIE! CHIE! CHIE! CHIE!
CHIE!
I am Meeme the Scourge
Okeeme my kinsman is on his way here.   140
It's been long since I arrived Abba today, and I am hungry. I have
come looking for articles
For the rites of the king, *and haven't found them yet.*
COME MY FRIEND (Odogwu), haven't you been told
That I am after Onukwu's wife?
What has kept you since morning? Do you want me to starve to
death, or Ogwashi to come after me?"   145
(*Laughter*)

First per-		
cussionist:	Pardon me	
	Pardon me, sir	
	Er . . . that article the king . . . uses . . . for his rites	
	Isn't it . . . a human head?	
Bard:	We are still on our way.	150
Audience:	Right!	
Okpewho:	The little antelope is breaking his limbs, when the real dance is yet to come!	
Bard:	SHORTLY AFTER, the meeting turned calm and cool.	
	It's lying that causes war.	
	Our man caused a division among them, and the councillors dispersed saying, "Well, Odogwu, you had called us to a meeting. 155	
	Since . . . your home is . . . beset with a horde of ants,	
	We must get out of the way, for we cannot cope	

Attend to your guest and let him go.
We don't want any trouble.''

(*Laughter*)

First per- cussionist:	THEY HAVE SEEN THE FIRE!
Okpewho:	Of course.
Bard:	They departed. Was he there unprepared?
Okpewho:	Of course not.
Bard:	The chick cries after its mother.
	Our man shut the door nicely
	And said to Odogwu, "You, little man —

(*Exclamations and side comments*)

Bring out the person you brought here!''
Shortly after . . . A great clamour chastens the earth!

First per-
cussionist: WHAT!

Bard: He (Odogwu) brought out that fellow,
That woman, handed her over to him, and shook hands.

(*Side comments*)

First per-
cussionist: There's no end to procrastination!

Bard: He (Meeme) told her, "You may wait for me at Eboka's place and
go home awhile with the goats theres.''
When she got home, Eboka handed over the goats to her.
The woman took the goats. Looking out on the way, she saw
Okeeme coming.
He said, "Lady . . . who . . . where are you coming from?'' She said
she was Onukwu Agbada's wife.
HE SAID, "SO IT'S YOU?'' *She said, "Yes.''*
He said, "Whose goats are these?'' She said
They were . . . given to her by . . .
By . . . by . . .

First per-
cussionist: Odogwu of Abba.

Bard: No!
They were given to her by . . .
Meeme.

Audience: Meeme.

Bard: (*Bard whispers warning to First Percussionist*)
It was Meeme who gave them to her.
He said to her, "And where is . . . that Meeme Odogwu?''
She said he was at Odogwu (of Abba)'s place.
He said, "All right.
Have they risen from the meeting they were said to be holding?
Is anyone still there?''
That fellow said —

160

165

170

175

180

185

190

(*Tape runs out. Spools are adjusted. False starts. Music is cued in*).
Man,

Okeeme set out.   195
Went on and on, right up to the house of a friend.
Told him, "They say you went for a meeting today. Have you
finished?" He said, "Yes." He said he had come after a cow
for the rites of the king.
What! He said, "Meeme is still at... Odogwu's place
No cooking, no eating!
He has refused all pleading.   200
We don't know what he plans to do to Odogwu,
But we are totally at a loss how to help.
That was the state in which we left them both."
He said, "I am not concerned with Meeme. I have come after a cow
for the rites of the king."
DASHED OUT, appeared at their market place.   205
What was a single bull to him?
With a rope fetched from the thicket, good for tying cows
He circled the waist of a bull
Wound it round his wrist
Set off.   210
Came to Odogwu's compound, called out to...Meeme Odogwu.
"I AM ON MY WAY HOME!"
Meeme said...
Meeme... "Odogwu, you are coming home with me.
The person I came to fetch has reached home already.   215
Give me the articles for the rites of the king
For you have not settled the problem.
OR DO I SEIZE THEM MYSELF?"

First per-
cussionist: Only a man can tell a man!
Bard: Packed his rifle, aimed it at Odogwu's shrine: 220
                  GALILILILILILIM! Blasted the shrine to bits.
                  Performed the funeral rites for him
                  Leapt outside, appeared at their market place
                  Grabbed a bull
                  Strapped a rope to its neck.   225
                  Mm hm hm, mm hm hm
                  Mm hm hm, mm hm hm
                  Oh ho ho, we've been to Abba, there's no war there
                  Alas Odogwu, I've been to Abba, there's no one there
Chorus: Mm hm hm, I've been to Abba, there's no one there   230
              Oh ho ho, I've been to Abba, there's no one there
Bard: Oh ho ho, we've been to Abba, there's no one there
              Woe, Odogwu, we've been to Abba, there's no one
Chorus: there
              Oh ho ho, ho ho ho   235
Bard: Oh ho ho, we've been to Abba, there's no one there
              Oh ho, Odogwu, we've been to Abba, there's no one there

Chorus: Odogwu, woe is me, I've been to Abba, there's no one there
Oh ho ho, I've been to Abba, there's no one there
Odinigwe Nwoha, my man, we've been to Abba, there's no
one there.

Bard: THEY SET OUT ON THEIR WAY . . . THE CHICK CRIES
AFTER ITS MOTHER. 240
WENT ON AND ON, right up to the king's palace.
(Meeme) Laid his cow to the tether.
Said . . . "Okeeme, we shall take yours to the king's palace."
The wife of . . . Onukwu was waiting for him at (Okeeme's) place,
with the seven goats,
Goats claimed in payment for a man's wife. 245

(First Percussionist moans wistfully)
She had herded them home.
TOLD HER, "If you lose any of them; you will be the victim at the
rites of the king."

(Laughter)

**First per-
cussionist:** Those men of old, they spoke only with matchet-point!
Bard: THAT WOMAN LABOURED ON, till she got home
And entered Meeme's place. 250
When they got home . . . from Abba
They shared the goats
He and . . . Okeeme.
Having shared the goats they had made the woman bring home
They took on the bull . . . that Okeeme had brought over 255

*(Bard snatches bottle from Second Percussionist to correct the
rhythm, saying, "Kogom-kom-kogom. We're not doing the
samba." Laughter. Second Percussionist resumes striking).*
MAN, THEY WENT ON TO THE PALACE,
On and on till they got to the palace.
Told the king, "We're home.
Where is Onukwu?" "Here he is," said (the king).
(Meeme) said to Onukwu, "Get up, 260
And declare your achievement.
For . . . you will marry this woman afresh before the nobility of
Ogwashi.
Produce the ransome-money for your wife."

(Laughter)

**First per-
cussionist:** THAT'S THE FEE FOR COWARDICE!
Bard: Picked up his rifle and blasted it beside the entrance, saying, "Only
those who declare their achievements will drink the wine
here. 265
Onukwu, I have been . . . have been to Abba to bring home articles
for the rites of the king.

You declare your achievement.

> *(Side comments)*

THIS DAY WILL BE YOUR LAST at the meetings of the nobility
of Ogwashi, for you will come no more.''

> *(More side comments)*

And so they returned Onukwu's wife to him at the king's palace

And asked him to leave.   270

And he left . . . and he left the nobility.

He did not return, and from there I returned home, having given
him back his wife.

> *(Percussionists sign off).*

Audience:	Welcome.
Bard:	Welcome to you. Welcome, my friend.
Okpewho:	Thank you.
Bard:	Thank you.

Part Three

Text and Context

The Narrator, Narrative-Pattern and Audience Experience of Oral Narrative-Performance

Ropo Sekoni

ORAL narrative performance, like all other speech acts, is a communication system in which a social discourse takes place principally between a narrator/performer and an audience. All instances of such discourse are designed by the performer for an examination of the dominant concerns of the artists' immediate community in particular, and human behaviour and the human condition in general.[1] The nature of communication or the exchange of ideas in oral narrative-performance may be similar to other processes of communication in which the communicator transfers some message to his listener. However, the additional factor of entertainment or the creation by narrators of a product that is pleasant to experience by the listeners, calls from the narrator and the audience, as well as the student of verbal art, a special attention to the composition and delivery of the product itself, in contradistinction to the message or the cognitive aspect of the narrative.

The discussion of the aesthetics of oral narrative-performance in Africa, especially West Africa, has been sparse and general. For example, Ruth Finnegan[2] in a casual reference to the oral narrative-tradition of some West African communities, emphasizes, without any convincing illustration, that phenomena of audience behaviour such as "spontaneous exclamations, actual questions . . . emotional reaction to the development of yet another parallel and repetitious episode" are sources of beauty in oral literature. In a more detailed discussion of the aesthetics of Krio narrative, Modupe Broderick identifies some specific aesthetic phenomena and devices in Krio narrative-tradition. Broderick, in a combination of Lévi-Straussian obsession with synchrony and his opponents' preoccupation with diachrony in myths and similar forms,

139

demonstrates with erudition the thematic implications of an interplay between content and its ordering in Krio narratives.[3] While Broderick's work on Krio narrative tradition is one of the most sophisticated discussions of structure as a source of aesethetic experience in oral narrative-performance in West Africa, his silence on what specific aesthetic states narrative structuring evokes, creates a major gap in the study of the nature and provenance of aesthetic experience in oral narrative-performance.[4]

It is thus the purpose of this paper to discuss the fundamental problems of the nature and process of aesthetic experience in oral narrative-performance. The paper will focus on Yoruba narrative-tradition and the author hopes that legitimate generalizations can be made from the findings for oral narrative-performance in other cultures.

Using Broderick's view of aesthetics in oral narrative as derivable from, and manifested in, the manipulation of narrative patterns for the purpose of communicating meaning and attaining aesthetic experience,[5] this writer takes the theoretical position that aesthetic experience in oral narrative-performance is made up of three inseparable components: captivation of audience, retention of audience and the transfer of cognitive experience to the audience. These three dimensions are, unlike Broderick's separation of cognition and aesthetic experience, inseparable from each other; they are proverbially, three elements of a triadic, mosaic or siamese triplets that can only survive in their jointness.[6]

Since oral narrative-performance is, like stage productions, characterized by an immediate interaction of narrator and audience, the first contact between both parties initiates the first effort by the narrator to achieve aesthetic harmony with his audience. Apart from such preliminary formulae as for example in Yoruba, "My story spins and spins and falls on the heads of two jealous co-wives", often used in announcing the shift from the factual world of the narrative community to the fictive experience to be subsequently evoked by the narrator, the initial attraction of the audience to narrative experience depends on three factors which are external to the narrative itself. The first of such factors is the possession of a good and charming voice by the narrator. The others are the narrator's facility with the language of narration and his ability to use his body—face, trunk, arms and legs—as materials for the evocation of a fictive experience for his audience. If a storyteller/performer is to establish a rapport with his audience, he must be consistent in his mastery of the language and should possess an effective voice that can charm the audience. Since most members of the audience are usually much younger than the narrator, the narrator's use of language should be good enough to provide an enviable language-performance model to which members of the audience may aspire in their own use of language. The same condition holds for the narrator's use of extra-verbal devices such as gestures, gesticulations and spatial relations.

The narrator's ability to use his voice and body to convey the emotions of characters, to delineate his characters and comment on specific actions of such characters, is basic for the achievement of initial aesthetic harmony with the audience. These skills serve as devices for diverting the attention of the audience from their private thoughts and preoccupations to the experience of images that are being selected and organized by the narrator with the hope of transferring to the audience ideas about some aspects of the recurrent concerns of the narrator's community. After the narrator's beautiful voice, skillful use of language and effective manipulation of his body have attracted the attention of the audience to the narrative experience, the narrator still needs to retain or hold this attention till the end of the story. Although a good voice and facility with language are devices for retaining audience attention, a more important factor in this respect is the organization of the story itself.

The story must be told in a manner that assists the narrator in retaining the physical attention of the audience as well as in gaining the emotive and cognitive attention of the audience. A charming voice and good mastery of the language become, as the story progresses, secondary sources of aesthetic harmony. The patterning of images or episodes of the story is the most important single factor in the attainment of the other two elements of aesthetic harmony: the emotive and cognitive satisfaction of the audience. These two elements are intricately intertwined and can thus be treated together even at the risk of sacrificing clarity.

Cognitive satisfaction refers mainly to the ability of the narrator/performer to relate individual images to a theme or a comment on a specific aspect of human behaviour in his community. In other words, the diverse images in a story must in their totality achieve either clarity of meaning or the suggestion of meaning.

Thus images or the units of behaviour externalized by characters in stories must, in their combination, be capable of suggesting to the audience the narrator's statement(s) about some of the recurrent concerns or values of the community. Some of these concerns and values are such social issues as justice, honesty, order, peace and respect for duly constituted and socially accepted authorities. Others, for instance, could be such ontological considerations as death, the purpose and dilemma of man's mission, the origin and ultimate end of man, etc.

In any instance of narrative-performance, the narrator and his audience are not only concerned with the examination of the dominant values of their community but are also interested in the encapsulation of such discourse in an aesthetic form.

Emotive satisfaction, on the other hand, refers to the capacity of the narrator to manipulate the feelings of the audience during performance in such a manner that the members of the audience will feel encouraged to continue to direct their attention to the narrative experience while it lasts. The retention of audience attention is however only attainable through the performer's manipulation of the emotions of the audience. Manipulation of audience feelings or sensations is manifested in narrative-performance through the patterning of narrative images or episodes. For audience emotion to be successfully manipulated, the performer must arrange his images in such a way that subsequent images vary audience emotion. The elimination of boredom is thus a crucial factor in the performer's effort at varying audience sensation. While such non-plot related elements of a story as songs or authorial comments are means of eliminating boredom, effective and subtle elimination of boredom can only be achieved through the interlarding of such plot-related materials as images or episodes that refer directly or peripherally to the behaviour of characters in stories. Narrative images or episodes should accordingly be organized into patterns that manipulate audience emotions during performance. More specifically, narrative units should fluctuate audience sensations or feelings during performance by intermittently activating, stabilizing or depressing audience sensation.

The fluctuation of audience sensation is attempted through the relationship existing between two images or sets of image which the audience is confronted with as a performance progresses. For example, a story in which a jealous co-wife sends her husband's son on a dangerous errand is capable of activating the sensation of audience members by raising their expectation. The story may either further activate this with the image of the boy's willingness to go on the errand or depress such a sensation with the boy's refusal to obey the jealous co-wife's instructions. However, the fluctuation of audience sensation will be meaningless if different images or episodes fail to circumscribe the perception of the audience. In other words, while in their diversity images should vary audience sensation, they must also combine not only to move the story towards a complete closure but also to create a cognitive focus for the audience vis-à-vis the performer's preoccupation. Correspondingly, on the emotive side, the performer must align the images constituting his story in such a manner that he moves the sensation of his audience back and forth on a spectrum of expectancy that can be characterized at the one extreme by activation, in the middle by stabilization and at the other extreme by depression. Audience sensation is activated when its feeling is aroused or excited by the conception of a conflict requiring resolution. Sensation is stabilized when a new image that is given to the audience only succeeds in giving additional, but not conflicting, information about an already activated or depressed sensation. In other words, the sensation of the audience at a particular point during the narrative is stabilized when it remains exactly as it was before the supply of a new image. Finally, audience sensation is depressed when narrative-images are given only for the purpose of forestalling or defusing conflict.[7] In other words, conflict-producing images activate sensation while conflict-resolving images depress sensation.

Conflict is the major source of tension in oral narrative-performance just as it is in most other forms of fiction. The substance of any oral piece of fiction lies in the movement of images or episodes from the conception of conflict to the resolution of the conflict conceived at the initial part of the story. While a story is successfully completed when its major conflict is resolved, tension is increased and diminished in the course of a story by the creation of minor conflicts and resolutions within the larger framework of the major conflict that serves as the main axis of the story. The conception and resolution of such minor conflicts are devices for the manipulation of audience experience during a narrative-performance.

For any narrative-performance to provide full aesthetic satisfac- , tion for the audience, the performer must produce within each narrative experience at least two of the three sensations identified above. Indeed, in all stories, the audience must have their sensation activated as well as depressed while stabilization of sensation may only occur in highly successful and complex narratives. The occurrence of these three sensational states does not depend on the status of the characters in stories; images capable of activating and depressing audience sensation occur in animal as well as human and supernatural stories. Thus, each narrative-performance is composed of clusters of images that are capable of activating, stabilizing or depressing audience sensation.

By image we mean a unit of anthropomorphic behaviour such as a character —God, human, or plant—performing an act that is comprehensible within the framework of human experience. An example of an image is when a character performs or receives an action, for example when one character beats another character or sends another character on an errand or asks another character for a favour. Image-cluster refers to a combination of closely tempo-causally related images or a sequence of images that inevitably lead to the conception and resolution of discrete conflicts within the larger framework of the main conflict serving as the axis of a story. For instance, a story in which a wicked senior wife sends the only son of her deceased co-wife on a dangerous journey to the land of monsters will evoke two sets of conflicts: major or continuous, and minor or discrete. The major conflict will be the boy's problems in performing the Herculean tasks ahẹad of him and either succumbing to or surviving the dangers inherent in them. This major conflict persists until either the boy is killed or returns home safely to shame his step-mother. However, discrete conflicts can occur within the larger conflict. For example, the boy may meet an old man on the way who requests him to perform a specific task for him. The boy's performance or non-performance of this task constitutes a discrete conflict. Thus, acts that contribute to the creation and resolution of a discrete conflict can be combined into an image-cluster.[8]

By way of illustration, one of the common Yoruba co-wife stories manifests the three characteristics of aesthetic harmony that we have identified above. A narrative titled "The Story of Two Wives"[9] evokes an experience of which the cognitive focus is on problems of social maladjustment. The junior wife is projected as a positive model of the community's values which foster good human relations: modesty, kindness, generosity, obedience, respect and consideration for others' concerns and interests. On the other hand, the senior wife is portrayed as a model of social maladjustment possessing characteristics opposite to those of the junior wife.

However, for the performer to meaningfully engage the audience and ensure the apprehension of his message, he must pattern his images with the hope of elimininating boredom by making the sensation of the audience fluctuate between activation and depression. In this narrative, there are about nineteen images of behaviour all of which are aligned with the manipulation of audience emotion in mind. Schematically, this story (Story I at the end of this chapter), can be broken down as follows:

IMAGE PATTERNS IN "THE STORY OF TWO WIVES"
Progression and Characterization of Images

Activation-Images	Stabilization-Images	Depression-Images
Image I Jealousy and conflict between co-wives = conflict	—	*Image II* Exchange of property between the two wives = temporary truce, partial resolution of conflict.
Image III Loss of senior wife's property = restoration of conflict.	—	*Image IV* Offer of replacement of lost *igbako* = partial resolution of conflict.
Image V Senior wife refuses offer of replacement and·insists on having her original *igbako* back = conflict restored.	—	*Image VI* Junior wife sets out to look for the original *igbako* = partial resolution of conflict.
Image VII Requests made of junior wife; crisis of choice = conflict conceived within the individual.	—	*Image VIII* Requests fulfill partial resolution of conflict.

145

*Images IX
and X*

Repetition of old
conflict and
resolution

Image XI
Injunction to
pluck non-juicy
fruit = conflict
conceived from
crisis of choice.

—

Image XII
Retrieval of original
igbako and acquisi-
tion of new wealth =
partial resolution.

Image XIII
Senior wife refuses
offer of wealth =
new conflict con-
ceived.

Image XIV
Senior wife jour-
neys to the stream
in order to "lose"
her *igbako* = con-
flict restored.

Image XV
Senior wife's
feigned loss and
search for the
igbako, requests
made, requests
rejected = conflict
intensified.

*Images XVI &
XVII*

Meeting with two
other women who
request for help in
vain = repetition
of old conflict.

Image XVIII
Non-compliance
with final injunc-
tion; taking all
the fruits home.
Disjuncture between
senior wife's and
junior wife's ap-
proach capable of
exciting audience =
conflict climaxed.

Image XIX
Senior wife is killed.
Agent of disorder is
eliminated and total
order restored =
final resolution of
conflict.

The introduction or initial exposition, in which the note of discord and jealousy between two co-wives is suggested, provides the initial activation of audience sensation. With this, the audience's expectation of a relationship riddled with conflicts is raised. The second image—junior wife borrowing *igbako* from the senior wife and the senior wife's positive response—quickly depresses audience sensation by suggesting the possibility of peace and mutual acceptance between the wives. The third image —the loss of the *igbako* by the junior wife—returns to the activating of audience sensation produced by the initial image. The possibility of conflict is further aggravated by the loss of the senior wife's property by the junior wife while the fourth image—junior wife's offer of replacement—is capable of depressing audience sensation; it suggests the possibility of peace or of avoidance of conflict. The fifth image—senior wife's rejection of the offer of replacement —returns. audience sensation to its activated level as it further sharpens the ensuing conflict between the two wives. The junior wife's decision to search for the *igbako* is capable of depressing sensation, especially as it suggests the possibility of conflict avoidance. Image seven—the first old woman's request to the junior wife—activates sensation. it creates the tension that accompanies choice. However, the junior wife's fulfilment in the eighth and ninth images are stabilizing in that they simply reinforce an old attitude. The junior wife's obedience to the old woman in the tenth image is likely to depress sensation, especially as it is followed by the announcement of a possible retrieval of the lost *igbako*. Furthermore, the plucking of the fruits in the eleventh image and the junior wife's return journey home are images that are capable of activating sensation; the audience's expectation is raised as their certainty of the successful outcome is made to dangle with this image of movement in space. Image twelve—the recovery of the original *igbako* and the appearance of wealth—is one capable of depressing sensation; the audience is likely to feel relieved by the resolution of a protracted conflict.

However, this sensation is quickly activated by the conception of a new conflict in the senior wife's refusal of the offer of wealth from the junior wife in the thirteenth image. This activation is continued by the senior wife's decision to take her *igbako* to the stream as well as by the feigned loss of her *igbako* and her search for it in images fourteen and fifteen. This activation of sensation is also produced in the senior wife's refusal to carry out the instruction of the old women in images sixteen and seventeen. Images sixteen and seventeen are sensation stabilizers—they merely recreate an old structure. The senior wife's plucking of the wrong fruits in the eighteenth image first stabilizes sensation because it shows the senior wife behaving true to type. However, the image may also activate sensation later as the movement in space is capable of producing doubt in the minds of the audience as to what might happen at home.

Finally, the last image produces an increasing depression of audience sensation. The smashing of the two fruits in the house, that were to be smashed on the way, and the resultant appearance of bees and scorpions presage the final defeat of an agent of disorder that is later achieved by bites from the snakes from the third fruit. The massive attack by these deadly creatures of an avaricious and uncompromising character supplies the final resolution to the major conflict of the jealousy/envy of junior wife by senior wife. With the death of the senior wife, the performer's comment on social maladjustment is underscored. Tolerance, understanding, flexibility are rewarded in the junior wife while their opposite are punished in the senior wife.

Similarly, an animal story by a different performer hundreds of kilometres away from the home of the performer of the co-wives' story shows the same degree of interest by the performer in manipulating audience emotion by interchanging between activation and depression of audience sensation. The cognitive focus of the story, "The Tortoise and the Iroko",[10] is on the notion of the evasion of justice or utter Machiavellianism. The Iroko is portrayed as the custodian of justice, while the tortoise is projected as an evader of justice. In their juxtaposition, the performer suggests the problems—either as delay or denial—that characterize the delivery of justice. The performer also suggests, with the final triumph of Iroko, that the fulfillment of contractual obligations and the punishment of the guilty are necessary conditions for upholding order in any community.

In terms of the emotional experience of the narrative, the performer patterns the images of the story in a way that suggests the elimination of boredom as a key device in the retention of audience attention. The images in this story can be broken into eighteen units of action:

IMAGE PATTERNS IN "TORTOISE AND IROKO"

Activation-Images   Stabilization-Images   Depression-Images

Image I
General famine, Iroko's
survival, conflicts with
Tortoise's starvation.

—

Image II
Tortoise requests for
Iroko's assistance = con-
flict further individualized.

—

Image III
Iroko accepts to help
Tortoise = partial reso-
lution of conflict.

Image IV
Invitation of Goat into the
picture without full knowledge of Iroko/Tortoise
deal = potential conflict
between Goat and Tortoise
or Goat and Iroko.

—

Image V
Goat fulfills obligation
for Tortoise and is kill-
ed by Iroko = partial
resolution.

Image VI
Tortoise makes a new deal
with Iroko = conflict
restored.

—

Image VII
Iroko accepts Tortoise's
conditions of two years
for two blows = partial
resolution.

Image VIII
Sheep is invited to sleep in
Tortoise's house = con-
flict restored.

—

Image IX
Sheep fulfills obligation
and is killed by Iroko's
blows = partial resolu-
tion.

Image X
Tortoise makes a bigger
demand = conflict restor-
ed.

—

Image XI
Iroko accepts Tortoise's
requests = partial reso-
lution.

Image XII
Invitation of Wild Pig =
conflict renewed.

—

Image XIII
Wild Pig is killed by
Iroko = partial resolu-
tion.

Image XIV

Tortoise asks for seven yams = conflict restored.

—

Image XV

Iroko accepts = partial resolution.

Image XVI

Invitation of Civet Cat = conflict renewed.

—

Image XVII

The rain washes Civet Cat away thus allowing a frontal meeting between Iroko and Tortoise = conflict intensified.

—

Image XVIII

Iroko kills Tortoise after several abortive attempts = final resolution of conflict.

The performer organizes these actions to make audience sensation fluctuate and thereby further his interest in the achievement of aesthetic harmony with his audience. While he engages his audience cognitively with the notion of justice, he occupies them emotionally by varying their sensation with images that are capable of producing different sensations.

The initial situation of serious famine and total desiccation supplies the first image of activation of sensation. The extreme situation of mass starvation suggests the need for urgent or desperate solution by Tortoise. Similarly, activation is suggested in the second image—Tortoise's request for assistance from Iroko—while Iroko's willingness to assist the Tortoise in the third image, as long as the latter obeys his injunction, is capable of depressing audience sensation. With Iroko's assistance, the initial conflict is resolved—Tortoise's starvation is temporarily stemmed. However, in the fourth image Tortoise's invitation to Goat to sleep in his ante-room and answer early morning calls by visitors is a sensation-activating unit: it introduces the possibility of another conflict, either between Goat and Iroko, or Tortoise and Iroko. But Goat's response to Iroko, together with the subsequent killing of Goat by Iroko, is a sensation-depressing image. The first conflict between Iroko and Tortoise, vis-à-vis food, is not resolved. Furthermore, Tortoise's food supply is greatly improved with the protein that he now gets from Goat's meat.

Tortoise's second visit to Iroko with the request for more yams and hence more blows reintroduces the activation of sensation with the concept of a new conflict between Iroko and Tortoise. This activated sensation is quickly replaced with depression as Tortoise successfully invites Sheep to come and sleep with him and answer calls for him. The fact that the Sheep is a symbol of stupidity among the Yoruba makes its eventual death almost a *fait accompli* and thus predicts the subsequent killing of Sheep by Iroko. Tortoise's third visit to Iroko again activates sensation in that it re-establishes a new conflict between Iroko and Tortoise. Furthermore, Tortoise's invitation to Wild Pig supplies another image of sensation-activation. Wild Pig's characteristic unruliness and intractability increase the doubt of the outcome of the Iroko/Wild Pig encounter the following morning. However, with Iroko's killing of Wild Pig, the performer supplies a sensation-depressing image.

Another activation of audience sensation is attempted in Tortoise's fourth visit to Iroko, now that a new and more formidable conflict is conceived with the increase in the number of blows to be given by Iroko. This activated sensation is however quickly depressed by Tortoise's invitation to Civet-Cat to be his guest. The fact that this is an animal known for its excessive smell and love of sleep predicts the outcome of the Iroko/Civet-Cat meeting the following morning. Surprisingly, however, sensation is quickly activated by the incident of the heavy down-pour that washes the slumbering Civet-Cat away from the outpost. This activation is then quickly followed by the final depression that accompanies Iroko's killing of Tortoise. This final depression of sensation, reflective of poetic justice, shows the final sense of satisfaction and fulfillment of the initial expectation of the audience raised by the series of violated contracts made between Iroko and Tortoise.

Thus, in these two stories, the organization or patterning of images is a crucial factor in the production of a full and harmonious experience of the narrative for both narrator and audience. It is at the level of organization or composition that the performer holds the audience's attention long enough to make them grasp, in a way pleasant to experience, the cognitive aspect of his performance. Accordingly, a performer's achievement of artistic spacing of images in relation to one another is a key factor in the attainment of a form capable of establishing aesthetic harmony with his audience. The elimination of boredom or the variegation of sensation in the audience, a crucial obligation on the part of the narrator, is manifestly attainable through the narrator's capacity to alternate between sensation-activating or conflict-producing images and sensation-depressing or conflict-resolving images.

The analysis of beauty in oral performance will be an on-going enterprise among folklorists and scholars of oral literature for some time to come. However, the need for the development of rigorous and yet flexible ways of determining and describing salient features of aesthetic experience in such a temporal art form as narrative-performance is an urgent one. The fulfillment of this need has been partly attempted in this short study.

STORY I

THE STORY OF TWO WIVES

Performer:	Musa Ayinde
Ethnic Group:	Yoruba
Profession:	Tailor (Age 29)
Place:	Akodudu, Ilorin
Audience:	Three members
Time:	8.00 p.m.
Date:	28th December, 1979

Performer: Alo o!
Audience: Alo o!
Performer: Ni ijo kan
Audience: Ijo kan kitan l'aiye
Performer: Ni igba kan
Audience: Igba kan nlo, igba kan nbo, sugbon aiye duro titi l'aiye. [11]

Once upon a time, there were two wives who lived in discord because the senior wife was jealous of the junior wife. However, since they were married to the same husband, they were forced to live together. One day the junior wife borrowed the senior wife's *igbako* because she had misplaced hers. Later, she went to a nearby stream to wash it together with other household utensils. As she was washing the *igbako*, it accidentally fell into the stream and floated away. She returned home and reported the incident to the senior wife. The senior wife, who because of jealousy hated the junior wife, said, "You must go and find my *igbako*". The junior wife believed that the *igbako* was lost forever, so she searched her room and brought out her own. She offered it to the senior wife as a replacement for the lost *igbako*. The senior wife refused it. She said, "I want my very own *igbako*."

The junior wife then left for the stream. She followed the stream, crying and singing.

152

Performer: Where is my senior mate's *igbako?*
Audience: Slowly it floats down the stream, slowly.
Performer: Where is my senior mate's *igbako?*
Audience: Slowly it floats down the stream, slowly.

She continued along the stream bank, crying and singing. Then she met an old woman. The old woman asked, "Why are you crying, lady?" The woman replied, "The stream carried away my senior mate's *igbako.*" The old woman then said, "If you clean the sores on my feet, I will tell you where to find the *igbako.*" The junior wife did not hesitate. She cleaned and dressed the old woman's sores. The old woman said, "Continue along the bank, you will meet another old woman. She will tell you where to find the *igbako.*" The junior wife left the old woman. She continued along the bank of the stream, crying:

Performer: Where is my senior mate's *igbako?*
Audience: Slowly it floats down the stream, slowly.
Performer: Where is my senior mate's *igbako?*
Audience: Slowly it floats down the stream, slowly.

She continued along the stream bank. She continued walking, crying and singing. Then she met another old woman. The woman had boils all over her face. The old woman asked, "Why are you crying, lady?" The junior wife replied, "The stream carried away my senior mate's *igbako.*" The old woman then said, "If you squeeze my boils for me, I will tell you where to find the *igbako.*" The junior wife honoured the old woman's request. The old woman then said, "Continue along the bank, you will meet another old woman. She will tell you where to find the *igbako.*"

The junior wife left the old woman. She continued along the stream's bank, crying and singing:

Performer: Where is my senior mate's *igbako?*
Audience: Slowly it floats down the stream, slowly.
Performer: Where is my senior mate's *igbako?*
Audience: Slowly it floats down the stream, slowly.

She continued along the stream's bank. She continued walking and crying. Then she met another old woman who had skin rashes all over her body. The old woman asked, "Why are you crying, lady?" The junior wife replied, "The stream carried away my senior mate's *igbako.*" The old woman then said, "If you scratch my rash for me, I will tell you where to find the *igbako.*" Willingly, the junior wife carried out the old woman's wish.

The old woman then told her to go to a nearby orchard to pluck three fruits. "Do not pluck the juicy ones," instructed the old woman. After she had plucked three unripe fruits, the old woman then instructed her to smash one on the ground on her way home, another nearer home and the third when she reached home. The junior wife thanked her and left. On the way home, she smashed one fruit on the ground and there appeared the senior mate's *igbako.* Nearer her home, she smashed the second fruit and riches appeared. On getting home she smashed the third fruit and a beautiful new house appeared. The junior wife was happy. She returned her senior mate's *igbako* to her. She also offered to give some of her wealth to her senior mate who declined.

The senior wife was not happy and she became jealous of the junior wife. She then took her *igbako* to the stream, not to wash it, but to throw it into the stream. She threw it in the first time, but a wave pushed it back to her. She threw it in a second time, and again a wave pushed it back to her. She threw it in a third time with all her might, and then it floated away. She then started to walk along the stream's bank, pretending to be crying and singing:

Performer: Where is my *igbako*?
Audience: Slowly it floats down the stream, slowly.
Perfermer: Where is my *igbako*?
Audience: Slowly it floats down the stream, slowly.

She continued along the bank of the stream. She continued walking and crying. Then she met an old woman. The old woman asked, "Why are you crying, lady?" The woman replied, "The stream carried away my *igbako*." The old woman then said, "If you clean the sores on my feet, I will tell you where to find the *igbako*." The senior wife replied, "No, I cannot touch those horrible sores of yours." The old woman then said, "Continue along the bank, you will meet another old woman. She will tell you where to find the *igbako*."

The senior wife hissed contemptuously and then left the old woman. She continued walking along the bank, shedding crocodile tears and singing:

Performer: Where is my *igbako*?
Audience: Slowly it floats down the stream, slowly.
Performer: Where is my *igbako*?
Audience: Slowly it floats down the stream, slowly.

She continued along the bank. She continued walking and crying. Then she met another old woman. The old woman had boils all over her face. The old woman asked, "Why are you crying, lady.?" The senior wife replied, "The stream carried away my *igbako*." The old woman then said, "If you can squeeze my boils, I will tell you where to find the *igbako*." The senior wife said, "No, I cannot touch that horrible face of yours." The old woman then said, "Continue along the bank, you will meet another old woman. She will tell you where to find the *igbako*."

The senior wife spat and left the old woman. She continued along the bank, shedding crocodile tears and singing:

Performer: Where is my *igbako*?
Audience: Slowly it floats down the stream, slowly.
Performer: Where is my *igbako*?
Audience: Slowly it floats down the stream, slowly.

She continued along the bank. She continued walking and crying. Then she met another old woman. The old woman had skin rashes all over her body. The woman asked, "Why are you crying, lady?" The senior wife replied, "The stream carried away my *igbako*." The old woman then said, "If you scratch my rash, I will tell you where to find the *igbako*." The senior wife said, "No, I cannot scratch your horrible body." The old woman then asked her to go to a nearby orchard to pluck fruits. "Do not pluck the juicy ones," said the old woman. But the senior wife disobeyed the old woman's instructions by plucking three juicy fruits. The old woman then told her to smash one on the ground on her way home, another nearer her home, and the third when she reached her home.

The senior wife left the old woman without thanking her. Instead of smashing one of the fruits on the way home and another nearer her home, she carried the three fruits right into her bedroom where she locked herself up. She then smashed the first fruit and there appeared bees which started to sting her. She quickly smashed the second fruit and there appeared scorpions which also stung her. Desperately, she smashed the third fruit and there appeared snakes which bit her to death.

Performer: This is the end of my story. What does it teach us?

1st Member of Audience: It teaches us not to be jealous of others.

2nd Member of Audience: It teaches us not to be greedy.

Performer: And what else?

3rd Member of Audience: It teaches us not to tell lies and to be respectful to our elders.

Performer: Good.

STORY II

THE TORTOISE AND THE IROKO TREE:

Performer:	Monisola Fifo
Ethnic Group:	Yoruba
Profession:	Petty trading
Place:	Oke Agunla, Ondo
Audience:	Fifteen.
Time:	7 p.m.
Date:	March 20, 1979.

Once upon a time, there was a very serious famine in which trees dried up, leaves dried up, and birds and animals had nothing to eat. The soil also was dry. After a while, human beings as well as animals and trees began to die. It was only *Iroko* that was feeding well and remained fresh and green. It seemed as if he was taking vitality drugs. Tortoise, the animal full of tricks, looked at him for a while and asked himself how *Iroko* was feeding and managing to keep fresh. He then got ready and went to visit *Iroko*. When he arrived, he greeted *Iroko* and paid all due respect to him. He introduced his reason for coming. He said he had come to ask how *Iroko* was able to survive the famine and to be so fresh. He asked *Iroko* to let him into the secret and promised to pay whatever it would cost him. *Iroko* then smiled and said that it was not too difficult but asked whether Tortoise would be able to fulfil the one condition. Tortoise said he would. He then told Tortoise that he had yams and that he was ready to give Tortoise some, provided Tortoise was able to fulfil the condition to be laid down by him. Tortoise promise that he was ready to fulfil any condition at all, if only he would be given the yams. The *Iroko* laid down the condition that if Tortoise was given a yam, he should expect a blow of the club the following morning. Tortoise said that that condition seemed too simple for such a favour and that he was ready to receive the club on any part of his body.

Then *Iroko* gave one yam to Tortoise and Tortoise left *Iroko's* house. As he was going along he began to think of how to escape the danger from the blow of the heavy club. He later arrived at a possible solution. He decided to invite the first animal he met to his house. In short, as he went further, he saw Goat, then he saw Sheep. They both cried out in surprise. At last Goat approached him and asked from where he had got the yam he was carrying. Tortoise said it was from his own farm. He said he had plenty of yams in his farm. Goat asked whether she could follow him home and take part of the yam. Tortoise expressed sympathy for Goat's condition and asked her to follow him. Goat was very happy. She then followed Tortoise home. When they got home they prepared pounded yam. When they were about to start eating, Tortoise called out to Goat and said, "You know what? You cannot just eat the pounded yam like that. You have to do something for me. The job is not tedious to do. It is this: very early in the morning tomorrow at cock-crow, I shall have a visitor; when he comes he will knock at the door. If he calls me, you just answer. Tell him that I am asleep or that I am not home." Goat replied that that was not difficult to do. She asked if they could start eating. They finished the food at once. They rested a while and went to sleep. Very early on the following morning, *Iroko* took his club and went to Tortoise's house. Tortoise slept in the inner room but asked Goat to sleep in the parlour behind the door. When *Iroko* came and knocked at the door, Goat answered the call and opened the door for him. When *Iroko* saw her, he immediately gave her a heavy blow. It sent Goat sprawling on the ground and finally she died. When Tortoise saw the body, he was very happy. He then took it and prepared it for eating. He began to roast it.

In the afternoon of that day, Tortoise went to *Iroko* again. He told him that he had not felt his club at all, and asked if he had really beaten him. If that was the case, he would now ask for two yams, because one stroke of the club was nothing to him; it was just as though his body had been scratched. He asked *Iroko* to give him two yams and to come and give him two blows of the club the following morning. *Iroko* was annoyed and asked sternly if Tortoise would be able to receive two blows from his club. Tortoise said that there would be no problem. At once *Iroko* gave Tortoise two yams and Tortoise set off to his house. As he was going along he met Sheep. Sheep expressed surprise at seeing Tortoise with such heavy fat yams. He offered to follow Tortoise home so he could take some of the yam. Tortoise asked him to follow. He explained that he had got the yams from his own farm. Then Sheep followed Tortoise home. When they got home, they prepared pounded yam with delicious soup made with the goat meat. As they were about to start eating, Tortoise said, holding Sheep's hand, "Shouldn't we make some agreement about what you will do for me in return for the pounded yam?" Sheep asked what kind of agreement they were to make. Tortoise said it was not difficult. It was only that he always got up late. He always wanted to have a good night's sleep. His sleep must be interrupted. He said that a friend was going to call on him very early in the morning. Sheep should answer and tell him that Tortoise was not in. He asked Sheep to sleep behind the door so that when his friend knocked, he could open the door for him and tell him that Tortoise had gone out. Sheep said there would be no problem doing that. Then they ate and went to sleep.

Very early in the morning, *Iroko* had come again with his club. When he got to Tortoise's house, he knocked at the door as before. Sheep opened the door im-

156

mediately, and before he could utter a word, *Iroko* had given him two blows with his heavy club. Immediately after, Sheep died. *Iroko* did not know. He thought it was Tortoise who had opened the door. He went back to his house. When Tortoise still in bed, heard what had happened between Iroko and Sheep, he smiled. He felt happy. He had not finished the goat meat of the previous night but now he had Sheep meat as well. He said to himself that that was how he would survive the famine.

In the morning, he prepared the body of Sheep as he had done for Goat the previous day. He then went to *Iroko's* house. *Iroko* was very surprised to see him after the two heavy blows of the club. He thought it might be Tortoise's ghost, but Tortoise said it was not. He said *Iroko's* club had no effect on him. He then asked whether there were still any yams left. He asked for three yams this time and asked *Iroko* to come the following morning to give him three blows of his club—maybe he would feel it this time. Iroko agreed and gave him three yams. Tortoise took the three yams and began to go home again. As he was going along, he met Wild Pig who had become very lean because of the famine. When he saw Tortoise, he was surprised and he asked how he had got such fine yams. He asked Tortoise whether he could follow him home to take some of the yam. Tortoise told him that he had got the yam from his own farm. He said he had plenty of yams in his farm. Wild Pig asked Tortoise to do him a favour and Tortoise agreed. They went together to Tortoise's house. When they got there, they cooked the yams and prepared pounded yam with delicious soup. They cooked part of Sheep's meat. When they were about to start eating, Tortoise took hold of the hands of Wild Pig. He said that they should conclude a certain agreement before eating. Wild Pig asked what agreement they should make. Then Tortoise told him that he usually stayed late in bed but a friend was coming to call on him very early in the morning. Wild Pig should open the door for him when he knocked, and say Tortoise had gone out. Wild Pig considered this a very simple matter and agreed. After the meal, Tortoise went into the inner room to sleep while the Wild Pig slept in the parlour behind the door.

Very early in the morning, *Iroko* took his club as usual and came to Tortoise's house. When he got to the gate of Tortoise's house, he knocked as usual. Wild Pig heard and came to open the door. When *Iroko* saw Wild Pig, he gave him three heavy blows with his club. Before the third blow, Wild Pig had fallen dead. *Iroko* went back home. He thought he had killed Tortoise this time. Tortoise heard what had happened and again he was very happy. When he got up, he took Wild Pig's body and prepared it for eating as he had done with other animals. He then left for *Iroko's* house. When *Iroko* saw him, he was sad. He asked himself whether Tortoise would be able to cheat him like this for ever. He recounted how he had been giving yams to Tortoise and trying to kill him without success. He was surprised. Tortoise boasted again that his club could not do anything to him. He even advised *Iroko* to look for a better club.

The following day Tortoise went to *Iroko* again to ask for seven yams with much boasting. Iroko gave him seven yams and Tortoise went home again. As he was going along he met Civet-Cat (*Eta*) an animal with an acrid smell and a propensity for sleeping. He had become lean as a result of the famine. When he saw Tortoise with the yams, he approached him and Tortoise asked him to follow him to his house. When they got home, they prepared pounded yam as usual. When they were about to start eating, Tortoise asked Civet-Cat to enter into a certain agreement with him so he could eat. Tortoise said his friend was coming to call on him very early in the morning. He said to Civet-Cat what he had said to the other animals before him. He asked him to sleep behind the door so that when his friend knocked, he could open for him. Civet-Cat agreed and they ate the food. Shortly after, they went to sleep. Almost immediately, heavy rain started. Civet-Cat was noted for sleeping soundly. He went to sleep immediately. A torrent of water entered the house and carried Civet-Cat away. Tortoise did not know this. Very early in the morning, *Iroko*, who was so angry that he was unable to sleep all night, came to Tortoise's house and knocked as before. Nobody answered. Tortoise heard his knock and began to call Civet-Cat to open the door. When *Iroko* heard Tortoise calling Civet-Cat, he became very annoyed. He knocked again angrily. Tortoise continued to call Civet-Cat softly to open the door. *Iroko* then kicked open the door and went to Tortoise in the inner room. He found Tortoise and gave him heavy blows with his club with all his might until Tortoise fell down dead. *Iroko* went back home expecting Tortoise to come to boast as usual. He waited for Tortoise for about four days. At last he went to Tortoise's house to check up. When he got there he found him dead. That was how Tortoise died.

This story teaches us not to be hypocritical. He who is a hypocrite will die treacherously. If one sees a danger coming, one should not turn it on another man' head. Instead, one should try to prevent it or else one will suffer for it in the end.

NOTES

1. Seymour Chatman, Story and Discourse. (Itahca, 1978). Bennison Gray, *The Phenomenon of Literature*. (The Hague, 1975).

2. Ruth Finnegan, *Oral Literature in Africa:* (Oxford, 1970). Especially the chapter on Prose Narrative II: Content and Form.

3. Modupe Broderick, "The 'Tori': Structure, Aesthetic and Time in Krio Oral Narrative-Performance," Ph.D. Thesis, University of Wisconsin, (1977)

4. See for example, Modupe Broderick, "Social Significance of Binary Oppositions and Narrative Patterns in Three West African Oral Narratives". Paper presented at the 1981 African Literature Association Conference in Claremont, California, U.S.A.

5. Ibid.

6. See Ropo Sekoni, "Cognitive an Aesthetic Process in Yoruba Oral Narrative" **Proceeding of MLAN Conference Papers, 1980,**

7. For more information on image-patterning as a means of making audience emotion, fluctuate, see Ropo Sekoni, "A World in Search of Leadership: a study of Structure and Communication in Soyinka's scripts", Ph.D thesis, University of Wisconsin-Madison. 1977

8. **For a different conception of image-cluster, see Harold Scheub, *The Xhosa Ntsomi*. (Oxford, 1975).**

9. Modupe Broderick had at Bayero University, Kano, been conducting research into narratology in such cultures as Krio, Mende, Yoruba, Hausa and a few other smaller cultures. This narrative, Story I above, is from Broderick's data bank.

10. See Story II above. Story II is from Ropo Sekoni's collection.
11. This Yoruba formula for commencing a narrative-performance can be translated thus:

    Performer: A story!
    Audience: Yes, a story!
    Performer: One day . . .
    Audience: One day never ends.
    Performer: Once upon a time . . .
    Audience: Time goes, time comes, but life endures for ever.

Performer: A story.
Performer:
Audience:

The Oral Performer and his Audience:
A Case Study of *The Ozidi Saga*

Isidore Okpewho

ALTHOUGH in oral literary studies it is widely accepted that the audience of an oral performance generally exerts a dynamic influence on the performer's work, whether in a participatory or a critical capacity, case studies of this influence are somewhat rare. This is largely because the business of transcribing with absolute faith the relevant contingencies of an oral performance is a very expensive one; there are very few books in which these contingencies are recorded at the appropriate points, because there are equally few publishers willing to commit their money to the volume of material that would result from such meticulous documentation. Consequently, we have mostly been content with platitudes about the integration of the audience in the performance of a song or a tale; seldom have we been exposed to enlightening insights because this integration seems generally accepted as an article of faith. It is therefore with considerable joy that one receives the publication of J. P. Clark's edition of *The Ozidi Saga* which, by meticulously documenting the statements interpolated by various "Spectators" into the narration of the tale, invites us to critically examine the role of the audience in one particular performance and thus abandon our smug acceptance of well-advertised positions on the subject.

We can identify roughly two positions with regard to the role of the audience in an oral performance. The first sees the performer as one member of a society of which his audience is only a random portion. Though he is an artist blessed with uncommon skill in executing a song or a tale before an audience, sometimes to the accompaniment of music played by himself or attending instrumentalists, his outlook and sensations are not different from those of the rest of the society. The images of his tale are simply the same as those experienced by other members of his community, and at the moment of performance he merely bears with him the charge to convey to a wider public a world-view which he shares with his fellows. The reason why the audience is able to participate actively in the performance of a tale is that there is no division whatsoever between the narrator's apperception of the *world* of the tale and their own.

Such a view of total harmony between artist and audience may be seen in Harold Scheub's report of performances by women among the Xhosa of southern Africa whom he has scrupulously researched. "There is full participation," he tells us, "by the members of the audience in the unfolding story. No proscenium arch exists, there is no safety in distance or darkness. Everyone is known: the artist emerges from the audience and, her narrative complete, is again swallowed up by the audience. The separate emotions and experience of individual members of an audience are woven into the narrative being evoked. The artistic experience is a complex one. The members of the audience know the images. They have experienced them scores of times. They know the performer intimately and she knows them. The artist seeks in a variety of ways to involve the audience wholly in her production."[1]

The implication of this emotional-intellectual harmony between the artist and his audience is that there is no point at which the artist may be seen to be contravening or rebelling against the outlook of his society of which the audience is a random sample. The success of a performance is judged fundamentally by the degree to which the artist mirrors the outlook and expectations of this society; and the audience of the performance seems obliged primarily to aid the artist in this task of mirroring. The extreme corollary of this view of an artist-audience harmony is thus that, where in the course of his story a narrator commits a gaffe or seems to deviate from a communal point of view, the audience will simply accept the event as an aberration to which the rest of the society are liable and thus save the artist the unnecessary embarrassment of a correction. This at least would seem to be the view of Daniel Biebuyck when he tells us, from his research among Zairean story-tellers, that "the Nyanga listener is not at all disturbed by such apparent inconsistencies"[2] as may from time to time crop up in the performance of a tale.

A somewhat different position on this subject accepts that *some*

161

line is discernible between artist and audience. Something of this position has been articulated by Ruth Finnegan in her comparative survey, *Oral Poetry,* in the section where she treats the various kinds and roles of an audience at oral performances. After discussing the category of "participatory" audiences, she goes on to speak of a different kind: "In other cases, which need to be distinguished, the occasion is a specialist one in that the demarcation between performer(s) and audience is clear, and the audience is functionally separate". In discussing this category of artist-audience relationship, Finnegan leads us through a comparative survey of situations among the Kirghiz of Turkey, the Chinese, the Yoruba and various other communities. The Yoruba example is particularly enlightening, perhaps because it is closer to us. She quotes from Babalola's study of *ijala* performances, showing how members of the audience (some of them *ijala* artists present at the occasion) may dispute details in the performer's song and how the performer in turn responds, to assert either his correctness or his poetic licence. She then concludes this part of her discussion by saying: "Such cases are interesting for what they show about the old theories about the possibly 'communal' nature of oral literature, and the part played by the 'folk' in its creation . . . There are participatory audiences, for one thing, and then, over and above the way in which any *face-to-face* audience is likely to affect the manner and content of the poetry, there is the accepted convention in some contexts that members of the audience can intervene directly."[3]

The implication of this latter position is that there is a sense in which the artist and his audience may not be seen in terms of a harmonious equivalence. He may be a member of the larger society, but at the moment of his performance, he is engaged in an activity which puts him in a special light and indeed encourages a certain atmosphere of confrontation between him and his listeners. There is no doubt that in the final analysis this confrontation will result in an overall gain in excitement for the performance and may indeed bring out the best in the creative artist. But the situation does invite us to query the old assumption that in his performance the artist is simply mirroring the outlook of his society at large.

In the following study I would like to use the *The Ozidi Saga*[4] as a way of testing the various levels of interaction between the sensibilities of the artist and his audience. But first it is important to know something of the circumstances in which this version of the

Ozidi tale of the Ijo was recorded. This story of a posthumously born hero, who avenges the assassination of his father by fellow-warriors and never stops his slaughter until he eliminates all the forces in his community and reigns in uncontested supremacy, is traditionally told during a festival among the Tarakiri Orua, a sub-group of the Ijo of the Niger Delta (in the Bendel State of Nigeria). Traditionally the performance spans a period of seven nights. In this particular instance, the story was performed in Ibadan, in the Yoruba west of Nigeria, several hundred kilometers away from its origin. In spite of this remove, however, the atmosphere of the recording managed (and here J. P. Clark deserves full credit for his imagination) to retain something of the traditional setting. Though there were a number of European and other non-Ijo colleagues who accompanied Clark to the event, the audience was essentially made up of Ijo residents at Ibadan; the performance itself was hosted by Madam Yabuku, an Ijo matron who has led Ijo groups in the performance of traditional songs for Radio Nigeria; the recording was done by Clark, himself an Ijo; and the entire business was accomplished in a total of seven nights as dictated by tradition. We can safely say therefore that, though the story was performed far from home and outside of the festival circumstances in which it was regularly enacted in the home setting, the artist (who was also backed by a group of musical accompanists and cheer-leaders), had an adequate socio-cultural climate for the performance of the story. Let us now examine the performance in the context of the behaviour of the audience.

Approbation and encouragement

Perhaps we should start by observing those instances in which the audience seems to take a positive and appreciative view of the bard's performance. There is no question that traditional performers like Okabou Ojobolo, who did this version of the Ozidi story, attract the patronage of scholars like J. P. Clark precisely because their art has won the approval of their fellow citizens who consequently recommend them to the curious field researcher. One of the most effective ways whereby an aritist achieves this measure of approbation is by his skill in manipulating traditional turns of phrase and the histrionic resources of speech and act to good, affective account.

There are, accordingly, countless instances in which Clark

records the "laughter" and "appellation" (with praise-names) by which various members of the audience greet the success of Okabou in executing a scene or a phrase. Once in a while, for instance, Madam Yabuku, the hostess of this performance, comes in to cheer the bard with his peculiar praise-name for doing a good job, and of course the bard relishes this approbation to the full. The following digressive dialogue, which comes at the end of the narration of the struggle in which Ozidi destroys an early opponent, Ebeya, is typical of the exchange of courtesies between Madam Yabuku and the bard Okabou:

(Appellation)

Yabuku:	Agada kpa yan yan!
Okabou:	It's fire!
	Don't touch it!
	Touch it and you get burnt.
Yabuku:	Now on with it!
Okabou:	Agreed
	Fast runs the tide.
	And see how I breast it. O voice, pity!
	Seven days goes the narrative.
	And the voice is beginning to patch.

(Laughter) (p. 169)

Another notable exchange comes towards the very end of the performance on the last (seventh) day. Having executed that last episode in which Ozidi destroys the Smallpox King and embraces his mother (or grandmother) in a final show of triumphant joy, the bard earns one more appreciative appellation from a hostess whom he has surely done proud (p. 387).

Much more frequent in this performance, however, are those instances in which the bard seems to carry the audience along by the affective force of his speech and act so that they react favourably with expressions such as laughter, gasping and ululation. Whether in these instances the bard touches them with an empathic recognition of images which are part of the stock of their cultural life, or successfully sweeps them off the ground of reality so that they accept the fantasy of his portraits, there is no doubt that he has made a positive impact on their senses. For intance, when night falls on the battle between Ozidi and the "half-man" Azezabife and the latter pleads for suspension of hostilities on the grounds that "I do not in the dimness and darkness of night seek fights; one

164

eye it is I have", there is laughter from the audience (p. 80). The audience also greets with laughter the touch of humour in that scene in which Azemaroti, all hot and agitated with the prospect of cooking the captive Ozidi and his witch-grandmother Oreame for dinner, is seized with lust at the sight of the rejuvenated sorceress:

> But though he paced about wildly, the moment he caught sight of those breasts of Oreame, he gulped, ogled, and grew completely distracted.
>
> (*Laughter*) (p. 348)

Indeed, the "speaking picture" conjured up by these statements and descriptions is not so obvious to us from a straightforward reading of the printed text. We can well appreciate Ruth Finnegan's statement that "in the case of oral literature . . . the bare words can *not* be left to speak for themselves"[5]: in many of these instances we have to read the statement back again so as to realise or recognize the histrionic basis to the laughter from the audience, and in most cases, without the editor's notation of "laughter", the scenes would have fallen flat on the ground as simply unelevated moments in the rolling montage of fight episodes that constitute the Ozidi story. We are therefore immensely grateful to the editor for giving us a mental picture of the effectiveness of the artist in executing several episodes to the exhilaration of his audience.

Take the fight between Badoba and Ozidi in which the former, cowed by the latter, flees to a very distant place and stands towering: it is not immediately obvious why there is "laughter" from the audience at this point (p. 152), so we are simply left to conjecture a histrionic effort on the part of the bard. Again, in the following scene describing Oreame's preparations to surprise the enemy into whose hands she and Ozidi had fallen, the "laughter" from the audience seems to have preceded an elaboration of the bard's histrionic act:

> And taking herself to the backyard, you should see Oreame, all taut and tense.
>
> (*Laughter*)
>
> Up by her eyes the veins stood out, near bursting with strain.
> (p. 186)

The editor's annotations are perhaps most effective and helpful in that long episode describing the ponderous and bumbling movements of the Scrotum King as his giant scrotum gets in the way of his battle with the hero Ozidi (pp. 212-29).

165

Clearly, at these points of his performance, the bard has gained the approbation of his audience for a job well done. It is also arguable that they are congratulating him for representing well the acknowledged traditions of the Ijo; and this point is worth emphasizing. Take for instance that scene in which Oreame chants a spell on Ogueren and he is transfixed to the spot:

> Ogueren remained there anchored —
> > *(Laughter)*
> His eyes rolled —
> > *(Laughter)*
> and rolled. (p. 124)

No doubt the audience is moved to laughter here not only by the histrionic act of the bard in portraying Ogueren's plight, but also by the bard's successful recreation of the traditional belief in the effectiveness of magical spells.

Laughter and appellation represent one level of encouragement by the audience of the bard's creative act. A much deeper level of encouragement is shown by those instances in which individual spectators do actively help the bard's mythopoetic effort, and *The Ozidi Saga* reveals a variety of ways in which this can be done. To start with, the bard may sometimes be forced to incorporate a word or idea from a spectator's comment into the sequence of his own narration at that particular point either because it gives a more vivid expression of what he is trying to say in his story, or at any rate because it is apt and appeals to his alert imagination. An interesting example can be seen in the following passage relating to the tedious battle between Ozidi and Ofe, the principal assassin of the hero's father:

> So they held on to each other, and now Ofe, I mean, the number of times Ozidi thrust into Ofe was quite beyond counting. After being cut, he (Ofe) turned into something else. After being mown through, he formed into a new thing. After being carved up, he emerged a fresh creation. Whatever form he took on, when Ozidi had cut up that figure, Ofe showed up again, swearing:
> "Never, I am Ofe!"
> So it went on, and that day's battle also passed. And once more Ofe went home and had a drink of water.
> *Spectator:* A tough affair!
> Said Ofe: "Well, this thing is really complex. If they are

unable to work out my taboo, they would find it tough collecting my scalp, but they are terrible lot." (p.194)

The toughness or complexity which the spectator observes is an apt
description of the fight between the two characters, and the bard
does not hesitate to incorporate it into the speech which he proceeds to put into Ofe's mouth.

A similar prompting from the audience occurs at that scene
where the sorceress Oreame transforms herself into a charming
young lady and poses as Ozidi's wife, prior to their confrontation
with the mother and son team of Azema and Azemaroti:

> Indeed with those breasts . . .
> *Spectator I:* She was like a young woman.
> *Spectator II:* A young woman.
>
> If you saw her Lagos blouse, or her headtie, you'd seen a
> spectacle:
> *Caller:* O STORY!
> *Group:* YES!
> Or if it was the wrapper she tied about her waist you saw, it
> flowed right to the ground. Indeed she looked like a young
> woman of Accra.
> *Spectator I:* Most graceful.
> *Spectator II:* And charming.
> If you saw her figure, it really was graceful.
> (p. 343)

In the above passage we see—thanks to the editor's juxtaposition
of the Ijo text with the English translation—the bard appropriating
words suggested by the spectators for "young" (*erewon*) and
"charming" (*doin*) in the description of the seductive appearance
of the transformed Oreame.[6]

We would not be far wrong if we argued that in such cases the
bard has been stampeded into using particular words and ideas or
making more of a scene than he may have been inclined to. There is
no doubt that throughout the performance of this story the atmosphere is lively and often tense; besides, at several points of his
act the bard reveals considerable self-consciousness and uneasiness
before the equipment by means of which he is being recorded.[7] It is
clear therefore that he needs all the help he can get from the attending crowd so as to justify both his reputation and the present
patronage. In fact, he does not hesitate to solicit actively the co-
operation of the audience when the situation calls for it, not only in
terms of songs directly related to the tale (as in the introductory

"theme" song for Badoba, which the bard confesses he has forgotten, p. 150) but also in the provision of the odd detail that would aid the narrative act. Take for instance the following scene describing the frantic efforts that Oreame is making to find taboo objects that would help Ozidi destroy Azemaroti:

> The young of a toad, she also brought with her a tadpole. Next, (you give me your ears there). That bird, what do we Ijo call it now — this bird ...
>
> *Spectator:* Is it somewhat red?
> Quite red. That one too, she added to the lot.
>
> (p. 368)

Here surely the bard counts on, and receives, the co-operation of fellow Ijo citizens who are no strangers to the images that he employs in telling his story.

But perhaps the most vivid examples of the spectators' co-operation can be seen in those instances where they subsume roles within the mythic drama and, as it were, engage with the narrator in dialogue. Clark is evidently right in seeing the performance far more as a "multifaceted piece" of folk opera than simply as "literature":[8] and these quasi-dramatic roles of the audience certainly buttress the point. An interesting example occurs in the long episode involving Oreame and Ozidi on the one hand, and on the other Tebesonoma's sister Egberigbelea and her child, who are ultimately murdered in cold blood. Tebesonoma has sent Ozidi off to his sister and her baby as a diversionary tactic to avoid being killed by the hero before he is quite ready for battle. Confronted with the innocent woman and child, Ozidi is (rather uncharacteristically) filled with pity and unwilling to obey the witch Oreame's orders to kill them off. Thereupon Oreame proceeds to apply to his eyes the drug that will fill him with blind murderous fury:

> Next, bringing out a drug, she ordered him to open his eyes. "Open your eyes quick, open your eyes quick. Boy, boy, my child, open your eyes, open your eyes!" Forcibly, she had her way.
>
> *Spectator I:* What a wicked woman!
> "Mother, it burns badly."
> *Spectator II:* "Hush, don't ever say it burns."
> When he opened his eyes wide apart, there was nobody again for whom he had pity.
>
> (p. 253)

In the second spectator's words we see vividly recreated Oreame's demonic effort to stamp out all resistance from Ozidi. And yet Ozidi does not immediately dispatch the woman and her child. Though he begins to rage with the usual killing urge—lizards, monkeys and hornbills stampeding in his bowels, and so on—and the whole town, realizing who is in its midst, is thrown into panic and frenzy, there is a little hesitation lingering in the hero until his mentor the witch prods him once again:

> "When the real fight (i.e. with Tebesonoma) we sought is waiting there to be finished, are you dilly-dallying here? I say do the job quickly."
> "Oh mother, I'm horrified",
> When he spoke in this strain Oreame darted away.
> "So this boy has eyes running with tears like this! Come on, come out quick!"
> *Spectator II:* "I won't come out."
>   (*General laughter*)
> "Come out! Come out!" (pp. 256-7)

Here again our second spectator assumes a dramatic role, this time representing Ozidi's resistance to the witch. Whether or not the narrator acknowledges this unsolicited aid, there is clearly some gain in excitement at this point in the performance (as confirmed by the "general laughter") which does enhance our appreciation of the myth.

Control of scope and movement of narrative

By now it should be clear that in a typical African oral narrative performance, the audience is a force to be reckoned with, and that to a large extent he is a lucky performer who can count on the empathy and co-operation of an audience of fellow citizens to execute a challenging task of this kind. Without this prop to the narrator's efforts, the performance is quite likely to be a rather dull affair not only for the audience but more especially for the narrator himself, as the following observation by the Herskovitses about the Dahomean situation reveals: "One usage that is as common to discursive speech as to narrative is the interpolated explanation from the listener, or listeners. So important is it for narrative tempo that in the absence of an audience, or where the interjection is too long delayed, the narrator himself pauses to exclaim 'Good'. While this pause serves stylistic ends in narration—to introduce a transition, as a memory aid, or to heighten suspense, among others—it is but part of the traditional complex of patterned responses from the listener, demanded by the canons of taste. A Dahomean views the silent European listener as either boorish, or incapable of participating adequately because of lack of feeling or understanding."[9]

What the Herskovitses say about *tempo* in the above passage is enlightening, for it implies that in the final analysis, it is this response from the audience that controls the movement of the performance. At many points of *The Ozidi Saga,* for instance, members of the audience as well as the bard's performing group would seem to be egging him on to execute the job with speed. Every once in a while, in the course of the actual narration of the tale, the bard and the general group sing a song which either has a direct connection with the relevant episode or else is used for interludial effect. At the end of such a song, a spectator or "caller" may urge the narrator to "take it forward" (i.e. get on with the story itself) and not be slowed down by the singing. There are also numerous points in the performance where a "caller" endeavours to ginger up the crowd or back-up group, either because he notices their attention is flagging or else because, once again, they are getting carried away by the largely interludial act of singing and are forgetting that the story remains to be completed. Usually the prompting comes in the form of:

> *Caller:* O STORY!
> *Group:* YES!
> *Spectator:* Tell it on, man.[10]

In some cases, in fact, there is more direct indication of the fact that energies are failing, and the caller/spectator takes it upon himself to cheer up the spirits of those concerned. For instance, towards the end of the sixth of the seven nights of this performance, in the face of the long and tiresome struggle between the teams of Ozidi/Oreame and Odogu/Agonodi and with spirits visibly flagging, a "spectator" urges the general group: "Let bodies not slacken!" (p. 314). Even the bard occasionally tires of his responsibility to acquit himself and is duly prodded by his mentors to press on, as in the following exchange, again at the end of that sixth night:

> By this time . . . (Oh, how immense the narrative!)
> *Spectator:* Don't get distracted, just pilot it to port![11]

> On this occasion . . .
> *Caller:* OH, WAR STORY!
> *Group:* YES!

(p. 320)

In these various instances the spectators are trying to ensure that
the performance does not lose its tempo of excitement and thus appear a failure.

Much of the excitement which marks an oral narrative performance of this kind comes from the fact that the audience not only
urges the onward propulsion of the tale, as we have just seen, but
also encourages a considerable expansion of the material of the performance in terms of both the narrative and the choral text. A particularly interesting example of this urge for amplitude comes on
the seventh night, in the episode dealing with Ozidi's final destruc-
tion of Tebekawene. At the end of the gruelling fight between the
combatants, Ozidi's bowels finally go into the tumultuous rage
which regularly precedes his killing of his opponents, and then the
killing song; this is how this episode ends:

SONG

Solo: Come out now and take it!
Chorus: Yes!
Solo: Come out now and take it . . . . .!
Spectator: One blow!
And then the cry: "Tebekawene is sacrifice! Tebekawene is
sacrifice!
Tebekawene is sacrifice!" And out there Tebekawene lay pro-
strate.
Spectator II: Oh, yes, yes, yes, yes, yes, yes!
Spectator III: Perform for the town.
Spectator IV: Even to die for your father-land Orua well
befits you.

(p. 338)

The rest of this denouement is taken up with some members of the
Ijo audience introducing and identifying one another and expressing a general sense of upliftment before a bard who has done their
culture proud. The bard himself volunteers in an aside, in reference
to one of the spectators urging him on: "Because it is the story of
Orua that I'm telling, she appreciates it so much that she's forever
at my back" (pp. 338-9).

We may well appreciate the insistence of the audience here for a
fuller performance of the Tebekawene episode than they have been

171

given by the bard. The entire sixth night was taken up with one episode relating Ozidi's contest with Odogu, and this occupies nearly 50 pages of the book (essentially, pages 275-318). But the Tebekawene episode which takes up the first part of the seventh and final night, covers only about 12 pages in essential terms (pages 326-38). The audience may therefore, with the memory of the previous night fresh in their minds, have felt somewhat cheated of their full fare. Besides, Tebekawene's demise seems all too abruptly executed: the "slaughter song" ("Come out and take it") has been sung all too briefly this time, as against previous occasions when it was sung many more times before the final despatch of the enemy. The fall of Tebekawene is not accompanied by the usual decapitation, the dumping of the head in the hero's shrine, the thrashing about and ululation of the multitude of heads in the shrine, the frenzied triumphant rampage of the hero in the bushy premises and his uncle Temugedege's frightened complaint about the boy's madness, and the various other events which generally round off the hero's victory over an opponent with the due amount of tumult.

Indeed it would not be an unfair assessment of the nature of an oral performance to say that, as far as the responsibility for determining the textual scope of the overall performance goes, the audience is the prime mover. The Ozidi story is, as we know, traditionally performed over a total of seven days or nights, and the responsibility for determining the sequence of fight episodes that constitute the story—which is far from rigid[12]—may well be that of the performer. But the volume of text which the narration of every one of these episodes achieves depends considerably on the response which the performer gets from the audience in the course of the performance. For instance, it is arguable that the episode relating Ozidi's fight with the Scrotum King (pp. 212-29) would have been far less copious than it has turned out to be were it not for the encouragement that the bard received, from the audience's frequent applause, to elaborate as much as possible the portrait of the bumbling monster. The same could be said of the various other episodes of the story in which the spectators' interpolations urge the bard to expand the odd detail of description into a more affecting picture, as the following from the fight with Ofe (which covers the entire fourth night, about 50 pages):

Indeed if you saw Oreame she was like a young woman.
Spectator: Quite transformed was she.

172

> *Spectator:* She had changed into a young girl.
> Her bosom hung between standing and falling.
> (p. 181)

As a prime mover, therefore, responsible for the volume as well as the pace of the narrative performance, the audience may sometimes claim the prerogative of determining how much detail they would tolerate in the performance: in other words, some member or other of the audience may feel at any one point that he has had enough of the elaboration of a particular scene. His objection may be politely framed as a comment on the efforts of a character in the tale but a more discriminating judgment would reveal that in actual fact the spectator would prefer that the bard moved on.

Take for instance that second flirtation scene between Ozidi and Odogu's wife (pp. 285-94). The bard has been building up this love affair for some time, emphasizing as much as possible—with some help, of course, from the audience—its sensuous underpinnings. He has also been developing—with the due amount of suspense, we must admit—the treacherous moves that Odogu's wife, in true Delilah fashion, continues to make to elicit from Ozidi the source of his mystical power for the benefit of her husband. Ozidi himself is continually led to the brink of bringing out his extra-ordinary sword (whether to reveal the secret to her or to slaughter her is not immediately clear), and the elaboration of this whole scene goes on until one spectator is forced to comment: "All this labour to lay a woman!" (p. 294). Of course, one way of looking at this statement would be to see it as a comment on the contending stresses within the hero Ozidi in the context of an ill-fated love affair. But it is equally arguable as an instinctive reaction by this spectator to the tedious over-elaboration of the episode. The bard himself may have picked up the warning, for soon after this comment from the wings, he terminates Ozidi's internal struggle: the hero pulls out his sword from the shrine for the last time, the "slaughter song" is sung once more, and the sword descends on the neck of Odogu's wife.

A more revealing comment from the audience comes later on in the story during the fight between Ozidi and Azemaroti, on the seventh and last night of the performance, when the stamina of both bard and spectators had been thoroughly stretched. Somewhere during the interminable exchange of physical blows between the now essentially fatigued combatants, the equally fatigued audience is beginning to anticipate the end of the episode. Banter follows between the bard and his spectators:

> With the sound of each blow . . .
> *Spectator I:* Why not rest!
> The blows!
> How could he pause for breath, when he was in the field of battle!
> However hard he hacked at him, he danced away
> *Spectator II:* Leave off when he hasn't killed!

(p. 367f)

It would appear from this passage that the bard has misunderstood the first spectator's comment as referring to the hero, and so has tried to educate the spectator on the inescapable urgency of battle action. But the second spectator makes the comment more pointedly: skip everything and get to the actual point of killing! The bard seems to have ignored this pressure from the wings, for he continues describing the exchange of blows. But this does not go on for too long. Shortly after, we are told: "At last, after a long fight, Oreame came back, levelling in from there to a screeching stop" and bringing with her various taboo objects that transfix Azemaroti and set him up for the final death blow (pp. 368-9). And yet Azemaroti does not immediately fall under Ozidi's deadly blows: he has enough magic left in him to reconstitute himself after being halved. With the prospect of yet another tiresome series of thrusts, a spectator is once again moved to comment "When two men fight, is there no running away?" (p. 369). Of course this spectator should know, being himself an Ijo, that the regular pattern is for Ozidi to kill every one of his opponents, so there is no talk of an escape; but his rather realistic, all-too-human comment simply reveals his subdued impatience at this endless fighting. Again the bard seems to have got the message, for soon after, the "slaughter song" resounds and Azemaroti is slashed to pieces. A relieved audience applauds the termination:

> *Spectator:* HIP, HIP, HIP, HIP!
> *Spectator:* HURRAH! (p. 370)

Much has been written, on the basis of internal evidence revealed by the artist's own manipulation of the structural and stylistic resources of the story, about the twin modes of expansion and contraction in the narrative art.[13] What the above instances demonstrate is the role of external factors, in the form of audience reaction, in determining these stresses. It may seem ironical that within the same performance the audience would alternately urge the narrator to expand and shorten his act, but this may be explained in a variety of ways: either as evidence of the uneven quality of the performer's art, or of the decline in spirits at a performance lasting such a long time, or else of the divergence of insights which such a varied gathering of *individuals* is liable to reveal.

Conflict of purposes

The potential for this divergence or conflict, at least as far as the relationship between artist and audience goes, can be seen in the very fact that, however encouraging the remarks of spectators may be to the artist, he has to make some effort to steady himself and not be diverted from his line of logic. The situation is somewhat analagous to that of the public speaker. Though he feels encouraged every time he gets applause from the audience, he surely does not want his concentration broken, so once in a while he motions to the audience to hold off the applause until he has reached a convenient point in his development of the argument. If there is so much risk value in a positive gesture from the audience, we can imagine how much more there is when the audience imposes directly upon the artist's chosen path of development of his story.

We saw something of this imposition above, in the audience's request that the bard curtail his development of the fighting between Ozidi and Azemaroti. There are further examples within the same episode of this tussle between bard and audience. One of these occurs before the actual confrontation between the mother and son teams of Oreame-Ozidi and Azema-Azemaroti. Searching for action, Oreame and Ozidi arrive at the enemy's town with the old sorceress disguised as a young consort to the hero and displaying none of her grim menace:

> All her bags, all her kit, had quite melted into her body.
> *Spectator:* Power!
>
> (*Laughter*)
> When at last they arrived at the town, there was no general scare since none recognized them.
> (p. 343)

The spectator's exclamation is clearly a reference to the frightening power of Oreame, even to the magical feat that caused her charms to disappear into her body. But the word "power" carried with it at that particular time, as Clark himself usefully points out in a footnote, a heavy semantic charge. The performance was recorded in 1963 in Ibadan, capital of the then Western Region and center of the ominous political crisis of that time; "power" was a popular slogan then shouted mostly in reference to one of the political combatants popularly known as "Fani Power". The significance of that word was therefore not lost on the bard who himself was living in Ibadan. In fact, in a much earlier episode he had used that word in circumstances relating to the fierce confrontation between Ozidi and one of his enemies, Azezabife. This scene portrays Azezabife's frantic struggle to crush under his foot a gourd containing a magical concoction and thus regain his failing strength:

> As it fell, and he squashed it like this underfoot, oh, power (*pawa*) showed again in Azeza.
>
> (*Laughter*)
>
> *Caller:* O STORY!
> *Group:* YES!
> As soon as Azeza's strength surged back into his body, all Azeza's body grew hot.
>
> (p. 94)

This idea of the surge of destructive energy within the body from its contact with magical charm, as well as the charged connotation of the word "power", may have occurred to the bard's mind when that spectator shouted "Power" in reference to the disguised Oreame. But the bard apparently had no intent at this point of playing up the image of confrontation, and so refused to be diverted from his line of development of the story by stressing that the citizens of the town took no fright when they saw the strangers Oreame and Ozidi. Where the spectator sought to relish the prospect of confrontation, or at least the appeal of terror, the bard considered such an image premature within the scheme of development of the plot. Clearly, there is here a certain divergence of interests.

Later on, however, the bard is to some extent diverted from his line of development. In the heat of the fighting between the two mother-son teams, Ozidi pulls out his magical sword and deals Azemaroti a blow which sends him into a distant forest far beyond the town (p. 355). His mother Azema takes up the challenge and

176

locks with Oreame in fierce combat, "biting off Oreame's hair and
tangling it into wild knots" (p. 356). By this time, Azemaroti has
been scampering through the forest back to town, and finally
makes it. We are now poised for combat between the two males, as
we are told:

> And Ozidi stood anchored like a tree, waiting for him.
> *Spectator II:* Your mother has had her hair all bitten.
> (*Laughter*)
> *Caller:* O STORY!
> *Group:* YES!
> Said Oreame: "Yes, never again!
> You Azemaroti, is it my hair you've torn apart like this and
> would want to tear up more?
> Yes, never again!"
> While pouring imprecations, she had already whipped out her
> fan, and was whisking about the place. Then she flew off into
> the sky.
>
> (p. 357)

The story continues with the fight against Azema, who is finally
killed (p. 359). But though we seem to have been prepared for a
tangle between Ozidi and Azemaroti in the above passage, Spectator II has let drop an observation which forces the narrator to
take leave of his intent and return to the Oreame-Azema tussle instead. Here indeed it would seem the interest of the spectator has
imposed upon the narrator's own path of development.

I am not trying to charge this spectator with a deliberately
disruptive intent; that a spectator expresses a fascination with one
detail rather than another does not necessarily constitute a
dissatisfaction with the narrator's line of development. As a matter
of fact, it has often been observed that narratives of the *Ozidi* kind
are largely built on a montage of episodes or a collage of affective
situations. This means that in the scheme of development of many
a story (especially one like *Ozidi* built on a sequence of fight
episodes following pretty much the same pattern), one event may
just as soon be picked on as another. But I think we have here a
good illustration of how this episodicity does or at least *can* come
about: from an occasional disalignment of interests between bard
and spectator.

A somewhat more significant instance of this conflict of purposes may be seen in the contending claims of realism and romance
in the story. We must understand that the bard is telling a story that

operates at a high symbolic level, with beings of unusual powers and proportions accomplishing the most unimaginable feats. Such a story has a high emotive charge and the narrator himself, bearing the burden of the charge, can hardly be said to be walking on the ground of everyday reality for as long as he is engaged in telling the story: indeed we can see something of the bard's claim to divine inspiration in the tribute to Atazi, Okabou's predecessor in the narration of the Ozidi story.[14] Though some of this emotive charge may overflow to members of the audience on whom the bard is making an impression, it would be fair to observe that the audience on the whole has a better chance of taking a realistic or rational view of the events in the story than the bard has. A good example can be seen in the bard's introduction of Badoba into the story. Ozidi has just disposed of Ogueren, a giant of twenty limbs and a formidable opponent. Next comes Badoba bragging that he will finish off Ozidi in no time; the reason these earlier figures performed so poorly against Ozidi was that they did not have the requisite resources. The bard then goes on to paint a formidable picture of Badoba's physique: his head touched the sky, and the reach of his sword was out of sight. The comparison with Ogueren thus seems inevitable, as the following exchange reveals:

Spectator: Was he greater than Ogueren?
Okabou: What, greater than Ogueren? The heroes and
       heroes there—how can they be compared? Each
       had his own might.
Audience: Right?

(p. 147f)

The general audience has here shown a remarkable sympathy with the bard's struggle to answer the spectator's distracting question. But the exchange is nevertheless significant. The bard of a heroic myth does not often draw a preferential line between one hero and another. As combatants, the confrontation between them is all the more exciting if they are seen as fighting on more or less equal terms, even when they have somewhat different characteristics. More often the narrator is simply interested in the independent appeal of the respective fight episodes.[15] But the rationalization of the respective merits of the characters is an inevitable urge in the spectator who takes an objective view of the facts of the story.

The spectator's preference for realism as against the story-teller's romance can be seen also in his reaction to the fate befalling various characters in the tale. In the course of the bard's description of the gruesome duel between Ozidi and Odogu, with their respective mothers urging them on in the interminable bloodbath, a spectator is moved to observe: "Look at them playing with children born with such labour!" (p. 303). It is clear that this spectator is a rational observer seeing the facts of the story in human terms, but the story hardly operates at such a level. The narrator, considering the extraordinary circumstances in which he puts the birth and life of the characters of the story (including Ozidi himself), would prefer to cherish the romantic quality of the story whatever the ulterior message it has for human society.

Even in the matter of setting, the bard would seem to prefer his story to operate in more romantic circumstances than his audience might be inclined to subsume. Clark in his introductory essay (p. xvii) gives us a useful insight into the practice, among these narrators of the Ozidi story (Afoluwa, Erivini and Okabou), of habitually setting the story in the mythical land of "Ado" or Benin, which "to the Ijo imagination, is the embodiment of all that is distant and mysterious, the empire of improbable happenings that together with the world of spirits help to explain the events of their own lives". But the Ijo crowd gathered around the scene of this recording, away from their ancestral.homeland, was a particularly patriotic one and evidently unwilling to award the credit for origins to Benin rather than to their own homeland. Clark goes on to state that our narrator "Okabou in fact was always self-conscious when, prodded on by Madam Yabuku of Inekorogha, leader of the recorded session at Ibadan, he toed the clearly patriotic line of preferring the local name to the foreign one of Ado". All through his narration of the story we constantly see this tension between the two settings of Orua and Ado; but one confrontation between Okabou and a spectator is particularly enlightening. This comes in the battle between Ozidi and Badoba:

> Believe me, while Badoba went seeking battle—pardon the slip of tongue (in earlier saying Ofe rather than Badoba)—the citizens of Ado that stood on the sidelines to learn by sight—
> *Prompter:* The citizens of Orua—
> Oh, yes, that city of Ado in the forest of Orua—a group of them there observing the fight, three score persons, were mowed down accidentally by the mere wind of (Ozidi's)

179

sword.

(p. 153)

"A brilliant double-take by Okabou!" is Clark's footnote observation on the narrator's rejoinder here. Okabou is clearly ill at ease with all this patriotic pressure; but it is significant that though he makes a concession, he puts the fight not in the familiar heart of town but in the more romantic setting of "the forest of Orua".

The matter of setting is indeed only part of the large struggle between the narrow constraints to time and place as demonstrated by the audience and the narrator's preference for a larger spatio-temporal context for his art. Throughout the seven nights of the performance the bard is constantly teased by the Ijo spectators over his use of English words instead of Ijo originals. "Don't speak English!" is a warning that resounds every once in a while from this patriotic audience. The poor narrator is of course forced to respect their feelings and make the appropriate correction, especially in the matter of "time" or "when" which he frequently renders with the loan word "tain" rather than the Ijo "seri" (pp. 104, 262, 274, 353, 361, etc). They also tease him for using other loan words like "kulude" (for English "cooled") instead of the Ijo "doode" (p. 117), or "bede" (for English "bed") rather than the Ijo "obine" (p. 28). Sometimes he even opts to check himself before his critics are upon him (e.g. pp. 240, 299). But once in a while he is somewhat impatient with all this nagging (e.g. pp. 284, 287, 303), and even pretends he has not heard the comment. To him it is all needlessly purist, and though as a tested performer he is no stranger to such occupational hazards, he is aware that they are just as liable to bring down his act as they are to enhance the excitement value of it.

Implications

The obvious meaning of all these efforts on the part of the audience is that they are, as oral literary scholars have often pointed out, an integral part of the creative act in an oral performance. To be sure, a greater concern for pattern over process might lead to a somewhat different conclusion. In discussing the relevance of contextual materials in traditional art, Lévi-Strauss tells us: "The essential problem for the philosophy of art is to know whether the artist regards them as interlocutors or not. No doubt they are always regarded as such, although least of all in art which is too professional and most of all in the raw or naive art which verges on bricolage, to the detriment of structure in both cases. No form of art is, however, worthy of the name if it allows itself to come entirely under the sway of extraneous contingencies, whether of occasion or purpose. If it did so it would rate as an icon (supplementary to the model) or as an implement (complementary with the material worked). Even the most professional art succeeds in moving us only if it arrests in time this dissipation of the contingent in favour of the pretext and incorporates it in the work, thereby investing it with the dignity of being an object in its own right."[16]

Lévi-Strauss is definitely right that if the artist does not handle the intrusion of contingencies (like audience comments or even the urge to refer to the physical environment of the performance, as Okabou frequently does with Ibadan locales), he will end up a failure in practical aesthetic terms. But Lévi-Strauss' concern with "model" or "pre-text" implies that this is the real stake. So long as he is not forced to abandon the performance entirely, the artist can with appropriate skill take in as much contingence as possible. If he is clever enough he can go into a more extended dialogue with his audience and still keep the story going right to the last fight with the Smallpox King; the performance in that case might indeed be considered a more successful affair for the greater excitement that is generated while the "model" of the story—whatever it may be —is in no way distrupted. The problem with Lévi-Strauss' claim is that whereas in his general disquisitions on "structure" he is concerned with the *mode* of human thinking processes, in the above case (which in all fairness to him comes very early in his long career of studies in mythology) he seems to be thinking in terms of specific aprioristic forms or some fixed form of the tale; as we pointed out earlier, field research has shown that in such multiple-fight narratives there is often no fixed sequence that the fights have to follow.

A less obvious implication, however, of Okabou's experience with his audience is the sociological judgement which it forces upon us. Harold Scheub's observation that "the artist emerges from the audience and, her narrative completed, is again swallowed up by the audience" has far more significance than Scheub seems to appreciate. The movement away from the audience is not only a spatial one but, even more importantly, an emotional one. As I have argued above, the act of performance imposes a greater emotive charge on the bard than on the audience, and many of the comments made by spectators are in fact designed, whether consciously or not, to bring the artist down to the earth of realism from which he seems to be straying. That question by a spectator as to whether Badoba is greater than Ogueren is not just a mark of naïveté or ignorance, but a logical interpretation of the gain in poetic afflatus which Badoba's portrayal invites; the poet's reply to the spectator wins approval only because he establishes the point that the world of myth cannot be equated with the world of reality. And it is precisely because he lends his uncommon genius to the portrayal of an equally uncommon world that the narrator, at least at the moment of performance, is no longer emotionally part of the ordinary world of men.

There is an even less obvious implication to the occasional comments made by spectators. We do not know the actual number of these "spectators" that we find indicated on the various pages of the text: it would clearly have cost Clark more time and money to identify them individually. Whatever the case may be, anyone who has had the experience of collecting oral narratives will have encountered spectators who volunteer information or throw in questions and comments every once in while: there is more often than not an effort at self-projection.[17] They are aware what special notice and respect the bard is enjoying from those magnificent men with their recording machines, and they want to share some of this recognition and be part of that sophisticated company. In one of my recent recordings, for instance, an apprentice of the bard came forward to give a fuller introduction of himself and his career because he thought himself insufficiently represented in the bard's general introduction!

Now I believe that something of this urge for individual attention is present in the comments volunteered by some members of the audience. In many ways they are saying that they too know the story and perhaps qualify to be recorded just as much as Okabou does. When they urge curtailment or expansion they seem to imply that they have a better sense of proportion than the incumbent narrator does. And when they criticize the bard's diction they may be far more inclined to impress the rest of the audience with their knowledge of Ijo speech than to help the bard tell a truly patriotic story. Whatever the case may be, they are in subtle ways trying to draw from the bard some of the attention which he is clearly enjoying as the centre of attraction. The bard is now effectively separated from them, both physically and emotionally, and this remove encourages some confrontation (however polite) between him and them. It is true that the story remains the general patrimony of the Ijo people; it is also true that whatever exchanges ensue between bard and audience contribute to the overall excitement. But the urge for the individual selfhood, or what Gwendlyn Brooks would peculiarly call a "singlicity", points to a somewhat greater degree of individual consciousness in the social fabric than some anthropologist are prepared to recongnize in their theories about a "collective consciousness."[18] Finnegan is surely right in her distrust of those "old theories about the possible 'commual' nature of oral literature."

NOTES

1. Harold Scheub, "Body and Image in Oral Narrative Performance" *New Literary History*, (1977), pp. 347. In his book *The Xhosa Ntsomi* (Oxford: Clarendon, 1975) pp. 12-14, Scheub acknowledges the potential for distruption as a result of confrontation between performer and audience, but seems to consider harmony the ideal relationship: "But our final judgement and critical evaluation of the *ntsomi* and ngamekwane traditions must be made at these moments of total harmony as the artist exploits this rapport and as she brings the many elements of the production to a single focus which then sustained to the climax" (p. 14).

2. Daniel Biebuyck. *Hero and Chief* (Berkeley: University of California Press, 1978), p. 157, note 67

3. See Ruth Finegan, *Oral Poetry* (Cambridge: Cambridge University Press, 1977), p. 232.

4. J. P. Clark, *The Ozidi Saga: Collected and Translated from the Ijo of Okabou Ojobolo* (Ibadan: Ibadan University Press and Oxford University Press, 1977).

5. *Oral Literature in Africa* Oxford Clarendon, 1970), p. 15.

6. See also my discussion of the "ring" device in *The Epic in Africa* (New York: Columbia University Press, 1979), pp. 200-201

7. Examples of this self-consciousness can be seen in *The Ozidi Saga*, pp. 84, 257, 348, 362.

8. *The Ozidi Saga*, p. ix

9. Melville and Frances Herskovits *Dahomean Narrative: A Cross-Cultural Analysis* (Evanston: Northwestern University Press, 1958), p. 52.

10. See examples on pp. 61, 285, 295, 298, 312, 316, etc.

11. See p. 320. It is somewhat painful to observe that part of the bard's problem comes from the pressure to fill the tape. See especially pp. 204 and 342. On p. 321. the narration strangly continues for a couple of pages more, despite

Okabou's statement that day had broken and that he was therefore stopping the performance meanwhile!

12. See *The Epic in Africa*, p. 175.

13. For the oral narrative, se M. N. Nagler, *Spontaneity and Tradition* (Berkely: University of California Press, 1974); Isidore Okepwho, *The Epic in Africa*. pp. 179-94; John Willian Johnson, Yes, Virginia, There is an Epic in Africa" *Research in African Literatures,* 1 (1980), pp. 318-9. For modern fiction, ses E. M. Forster's interesting discussion on "rhythm" in his *Aspects of the Novel* (Harmondsworth: Penguin, 1962, pp. 151-70.

14. See pp. 155 and 202 f. Compare S. A. Babalola, *The Content and Form of Yoruba Ijala,* (Oxford: Clarendon, 1966), pp. 46-47; Daniel Biebuyck and K. C. Mateene, The Mwindo Epic (Barkely: University of California Press, 1969), p. 12; Plato, *Ion* 530, 533 and 541.

15. See G. S. Kirk, *Myth: Its Meaning and Functions* (Cambridge: Cambridge University Press 1970: p. 39; Okpewho, Myth in Africa, p. 99

16. Claude Levi-Strauss, *The Savage Mind* (London: Weidenfield and Nicolson, 196), p. 29.

17. On self-projection, see further John A. Robinson, "Personal Narratives Reconsidered" *Journal of American Folklore* 94 (1987), p. 61.

18. On social structure as an "emergent quality" of performance, see Richard Bauman, *Verbal Art as Performance* (Rowley, Mass: Newbury House, 1977), pp. 42—45.

184

Wand or Walking Stick? The Formula and its Use in Zulu Praise Poems

Elizabeth Gunner

The background

IT IS fair to say that the formula has been the object of intense, anxious, even myopic scrutiny by scholars for several decades. Magoun stated firmly in 1953 that "oral poetry . . . is composed entirely of formulas, large and small, while lettered poetry is never formulaic" (1953:447). Lord's pronouncements on oral epic song, made in 1960, were equally uncompromising: "it consists of the building of metrical lines and half-lines by means of formulae and formulaic expressions" (1960:4). Subsequently, though, scholars such as Benson (1966) have demonstrated that the categorical oral/formulaic, written/non-formulaic distinction made by Magoun is invalid, others, such as Bird, have put forward a less rigid definition of the formula which allows more scope for the creativity of individual composers: "(it) may be roughly defined as a kind of abstract-pattern sentence into which the singer can substitute a great number of words, creating a line that will meet the metrical requirements of the poem" (1972:283). Yet even if we prefer a looser definition of the formula, the question remains: how prevalent is the formula in African oral poetry? And if it exists, how is it used?

As Finnegan (1976) has pointed out, African and other oral poetry often make use of conventional themes rather than formulae. Consider for instance the Hausa praise songs discussed by Smith which use set topics or themes (1957:33-4, 39) or the praise poems of the East African Bahima. Here the composer attempts to repeat identical themes with different and startling turns of phrase and achieves his effects in that way (Morris, 1964:25). To take a further example, Babalola makes only a brief mention of formulae in his study of Yoruba *ijala*, hunters' songs (1966:35). Writings on oral poetry from Southern Africa make little or no mention of the subject; the latter is the case in Fortune and Hodza's *Shona praise poetry* (1979). The works on Tswana praise poetry (Schapera, 1965), Sotho heroic poetry (Kunene, 1971; Damane and Sanders, 1974) and Zulu praise poems (Cope, 1968) are silent on the subject. There are, however, brief references to formulae in Xhosa praise poetry by Opland (1975:195) and by Wainwright (1978:98-100; 105), and although Cope does not mention formulae in his *Izibongo, Zulu praise-poems* (1986), he refers several times to shared praise names in various praise poems (and see Cope, 1978).

While it is reasonably clear, then, that African oral poetry is not completely formulaic-and in some cases, such as Somali poetry, not formulaic at all — the question remains: do formulae play any significant part in the poetic traditions in which they figure, or is formulae-hunting a harmless but idiosyncratic pastime which is best avoided? Finnegan warns against any exclusive concern with formulae:

> Why look primarily at repeated word patterns (as in the narrower definition) which form only part of the poet's conventional art and not to all the other accepted patterns like music, parrallelism, figurative language, use of soliloquy or address, themes known to be specifically evocative for specific audiences and so on? These often equally shape (and aid) the poet's diction written or oral, and form part of accepted convention. (1976:160)

While such a "primary" concern may give a false view of the techniques of a body of poetry, there is no reason why formulae should not be seen and discussed as part of the poetic diction of a tradition. Questions as to the role of formulae in composition and in performance can then be asked, together with considerations of style both in the formulae and in the genre as a whole. After collecting a large number of *izibongo* (praise poems) recited by bards and non-specialists in Zululand in 1976, and comparing this material with published sources, it became clear to me that the number of similarly worded units which occurred in *izibongo* from different periods, and in some cases from widely scattered districts, must be formulae of some sort. If they were not formulae, what were they?

Before looking in some detail at examples of these formulae in the praise poems, a few further points need to be made. Firstly, there is the question of metre and formulae. Even Bird's looser definition (see p. 185) mentions "the requirements of a poem". It is possible that the recent discovery of the rules governing scansion in classical Somali poetry (Andrzejewski, 1981) will lead to similar findings in other African poetic traditions which it has been assumed have no metrical systems. This may be the case with the various traditions of Southern African panegyric, including Zulu *izibongo* (praise poems). At present, however, there is no irrefutable evidence as to the existence of metre nor is there agreement on the subject (see Cope, 1968:40; Kunene, 1971; Nkabinde, 1976 and Rycroft, 1980). Secondly, it should be emphasized that although this paper focuses on the formula and its use in the praise poems, it is only a single element in the overall poetic diction and in the total performance situation. Thirdly, we need to remember that there are two modes of performance in *izibongo*, the call mode and the declamatory mode, the latter being the one used by bards who are known as *izimbongi*. Formulae are found in praise poems performed in both modes.

The formulae

Formulae in Zulu praises show a range of flexibility: whereas a very few recur in identical form, a far greater number are flexible. They are in many cases complete sentences having as fixed points a repeated verb (or verbs), an image or idea in a similar or identical syntactic pattern. The fixed point or points render them recognizably "the same" although the surface structure may vary somewhat. Another type of formulae usually consists of a phrase or clause. These are used to emphazise the narrative element in a praise poem, and sometimes to create a special atmosphere of grandeur; they are frequently either spatial or temporal in their reference. Others of this type have the effect of rounding off a line and are themselves balanced through antithesis, grammatical identity, or both. In general, formulae allow for a combination of the novel and the familiar, the general and the particular, and through devices such as expansion and substitution are free to include a measure of their own material.

Type 1: Fixed formuiae

There are fewer of this type as far as I can ascertain and even

187

these fixed formulae have limited possibilities for expansion. Many of the so-called fixed formulae are proverbs and they too allow for small changes: limited expansion can occur in the form of a patronymic inserted between the fixed words, as in Example I; also a different form of the same verb may be used to give another shade of meaning without altering the basic idea held in the formula, as in Example 4. A further feature of fixed formulae—and of many others — is the high frequency of imagery drawn from nature. Thus the characteristics or experience of the individuals are highlighted through metaphor: Example I compares the precocious competence of one who takes office at an early age to the stiff "umthente" grass, prickly even before it reaches full height. An individual's survival of a severe crisis is compared to the amazing resilience of the seemingly indestructible "dabane", a coleus-type weed. Strength and quick growth in a person are evoked through reference to the fast-growing eucalyptus trees, introduced to the Zulù coastal areas by white farmers; and the qualities of energy and selfless industry are evoked in the image of the antbear making nests for others to enjoy. The fixed formulae, like others, often encapsulate ideas or themes which are dominant in praise poetry as a whole. Thus resilience, strength and selflessness—the qualities focused on in Examples 2, 3 and 4 respectively—feature widely as admired qualities in *izibongo*.

Example I

    i. UMthente uhlab' usamila.
    ii. UMthente kaJama uhlab' usamila.
    i. The Young Grass stabs as it grows.
    ii. The Young Grass son of (royal) Jama stabs as it grows.[2]

Example 2

    UMafavuke njengedabane.
    The One who Dies and Awakes like the "dabane" plant.[3]

Example 3

    UGamthri umuthi wabelungu.
    Gumtree, tree of the white man.[4]

Example 4

    i. ISambane esimb' umgodi singawulali.
    ii. ISambane esimb' umgodi kasabesawolala.
    i. Ant-eater which digs a hole without sleeping in it.

ii.Ant-eater which digs a hole but will not sleep in it.[5]

Type 2: Flexible formulae

These constitute the greater bulk of formulae in the tradition. As a group they exhibit many of the characteristics in form and content of the genre as a whole. The following categories of flexible formulae are by no means mutually exclusive. In many cases a particular formula has the characteristics of two or more of the categories and it is often these multi-category formulae which carry the greatest poetic power. For instance, a formula may be couched in figurative language, contain an idea dominant in the genre. and in its structure and semantics make use of balance and contrast as in the case of Example 8, the "vanished moon" formula. It would be wrong to regard the flexible formulae merely as fillers, cementing together more important or more interesting sections of a praise poem. Rather, they often seem to confer authenticity and value on the praises and it is assumed that anyone using the formulae—so long as he is sparing in his use of them—knows the tradition well and is adept at its poetic shorthand. Categories of flexible formulae are:

    a. those using figurative language
    b. those with a dominant idea
    c. those with marked balance and contrast
    d. those with marked alliteration or assonance.

2a. Flexible formulae using figurative language

The following are a small sample of the wide variety of animal and natural imagery found in the formulae. Cattle imagery features largely in ordinary and in formulaic lines, and usually carries association of worth and value because of the importance of cattle in Zulu culture. It is interesting that the first cattle formula below did not occur in any of the older *izibongo* I recorded. It is possible that this is a recent formula composed to fit the group and individual skirmishing which often takes place after gatherings such as weddings. The second cattle formula on the other hand is recorded as a "typical warrior's praise" by Callaway as early as 1868 and features frequently in nineteenth century and modern *izibongo*. Each of these formulae also relates to a web of ideas returned to time and again in praise poetry as a genre. The idea of courage is expressed in the cattle image of one against many in Example 5 and in the equally popular and older "Peacemaker between the bulls", (Example 6). The idea of one against many, of having to use one's wits to survive, is encapsulated in the "Hare with two resting places" image in Example 7; the "vanished moon" in Example 8 links to the idea of resilience and the ability to survive when all seems lost.

Most formulae occur in the praise poems of members of ruling houses, royalty and ordinary individuals and this is the case with three of the formulae here. Only the "moon" formula seems restricted to those who are in some way eminent—certainly in this image the Western connotations of remote feminine beauty are entirely absent!

As I have mentioned, part of the attraction of many formulae is the way in which they combine stability and flexibility. In this group the metaphors themselves are stable: there is never any substitution of "cow", "bulls", "hare" or "moon". Moreover, these metaphors introduce the formula or—in the case of Example 6 —follow the opening word. There are a number of formal changes possible after the constant opening. A verb with similar meaning, identical length and in the same voice and tense may be substituted. This represents a minimal change with no alteration to the rhythm or syntax of the formula (see Example 5). A wider degree of flexibility occurs when, after the constant opening phrase, optional verbs and optional structure follow (see Example 6). Yet, even here, the variation in verbs used and in the underlying meaning is strictly limited. Variation within strict limits also occurs in other ways. For instance, in Examples 7 and 8, the principle of balance operates in the latter part of the formula. In 7, after the opening phrase "UNogwaja ozikhundlahundla" (Hare with two resting places) two parallel units always occur. The precise syntax of the paired units varies in different versions and the paired verbs vary slightly, but there is always grammatical repetition combined with semantic contrast in the two units. In this combination of variants and invariants, therefore, the latter part of the formula demonstrates in miniature the underlying principle of parallelism which in its various forms dominates the style of Southern African praise poetry, including Zulu *izibongo*. Contrast and balance are the essence of the form of Example 8, although it seems that there is no necessity for the neat grammatical patterning of the "Hare" formula (Example 7). In every instance which I recorded, the opening words "INyanga bath ifile" (The Moon, they said it had died) were constant. The contrastive conjuction "kanti" (whereas), which followed or was implied, introduced a brief contrary statement. Here limited flexibility allowed for different verbs and slightly different syntax, but in each case below (see Example 8 i-iv) the emphatic contrast with the opening statement is clear.

A feature of the flexibility of this group of formulae is the way in which expansion of the basic unit is possible. Expansion is of great value to composers, subsequent reciters and to listeners because it invariably particularizes a formula by relating the general statement to a specific event, place, person or lineage. The length and structure of such expansions vary according to the skill and inclination of the composers. Whereas a bard may add an elaborate expansion running to several lines, an ordinary composer will often be content with statement of a place and patronymic. Examples 5,7 and 8 contain instances of such simple expansion and Example 8 also leads to a four-line extension when it is used in the *izibongo* of the Nazarite prophet Isaiah Shembe (see Example 24).

Example 5

    i.INkomo esengwa iviyo.

    ii.INkomo ebanjwa iviyo kwaNomahengisi.

    i.Cow milked by a band of men.

    ii.Cow held fast by a band of men at Nomahengisi's place.[6]

Example 6

    i.UMlamula wezinkunzi ezilwayo.

    ii.UMlamula 'nkunzi ziyeke zibulalane.

    iii.UMlamula wezinkunzi ngabe waziyeka ngabe zabulalane ngabe phansi kwaTshani.

    i. Peacemaker between the bulls which fight.

    ii. Peacemaker between the bulls, they stopped killing each other.

    iii. Peacemaker between the bulls, if you'd left them they would have killed each other, they would have been under the Grass.[7]

Example 7

    i UNogwaja ozihundlakundla nesokulala. nesokwethamela.

   ii. UNogwaja ozikhundlahundla esinye sokulala esinye sokuthamela.

  iii. UNogwaja ozikhundlakhundla (kwesinye) uyalala kwesinye uyaphumula.

    i. Hare with two resting places both one for sleeping and one for basking.

   ii. Hare with two resting places one for sleeping and one for basking.

  iii. Hare with two resting places (in one) he sleeps in the other he rests.[8]

Example 8

   i INyanga bath' ifile kanti iyofa kusasa.

  ii. INyanga bath' ifile kanti icash' emafini.

 iii. INyanga bath' ifile kanti basho nje iduk' emafini.

 iv. INyanga bath' ifile (kanti) yethwasa kuMnyamana ozalwa nguMhlephuza.

   i. The Moon they said it had died whereas it will die tomorrow.

  ii. The Moon they said it had died whereas it was hiding in the clouds.

 iii. The Moon they said it had died whereas they meant it was lost in the clouds.

 iv. The Moon they said it had died (whereas) it was rising anew at Mnyamana's, son of Mhlephuza.[9]

2b. Flexible formulae with a dominant idea

The two formulae considered below make no use of striking metaphors yet are linked to one of the key values propounded by *izibongo,* that of courage. Example 9 refers directly to a man's bravery in a battle situation. It is extremely compact, containing two statements in its four words, and it occurs in closely similar form in a number of earlier *izibongo* and in a single contemporary one. It gains its expressive force from its cumulative emphasis rather than from any contrastive effect, stressing as it does that the bearer of the praise is both a leader *and* a fighter.

Izibongo frequently contain pithy references not only to character but also to appearance. Yet few references to appearance seem to have found their way into formulae and it is interesting to speculate why a comment on shortness should have done so.

Example 10 is found in the Ngoni (of Malawi) and in the Transvaal traditions of *izibongo* as .well as in Zulu *izibongo*. Possibly it has been retained in all three traditions because of its connections with the cardinal virtue of courage and also because of its usefulness as a compact corrective statement, i.e. stressing that shortness of stature does not mean that a man is less able or less courageous than others. The variations in form are also interesting. In each version the noun "izingubo" (clothes), adjective "-mfishane", and verb "-nyathela" are constant although the word order and syntax vary. The Transvaal Ndebele and Ngoni versions are fuller than the Zulu and contain contrastive parallel units which repeat the verb "nyathela" and balance "-mfishane" (short) with "-de" (tall), thus emphasizing the equality of the short and the tall! Perhaps the shorter Zulu version will in time shed its corrective implication and become merely a convenient line for pinpointing a feature of appearance.

Example 9

UMqh athi wempi abuya ayilwele.

He urges on the army and then fights himself.[10]

Example 10

   i. Izingubo zemfishane ziyanyathela.

   ii. Ungwasibindi ubemfishane l'ngubo ziyanyathela.

   iii. . . . kaMfishane kaNgubo ziyanyathelwa kanti nezabade ziyanyathelwa.

   iv. Hlatshwayo omfishane angahyatheli i'ngubo Ingani abade bayazinyathela.

   i. The clothes of the short of stature trail on the ground.

   ii. He is brave, short of stature, (and his) clothes trail on the ground.

   iii. The short of stature, his clothes are trailed on the ground whereas those of the tall are (also) trailed on the ground.

   iv. Hlatshwayo who is short, (yet) he does not trail his cloth whereas the tall ones trail theirs.[11]

2c. *Flexible formulae with marked balance and contrast*

Some of the formulae already cited (Example 7, for instance) show syntactic and semantic patterning but not to the same degree as those below. A similar use of contrast and balance is discussed by Nyembezi in his collection of Zulu proverbs (1954: 21-24) and is 'a characteristic of Zulu verbal art. Indeed, two of the syntactic patterns of the following formulae are among those most widely used in *izibongo*, and it is tempting to conclude that the combination of recognitions stemming from a known syntactic pattern and familiar words makes such formulae doubly attractive both to performers and to listeners. The formulae in this group exhibit a high degree of formal neatness coupled with a marked rhythm; they are an example of what Waldron, talking of a different poetic tradition, calls "'empty rhythmical-syntactical moulds' ready to be filled with meaning" (1957:792). Inversion features in Examples 11 and 12, where the second part of the line inverts the word-order of the first. A further combination of repetition and contrast is that the same verb occurs in both halves of the line but moves from the negative to the positive. This pattern of inversion combined with negative to positive verb repetition is particularly popular in the *izibongo* of ordinary people who compose their own praises and who have lines composed for them by others, but who have no skilled bards to compose, collate and expand praise on their behalf. Inversion is also a feature in Examples 13 and 14. In this case balance and contrast come firstly from the juxtaposition of paired opposing adjectives and secondly from the contrast in sense between the two halves of the formula. Thus in Example 13, "short"/"tall" or "young"/"older" feature as contrasts, as do "proposing to" and "being given a fever"! In Example 14, "large"/"small" provides the paired opposition and the contrast in sense is supplied by "chopper down" and "falls on its own". Both examples 13 and 14 have a limited flexibility and the variations possibly maintain the syntax, meaning and rhythm of the whole. In the former "short"/"tall" is sometimes replaced by "young"/"older" and the words of similar sound, sense and meaning, "umfehlane" "umkhunkane" (fever/cold), are interchangeable. Example 14 varies in number and tense but otherwise is constant.

Example 15 is built on another syntactic frame which is widely used in *izibongo* of ordinary people . Here repetition takes the form of identical word order and a repeated verb in the two halves of the line; contrast is supplied through singular/plural subjects and in the verb phrases "with a nail"/"with a pencil".

As regards figurative language, it is worth noting that the prominence of metaphor in other categories is found here also, adding once again to the richness of the poetic language' of the formulae.

The content of these formulae introduces a new element. Whereas the familiar themes of strength and resilience feature in Examples 11, 12, 14 and 15, Example 13 is more earthy and deals with the topics of sexual attraction and courtship, both of which feature prominently in popular praises in particular. Humour is an important element in the praises of ordinary people and often—as in the case of this formula line—comes from references to the opposite sex:

Example 11

   UMamba kayihlokozwa, ihlokozwa abanesibindi.
   The Mamba is not poked at, it is poked at (only) by the brave.[12]

Example 12

   UNtaba kayikh njwa, ikhǫn jwa ngamasalamuzi.
   The Mountain is not pointed at, it is pointed at (only) by wizards.[13]

Example 13

   i. UMqomis' wentombi emfishane, ende imbangela umfehlane/umkhuhlane.
   ii. UMthandi wentombi encane, endala imbangela umfehlane/umkhuhlane.

   i. Proposer to a short girl, the tall one gives him fever/cold
   ii. Lover of a young girl, the older one gives him fever/cold.

Example 14

   NMgawuli umuth' omkhulu, omncane uyaziwela.
   Chopper down of the big tree, the little one falls on its own.[14]

Example 15

   UMabhala ngozipho, abanye bebhala ngepensele.
   Writer with a nail, others write with a pencil.[15]

2d. Flexible formulae with marked alliteration or assonance

Much Zulu praise poetry is intensely alliterative over and above the concordial alliteration imposed by grammatical rules. In a few cases this general feature of the poetic language of *izibongo* is strikingly evident in a formula line. In the following example the front part containing the alliterative consonant is fixed (i.e. the first two words both of which contain the voiced alveolar lateral fricative "dl"). The second half of the line can be stated in two completely different ways, although both carry the same general implication of shameless behaviour. It is interesting to note that here too as in earlier examples, the opening words are constant and contain the distinctive features of the formula, thus making it easier for composers, performers and listeners to cue into it. The strong tone of censure regarding sexual misdemeanours which the formula displays is quite common in women's praise poetry but rarely occurs in men's *izibongo*. Also typical of women's *izibongo* is the way in which the line implies the virtue of the bearer compared with the lascivious habits of others.

Example 16

> UDlula bedlana, o'nto zawonina!/umfana ongenamhawu!
> Passer-by as they're having sex, the worthless privates of her mother!/the boy who knows no shame![16]

Type 3: Shorter formulae
3a. Those used by bards

A number of these formulae are found in *izibongo* performed by bards and therefore in the declamatory mode. They suit the more expansive, inspirational tone of the praises of people of high rank or status and they often add to the sense of expectancy and excitement which such praises generate; other short formulae denote that something important has already happened and create a sense of mysterious grandeur. These short formulae can be fixed onto a variety of lines or part-lines and as such are very versatile and of great use to bards when they compose and possibly when they are working with received praises from an earlier generation. A number of these formulae also contain alliteration, assonance or semantic contrast.

Example 17

> Kwaze kwasa—*until dawn*. This is often combined with

Example 18

> Bebikelana bengalele—*they spoke sleeplessly to each other*—
> and is also sometimes combined with

Example 19

> Lukhulu luyeza luyenyelela—*The great one is coming, gliding along...*
> The following show how they are sometimes combined:

Example 20

   i. USihlonono sakhal 'endlebeni yendoda—
     Kwaza kwasa amadoda bengalele bebikelana
     Athi'Kulukhulu luyasabeka luyenyelela ngalowo kaMenzi.'
     The Cricket chirpèd in the ear of a man—
     Until dawn men spoke sleeplessly to each other
     They said 'It is the great one, it is fearful, it is gliding
     along, descendant of (the Royal) Menzi'.

   ii. Here a formula reserved for royalty, *Gijimani . . .*is combined with *Lukhulu . . .:*

     Gijimani nge'ndlela zonkana niyobikela bangakezwa
     Nithi 'Lukhulu luyeza luyenyelela'
     Silufanis' nendlovu emnyama yasoBhalule.
     Run ye along all the roads, announce to those who have
     not heard,
     Say 'The great one is coming, gliding along'
     We compare him to the black elephant of Bhalule.[17]

3b. Shorter formulae used by bards and popular performers

The following two examples of this type of formula are widely used by bards and popular performers alike. In general, though, these formulae are less expressive and poetic than those in (3a) and they perhaps reflect the more limited expressive aims and techniques of popular composers. Example 21, for instance, has none of the assonance of Examples 17 and 19. It does not help to create an atmosphere of suspense or tension; rather, it has a more modest narrative function and serves as a means of filling out a reference to an event—usually a fight—a place or a lineage connection. It is also a means of making known one's mother's family, and its wide use illustrates the often tense relationship between maternal and paternal kin (Krige, 1936: 124, 128).

Like Examples 17-20, both 21 and 22 are versatile and can be attached to a variety of lines or part-lines.

Example 21

    . . . ekhaya konina kwa . . . . .
    . . . at his mother's homestead of the . . . . . .

The next phrase is used as a neat device for rounding off a line and giving it a sense of balance so appreciated by listeners and by those who perform. The balance comes from a simple antithesis of gender and the phrase is: abafazi namadoda—*women and men*. It can be used with a variety of antecedents as these examples illustrate. Also, as (i) below shows, it can be part of a wider patterning device—cross-linking in his case—as in lines 1-2. The first part of line 1 is itself a formula which uses alliteration ("ph") and assonance ("u" and "e") as foregrounding devices.

Example 22

abafazi namadoda—woman and men:

i. UPhunyuka bemphethe abafazi namadoda
   Amadoda ahayizana nasekhaya nangasenhle.
   U'nhlamwu azimshayanga ngoba zashaya abasekhaya
   konina kwaNtuli.
   Escaper as they grab him, the women and the men.
   The bullets didn't hit him because they hit those of his
   mother's homestead, the Ntulis.

ii. USidlukula-dlwedlwe besidlukula abafazi namadoda.
   The wild staff-shaker they shook her both, the women
   and the men.[18]

The formulae as poetic devices

The above examples should serve to illustrate that formulae, as they occur in Zulu *izibongo*, do themselves incorporate the poetic language available in the genre as a whole. Many of the formulae use metaphors which carry a high affective charge. This emotional charge of the formulae is perhaps doubly strong when they are set in a recognized syntactic frame. In their case also, "Age does not wither them/Nor custom stale their infinite variety." Some formulae use alliteration and assonance to a heightened degree; a number use semantic and syntactic patterning, thereby exploiting some—though by no means all—of the kinds of parallelism found in the wider body of the praise poems. In addition to all this, though, the formulae themselves constitute a poetic device, their very familiarity adding to their attraction.

Their use in composition

Okpewho (1979:160) has pointed out that scholars in recent years have been more interested in the potential which the formula has "for creative variation" than in "its role largely as a mnemonic tether in oral narrative composition". Yet is it necessary to make any sort of hard and fast distinction between memory and creative variation? Both may be facets of the same operation. The formulae in Zulu praise poems do in many instances allow for variation, as the above examples have shown. Both memory and creative variation would seem to operate in such cases.

There is another way in which memory and creative variation interact, and that is when poets—both the bards working in the declamatory mode and popular performers—use the formula as a base or launching pad for expansions. These vary in length. A nonspecialist may add only a single line to a formula, as in the following instance where the composer emphasizes his troubles by expanding the metaphor of "the rough rock" in line I through to a second line:

Example 23

Ng'uShishiliza kwelimaholo limshaye limbhedule
(expansion) Limphose phezulu ubuye sekumhlophe kuthe wa!
I am The Slitherer over the rough rock, it cut and grazed him
It tossed him up and when he came down he was (scraped)
dead white!

A more elaborate expansion is seen in the next example, from the *izibongo* of the Nazarite leader Isaiah Shembe. Here the formula "INyanga bath' ifile . . ." (Example 8 iii) leads to a description of Shembe's risen self sailing like the returning moon over his familiar haunts and over the gates of the Nazarite holy village, Ekuphakameni.

Example 24

(lines 105 ff) INyanga bath' ifile kanti basho nje iduk' emafini.
(expansion) Ugudlagudla i'ntaba zoMkhambathi
Uthe ngimbona eshona ngaleziya 'zintaba zakwaMadladla,
Uthi namhlanje unempilo eside simbona,
Waseqhamuka esekhazimula, esexhopha ngaphakathi kwamasango asEkuphakameni.
The Moon they said it had died whereas they meant it was lost in the clouds.
He skirts the mountains of Mkhambathi
And then I saw him disappearing in the direction of those far-

off hills of Madladla's place.
Even today he is alive, we behold him constantly,
He appeared shining, dazzling (the eyes) within the gates of Ekuphakameni.

Although many formulae cover a wide range in time and region, others seem more local in circulation. A formula may in fact begin by being simply a line borrowed from another praise poem, then borrowed again and so gradually becoming established as a widely known and useful line. Compact single-line or two-line praises are often passed from father to son and previously were also taken from the *izibongo* of the conquered and included in those of the victor (Cope, 1968). The regimental system, now defunct in all but name, must have contributed greatly to borrowing and to the creating of new formulae. One contemporary example of what was perhaps a formula in the making is the following from Ngoye. It has very local references and was heard three times over a period of several months in 1976:

Example 25

Waphuz' umuthi omubi ngoba waphuz' idibha eMlalazi,
Waphuz' uphoyizeni!
S/He drank horrible medicine because s/he drank the cattle dip at the Mlalazi River,
S/He drank poison![19]

One of the bearers of this praise maintained that she had slipped into the cattle dip while drunk and so had composed this line. As the second person who used the line was a young boy, it seemed unlikely that he too was commemorating a moment of drunkeness! It may be that he simply liked the line when he heard it and so included it in his own praises. Only time can tell whether the above example becomes established as a formula and then perhaps moves off to other districts to feature—possibly with slight differences—in the *izibongo* of other individuals. Formulae not only come into being from pleasing lines, they can disappear altogether or alter over generations and gather around them a different set of associations. Thus, for instance, Example 15,

UMabhala ngozipho abanye bebhala ngepensele
Writer with a fingernail, others write with a pencil,

has possibly grown out of an earlier line where the verb "-bhala" has its primary meaning of "scratch, make mark" rather than "write":

> UKlebe lobhalayo, UMabhala nganzipho.
> Hawk that makes its mark, Marker with a talon.[20]

Evidence would suggest, then, that the formulae are not static; they shift to include new words and new concepts, and young and old formulae exist together in the tradition of composing, listening and performing.

The significance of formulae in peformance

Although both bards and popular performers use formulae, thus demonstrating the essential unity of the genre, it remains true that bards performing in the declamatory mode tend to use the formulae for expansion rather more than others. This is due in part to the greater skill and craftsmanship of the bards and also possibly to the conditions of performance. Bards are expected to perform solo (or with one other performer) and their only interruptions are cries of excitement, agreement and encouragement from the audience. Composition in performance is not a standard feature of Zulu praise poetry, unlike Xhosa *izibongo* (Opland, 1975), and bards often recite praise poems which they have to a large extent memorised. This is the case with the *izibongo* of lineage ancestors. Other praise poems are a knitting together and elaboration of lines in praise of individuals gathered from diverse sources and a third category are freshly composed. But even those which a bard knits together or which he newly composes are prepared before performance. What, if anything, therefore, is the significance of formulae in a performance situation quite different from that described by Lord, whose analysis of Yugoslav oral narrative poetry synthesises the acts of composition and performance (Lord, 1960: 13, 101)? I would sugggest that formulaic lines or part lines serve both as recognition cues for an audience and as mnemonics for bards. Also the fact that formulae are widely known and in some cases carry considerable affective charge makes them particularly suitable as starting points for expansions likely to hold an audience's attention in a solo performance situation.

Praise poems are frequently performed in a second mode by those who make no claim to be bards. In the call mode, song, chant and dance feature as components together with the praise poem.

Delivery is entirely different from that in the declamatory mode. Whereas the emphasis there is on individual performance, here the emphasis is on the group. Many individuals call out at great speed a line or lines from the praise poem of a single "giya" dancer who leaps and prances as he pleases, giving an impromptu impression of fighting prowess. What is for the dancer a "multiform" whole is enunciated in numerous often repeated fragmented units by his comrades who call out the praises as he dances. Both the dancer and those who praise him "know" his *izibongo* and here too there is no stress on composition in performance. Yet in a way this is a more dynamic performing mode than that of the bards: new praises may be added by callers, the order of lines is arbitrary, and the amount and quality of praises called out for any individual may vary enormously from one occasion to the next. This is the performance mode where innovations in the shape of new formulae, modification to conventional subjects, and new metaphors are perhaps most likely to occur.[21] Perhaps, too, formulae are useful here because of their greater stability in the heat of utterance, and expansions are harder to find not only because of lesser craftsmanship but also because of the conditions of performance.

Both the *izibongo* which appear below demonstrate the general rule that formulae by no means dominate a single praise poem, yet one rarely exists without at least a single formulaic line or part line. The mode of performance for such *izibongo* also means that the examples given below are in one sense deceptive, because they are not faithful representations of any real performance with its multiple repetitions, overlaps and variations, and disregard for line stops.[22] Both are versions recollected in tranquillity by each of the bearers of the *izibongo*. To present them as I do here may emphasise the basic unity of the genre in the shared stylistic features of bard-performed and popular-performed *izibongo* but, unless accompanied by a commentary, it obscures the fundamental differences in the two modes of performance:

Example 26

The *izibongo* of Shishiliza Dube, Ngoye - (in both Examples 26 and 27, formulae are in italics);

I am The Slitherer over the rough rock, it cut and grazed him.
It tossed him up and when he came down he was *(scraped)* dead

202

white!
White are the shields, white the (shield) laces
Let (that bull) die, we want his hide for our shields
He rubs off (the soap) before he's washed at the riverside
Because he's afraid of the consequences of past deeds.
Hot-tempered Swiper, (yet) he doesn't eat a person, he eats
     (only) the tops of the sugar cane.
We dig holes all over the place and the empty spaces are red.
The fame of the soldiers who head for England.
Goblin of a little prostitute!
Ha! My mother-in-law, what has made you so hot-tempered?
Do you want to catch a fever?
Bride, you are ploughing here, what do you expect to get?
Hurrying one who tires himself out, Baboon of Ngoye (forest).

Example 27

The *izibongo* of Elias Mjadu, Richards Bay:

Constant attender at others' weddings
But when will he attend his own?
The newcomer there at Mdlebe.
The Constantly-Gazed-At-One like the sun.
Proposer to a girl — another came and he proposed to her.
The girl whose mother from KwaDlangezwa accepted marriage
     offers for her,
The girl who hit her mother-in-law.
You did wrong to hit the married woman at Ndlwanembila.
Wrestler with the little bull which had frightened off the
    Ntengas.
The man is making his complaint at the gateway of the Chief's
    place.
He escapes as they grab him, both women and men.
Men fight among themselves both at home and up-country.
The bullets didn't hit him because they hit his mother's people,
the Ntulis
I am being ruined because of a black man from the North,
Because I am being ruined by a man with a pot-belly.
He had sex with the girl that pestered and was never satisfied,
    whom he passed on to his brother.
His brother passed her on to the Mpukunyoni fellows with the

weighty private parts.

To conclude, it seems that it is not enough to speak of recurrent themes in Zulu praise poetry. The lines and phrases which are found to recur can be called formulae without this leading to undue agonizing over the place of metre in such formulae (although a careful perusal of formulae may unlock the key to metre, if it exists!). The formulae, moreover, can be regarded as both wand and walking-stick. On the one hand, their poetic features contribute to an awareness of language used in an intense and special way. On the other hand, their relative stability and their ability to provide a ready reference to a range of situations and attributes make them useful as an aid to composition, a walking-stick for bards and non-specialists alike. Moreover, the interplay of memory and creativity which the formulae allow for militates against any rigid view of the role of memory in the Zulu praising tradition.

NOTES

1. An earlier version of this paper was read at a symposium held at Wolfson College, Oxford University in June 1981 and organized by Veronike Gorog-Karady. I should like to record my thanks to the Commonwealth Foundation for their generous funding of my travel to Nigeria to attend the Ibadan Conference on "The Oral Performance in Africa".

2. (i) is from the *izibongo* of Chief Qokinsimbi Ntuli, Eshowe district. The recording is in E.G.'s tape collection and the reciter is Mboneni Ntuli. All the examples that follow are from *izibongo* recordd by E.G. unless otherwise stated.

   (ii) is from *izibongo* of Dinuzulu kaCetshwayo, d. 1913; the reciter is the *imbongi* Amos Gwala, bard of the late Bhekuzulu kaSolomon; my thanks to S.A.B.C., Durban and to Ernie Hilder for allowing me to make a copy of their recording.

   recited by Zizwezonke Mthethwa, Eshowe; also in the *izibongo* of Madlinyoka Hlabisa, of Hlabisa, recited by herself.

4. From the *izibongo* (a). of an unknown man, Hlabisa district.

   (b). of MaShekelela Dindi, Ngoye district. Recited by themselves

5. (i) From the *izibongo* of Zulu kaNogandaya, a renowned warrior of the early 19th century (Cope, 1968).

   (ii) From the *izibongo* of Isaiah Shembe, recited by the *imbongi* Azariah Mthiyane.

6. (i) From the *izibongo* of King Zwelithini kaBhekuzulu recited by the *imbongi* John Dlamini.
   (ii) From the *izibongo* of George Ngobese, Ngoye, recited by himself.
7. (i) Given as a typical warrior's praise in Callaway, 1968.
   (ii) From the *izibongo* of Mr Nzama, Ngoye, recited by himself.
   (iii) From the *izibongo* of Mavukefile Mdletshe, late 19th century, Mahlabathini district, recited by his son. The third "nggbe" make no sense grammatically and the reciter seems to be using it in his own idiosyncratic way for the effect of the repetition. This is perhaps his own creative variation of the formulae encapsulated in the *izibongo* of his father. There is a play on the word "Tshani" which means "grass" but also refers to the battle of 'Tshaneni where the bearer of the praise fought on the side of Dinuzulu kaCetshwayo against the rebellious Zibhebhu.
8. (i) From the *izibongo* of Halakashana Ntuli, Eshowe district, recited by Mzondeni Buthelezi.
   (ii) From the *izibongo* of a young girl, Ngoye.
   (iii) From the *izibongo* of King Zwelithini kaBhekuzulu.
9. (i) From the *izibongo* of Chief Mtekelzi Hlabisa, early 20th century recited by Sonduzabanye Hlabisa, *imbongi*.
   (ii) From the *izibongo* of Chief Nikiza Mkhwanazi, early 20th century Ngoye, recited by Masoswidi Mkhwanazi, *imbongi*.
   (iii) From the *izibongo* of Isaiah Shembe.
   (iv) From the *izibongo* of Chief Tshanibezwe Buthelezi, late 19th-early 20th century, Mahlabathini district, recited by Mgezeni Ndlela, *imbongi*.
10. From the *izibongo* of Chief Bambatha Zondi leader of the 1905 rebellion (Doke and Vilakazi, 1972); also from those of an early 20th century Zungu Chief, Empangeni, reciter Alpheus Luthuli, *imbongi*; also from those of Sonkeshana Buthelezi, late 19th century, Mahlabathini district, reciter Mgezeni Ndlela.
11. (i) From the *izibongo* of Chief Lindelihle Mzimela, Ngoye, recited by Phemba Mzimela, *imbongi;* also from the *izibongo* of Ernest Mkhwanazi and a Mr Dlamini, recited by themselves, Ngoye.
   (ii) From the *izibongo* of Zibhebhu kaMaphitha Zulu late 19th century recited by Amos Gwala.
   (iii) From the *izibongo* of Chief Silambo mid 19th century (van Warmelo, 1930:82).
   (iv) From the *izibongo* of Chief Hlatshwayo 19th century (Read, 1937:23).
12. From the *izibongo* of Mr Dube and of MaNtombela, Ngoye, recited by themselves.
13. From the *izibongo* of Bheki Dladla, Ngoye and Mr Zibani, Ngoye, recited by themselves.
14. From the *izibongo* of Chief Lindelihle Mzimela see Note II and Mr Dube see Note 12.
15. From the *izibongo* of Chief Zimema Mzimela, 19th century, Ngoye, recited by Phemba Mzimela, *imbongi;* also from the *izibongo* of MaMngema, Ngoye, recited by herself.
16. From the *izibongo* of MaMcasule Dube, Ngoye district, recited by herself; many others also have this line.

17. (i) From the *izibongo* of Chief Gatsha Buthelezi recited by INdodengemuntu Buthelezi, *imbongi*.
18. (i) From the *izibongo* of Elias Mjadu, Richards Bay, recited by himself. See Example 27.
    (ii) From the *izibongo* of MaMcasule Dube see Note 16 above.
19. From the *izibongo* of MaKhumalo and two others from the Ngoye district.
20. From the *izibongo* of Sonkeshana Buthelezi, late 19th century, Mahlabathini district, recited by Mgezeni Ndlela, *imbongi*.
21. The key innovative role of the popular praiser was first suggested to me by Rosemary Joseph during a symposium oat Wolfson College, Oxford University, June 1981.
22. In discussion of a recording of the *izibongo* of Shishiliza Dube which I played to delegates, even the endings used (Example 26 lines, 1-2) and based on only a fairly fast single-voice delivery were queried. "Why did you break the line there? There is no clear pause?" This raises the tricky question of how one represents "lines" in the often hectic recitation of oral poetry where, audibly, few breaks occur but where a pattern based on syntax can be discerned (or imposed?) during transcription. The breath-group-division principle is useful as a rule of thumb but even that is not as foolproof as it may seem at first!

REFERENCES

ANDRZEJEWSKI, B.W. 1981. "The Alliteration and Scansion of Somali poetry and their Cultural Correlates." Paper delivered at Africa Department Seminar, School of Oriental and African Studies, University of London.

BABALOLA, S.A. 1966. *The Content and Form of Yoruba Ijala*. Oxford: Claredon Press.

BENSON, L.D. 1966. "The Literary Character of Anglo-Saxon Formulaic Poetry." *Publication of the Modern Language Association*, 81, 334-41.

BIRD, C. 1972. "Heroic Songs of the Mande Hunters." *African Folklore*, ed. R.M. Dorson. Bloomington: Indiana University Press.

CALLAWAY, H. 1868. *Nursery Tales: Traditions and Histories of the Zulus*. Natal: Springvale Press.

COPE, A.T. 1968. *Izibongo: Zulu praise poems*. Oxford: Clarendon Press. 1978. "Towards an appreciation of Zulu folktales as literary art." *Social System and Tradition in Southern Africa*. Argyle, J. and E. Preston-White, eds. Cape Town: Oxford University Press.

DAMANE, M. and P. SANDERS, (eds). 1974. *Lithoko: Sotho Praise Poems*. Oxford: Clarendon Press.

DOKE, C.M. and B.W. VILAKAZI, 1972. *Zulu-English Dictionary*. Johannesburg: Witwatersrand University Press.

FINNEGAN, R. 1976. "How Oral is Oral Literature anyway?" *Oral Literature and the Formula*, Stolz, B.A. and R.S. Shannon, eds. Ann Arbor: Center for Coordination of Ancient and Modern Studies.

FORTUNE, G. and A.C. HODZA, 1979. *Shona Praise Poetry*. Oxford: Clarendon Press.

JAKOBSON, R. 1966. "Grammatical parallelism and its Russian facet." *Language,* 42, 399-429.

KRIGE, E. 1936. *The Social System of the Zulus.* Pietermaritzburg: Shutter and Shooter.

KUNENE, D.P. 1971. *Heroic Poetry of the Basotho.* Oxford: Clarendon Press.

LORD, A.B. 1960. *The Singer of Tales.* Cambridge, Mass.: Harvard University Press.

MAGOUN, F.P. 1953. "The Oral-Formulaic Character of Anglo-Saxon Narrative Poetry." *Speculum,* 28, 446-67.

MORRIS, H.F. 1964. *The Heroic Recitations of the Bahima of Ankole.* Oxford: Clarendon Press.

NKABINDE, A.C. 1976. *Zulu Prose and Praises: in Defence of a Living Tradition.* Empangeni: University of Zululand.

NYEMBEZI, C.L.S. 1954. *Zulu Proverbs.* Johannesburg: Witwatersrand University Press.

OKPEWHO, I. 1979. *The Epic in Africa: Toward a Poetics of the Oral Performance.* New York: Columbia University Press.

OPLAND, J. 1975. *"Imbongi nezibongo:* the Xhosa Oral Poet and the Contemporary Poetic tradition." *Publications of the Modern Language Association,* 90, 185-208.

READ, M. 1937. "Songs of the Ngoni People." *Bantu Studies,* 11, 1-35.

RYCROFT, D. 1980. "The Question of Metre in Southern African Praise Poetry." *Papers from the Third International Conference on African Languages,* (ed). J. Schultz. Pretoria: University of South Africa.

SMITH, M.G. 1957. "The Social Functions and Meaning of Hausa Praise-Singing." *Africa,* 27, 26-43.

WAINWRIGHT, A.T. 1978. "The Praises of Xhosa Mineworkers." M.A. thesis, University of South Africa, Pretoria.

WALDRON, R.A. 1957. "Oral-formulaic Technique and Middle English Alliterative Poetry." *Speculum,* 32, 792-804.

VAN WARMELO, N.J. 1930. *Transvaal Ndebele Texts.* Pretoria: Government Printers.

The Preservation, Transmission and Realization of Song Texts: A Psycho-Musical Approach

Daniel Avorgbedor

THE title of this paper, which focuses on song texts, should not prejudge the validity and strength of other modes of textual communication. The main purpose here is to illustrate the kinds and levels of transformation that the song-mode allows texts to undergo in order to effect communication in a special manner. An integrated analytical approach will be adopted, including relevant perspectives from music, psychology, and linguistics. It is hoped that this approach will create a meeting ground for those separate disciplines involved in the analysis of song texts. While most of the examples will be drawn from the Ewe society of southeastern Ghana, findings and speculations will have wider implications for the role of song and singing in establishing textual effectiveness in other cultures. Contextual factors, including individual and group idiosyncracies and kinesics, are integral to this analytical and theoretical presentation.

Song and human expression

Man is ontologically an expressive being, and both actions and reactions consequently permeate our modes of life and living. Artistic diversity, which is a distinctive and distinguishing mark of all cultures, provides indisputable evidence of our basic human need for expression. The song-mode is just one of the innumerable artistic avenues through which our latent response energies are released.[1]

A response is basically either an action or a reaction. While "reaction" will imply some confrontation and overtness, "action" is of no less status, and differences between the two should be sought from the emphatic qualities of the stimulus involved.[2] With regard to "action", it could be an original expression which is not

.irectly retaliatory in nature; it could take the form of a verbal proposition, or an independent initiation of a concrete project. Where an action is evident in terms of a concrete item, there is an overlap of "action" and "reaction" in terms of the origin and the concretization of that idea. In this case the idea represents the "stimulus", and the concrete item represents the maturation of that idea. The action-reaction chain can even ramify; an example of such an extended type will be the case in which one stimulus leads to the birth of an idea, and this idea is subsequently transformed into a pseudo-finite realization in concrete terms.[3] Even in the case of a song, which is composed of sound and physical stimuli, it is not independent of the diverse dispositions and responses of listeners or participants who influence one another through sympathetic affects, affects which are induced by the people's physical-aural proximities and general proxemics. Above all, individual temperaments, background experiences and projections also participate in the stimulus-response process.

Repetition reconsidered

Repetition, which is normally considered as an element of "redundancy", takes on an additional meaning and puts the very concept in doubt. Even at a superficial level of consideration, there is no literal repetition, as far as song texts are concerned in this paper. An initial analysis without the music reveals that when, for example, a sentence (or phrase) is stated and repeated, there are temporal factors that introduce a distinguishing mark between the initial statement and its repetition. The repetition constitutes, in temporal terms, a series of sequential events. The initial appearance of a sentence will carry with it some degree of "newness". Such newness is also subsequently altered when the sentence is repeated. The freshness with which we perceive the initial statement is altered by the degree of familiarity that the repetition introduces. Repetition also creates both differentiated and undifferentiated temporal segments that also introduce a tension between "familiarity" and "newness". Our expectations and projections are also constantly changing due to the repetition. The intensity of our involvement is contingent upon the quality and quantity of the listener-participant's background experiences that are recalled.

The differentiated temporal segments involve the linear time spans that the initial statement and its repetitions occupy. The "undifferentiated'' refers to the temporal adjustments that take place within the individual listener or performer before and after the repetition. Tension arises when a conflict-resolution transformational level is exigent due to the individual temporal span of each repetition that must be related to and mediated through the others. Such transformational level is also entertained according to varying individual modes of perception. Furthermore, as in performance situations, the spatial location of the singer (or performer) is as important as his posture. Among the Ewes, cantors (or lead singers) often move around the circumference of the performance arena, taking strategic positions for the delivery of the songs.[4] Sometimes a cantor would come as close as one foot to the spectator in order to confront him more directly with the song. While the song is directed in this manner to one specific spectator, it is also inevitable for the few immediate spectators to get involved because of their closeness to the original spectator.

When the song is finished, the cantor takes the next position, also at a direct communication distance with this next spectator. While the cantor is in this second position, the first spectator is still able to hear him repeat the song. With the help of the spatial distance and temporal gap, the first spectator is able to reflect more intensely on the first rendition of the song within the context of the second one. During this second rendition, the cantor's immediate physical confrontation with the first spectator is removed, and this is why the first spectator can now fully concentrate on the song which is being sung from a distance. In addition, the acoustic reverberation and distortion that result from that confrontation are also diminished; these acoustic phenomena are a hindrance to concentration on the song texts. There is an advantage in the second rendition because the sound (song) takes a longer time to reach the first spectator, and problems of intensity and distortion are also diminished due to the distance involved. The physical barrier created by the cantor's image is also thus removed. Even when there is a large audience and they all wear clothing which can absorb much of the extra acoustic presence, the particular spectators involved here are not easily spared the effects of the musical and sonic events within that close range.

An overall consideration reveals that the effects or results of the singing remain constant. This is so because all the spectators eventually receive the texts at the same strength. However, the emotional reactions vary because of individual backgrounds. A song performed in this fashion thus takes the spectators through subsequent repetitions, and places each spectator in slightly different receptive and perceptive attitudes. In all, these examples demonstrate different stages and levels of intensity in song transmission and reception.

In Ewe music one finds songs with elaborate texts which will take pages to transcribe, and songs based upon one or two lines of text. There are also the two types of repetition dealt with in this paper: the repetition of a whole song, and the repetition of one or more lines in a song. It is common practice to repeat a whole song which has repeated lines, as in music Example 1 below:

Example 1

Text	Translation
Gbomatodzui,	A hornless ram beats huge
efo agbogawo le ayeme ayeme.	rams through cunning.

Whenever this example is sung, a leader-chorus structure is adhered to. The leader always sings his part marked in the transcription, while the chorus responds with the "consequent" line. When an individual sings this song on his own, he naturally sings both the *leader* and *chorus* parts.[5]

In musical terms, this song is cast into a simple binary structure, made up of two related phrases. The first phrase is complete with the statement of the entire two-line text, and the second phrase repeats the text. The whole song can be sung or repeated several times. Textual repetition however carries a new meaning when we integrate the music. The second phrase is largely derived from the first in terms of contour and intervallic successions. However, the two phrases involve the use of two different sound registers—the second phrase exploits pitches within a lower sound register in order to effect a logical and artistic conclusion of the song.

In addition to the above details, the presence of a leader part introduces a psycho-dramatic feature into the performance of this song. Both phrases are introduced by the *leader* who is also responsible for the determination of the two sound registers of the song. While the two *leader* parts are not melodically the same, both invariably constitute a repetition—a textual one. Whenever the song is performed, the above characteristics and their relationships will always exist, despite minute internal differences such as different tonal area, volume, levels of excitement, and changes in performance contexts.[6] A multiple gestalt activity involving combinations, simultaneities, similarities, contrasts, separations and syntheses seizes the foreground in the individual sensory apprehension and perception at this point, and textual communication is constantly gaining strength.[7]

In Ewe song performance, especially within drumming contexts, the cantor-spectator confrontation described above assumes a widened dimension with the presence of at least two cantors and two cantresses. After a cantor has left one spectator and is attending to another one, a second cantor takes on again the spectator the first cantor has just left.[8] In this regard, a third dimension for perception, reception, and apprehension of the song text is created. Each new cantor brings to the same spectator a new artistic and personal aura. Individual modes of delivery and personal familiarities present the spectator with a configuration of communicative and affective surges, while at the same time confirming a previous delivery of the song. In addition, a cantress accompanies each cantor and they both deliver or sing together, the cantress singing at one octave above the cantor's pitch.[9] These three dimensions of song delivery which we would normally call repetitions actually allow the text to undergo multiple transformation, thereby intensifying, verifying, and diversifying the affective imports of the text. The three dimensions, which are made up of the close confrontation, distancing, and cantor rotation, unite with the more permanent ingredients (pitch focus, intervallic structure, sound register, sectional plan) for a total effect.

Repetition is then more than a device in maintaining stability, emphasis, structural balance, easy learning, and as a "corrective code."[10] A shift of sound register introduces the complex phenomenon of changing tone sensations with their emotional attendants.[11] To think of repetition without modification in meaning and affect will therefore be unfounded in Ewe song practice, considering the above evidence.

Example 2 illustrates the case of a long or an extended song. In the case of a short song, the minimal (short song) had to be re-experienced (i.e. repeated) and re-explained in order to achieve its maximum effect. Each repetition represents a confirmation and an extension of the minimal at a maximum level. In the long

Example 2

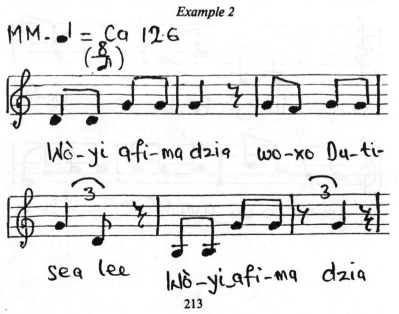

213

wò-xo Du-ti-sea lee, 'Me-kae te Duie

ne woa pa ɤo va ne wòa-xo

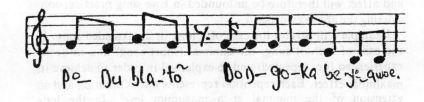

pɔ-Du bla-tõ Dɔɔ-gɔ-ka be yɛ qwoe.

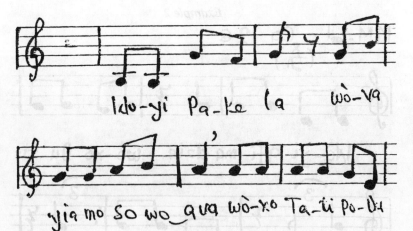

Idʋ-yi Pa-ke la wò-va

yia mo so wo qva wò-xo Ta-ũ pɔ-Dʋ

214

see, Ga-yi-me wò-tso, wò va

tso-tso ge va dɛ cɛ ŋjɩ be aŋe-ŋu-va-wo

koe Wo-koe yi ge Ɖɔ-ki-tae,

wo-va yiɑ do abi nɛ; wò-gbo va tsi

xo-mo Sa-ka-bo mi-dzu-dzɔ, e-ŋa-ma

song (Example 2), the text is elaborate, and there is hardly any repetition of any line. Even where a melodic portion is repeated, the accompanying text changes. Where the long song needs to be repeated, this is done once or twice. According to Ewe practice, one music club from a village would travel to perform in another village. As a form of appreciation and towards the enrichment of their own repertoire, members of the host village memorize and sing with renewed interest some of the songs sung by the visiting group. The long songs are therefore repeated to enable the hosts to digest them more carefully. This is the only chance the hosts have to familiarize themselves with the new songs, and they therefore carefully take due advantage of this one performance with the few repetitions.

Because a whole song can hardly be learnt within that brief performance period, the hosts learn the songs by singing the remembered portions, and in this manner the whole song is reconstructed as close as possible to the original as first heard. It is this participation from the individual learners that encourages the "renewed interest" earlier mentioned. Apart from those other functions that repetition performs, human mobility is an essential factor in the communication or transmission of song texts. The physical presence of cantors and cantresses enables the hosts to remember and learn the songs with ease: this is made possible by associating the songs with specific cantors and their individual kinesics. The importance of this human dimension cannot be easily glossed over as far as the transmission of song texts is concerned. The cyclic form of *hatsiatsia* also constitutes a type of repetition which gives an opportunity to the latecomer (or those who leave early) to hear songs which might have otherwise been missed.[12]

The lone singer

The personal psycho-dynamics of a song performance are also evident when one person is involved in singing. In a solo and secluded performance, the song psychologically and artistically transforms the soliloquy of a "mad" man into a true, lively, and significant experience.[13] The public assume no doubt or suspicion regarding the sanity of the singer. The melody artistically elevates the status of the text to an experience-renewing and experience-creating force. The solo singer uses the medium of song to temporarily escape direct involvement in normal social interactions, and the moral responsibilities of the singer are also transferred to the song itself. The singer, in his seclusion, becomes an intermediary between himself and the song. This is why he can *pour out* his feelings and emotions, uniting both words and music in order to sanction his neutral and yet dynamic role, so long as *he sings to himself who sings, and for himself who mediates between the song and the performer.* A person who sings by himself, whether in a room or outdoors, does so *through* himself, *for* himself, and *with* himself. In this case, the transmission, preservation, and realization of song texts do not happen in group performances only.

Even in a group performance the above solo characteristics will hold true to a large extent. The singing group essentially constitutes one *voice,* communicating one text with the help of a melody. The song-mode now unites and provides a single direction for the individual prescriptive and consequential reactions. The song does not reveal a bleak social and human identity; it provides a medium and a challenge through which many voices can *speak out* the same words (or ideas) unanimously. The group song provides a type of *hypnotic* effect whereby all the individual participants are submerged in an unconscious explicit act through the conscious manipulation of a crafted medium.[14] The old maxim, *Vox populi, vox Dei*, holds some relevance in the group song situation. The unanimous assertion of the text through group singing lends validity and strong appeal, and the text receives its efficacy. The message is transmitted, realized, and endowed with some values and realities of permanence. The elevated artistic status of song and singing, the effects of distancing and merging oneself in the song at the same time, the expressive-experiential involvement of many persons and their vocal and emotional unanimity—all interact to render the text socially established, well transmitted, and received.

Role of artistic license

There are two instances among the Ewe people where singing enables one to transcend social moral boundaries. The first instance involves song texts that are loaded with references to the genitals or sexual acts. The other instance concerns a body of *halo* songs that contain insults directed at specific persons.[15] The third and fourth examples below illustrate the contents of the songs referred to above.

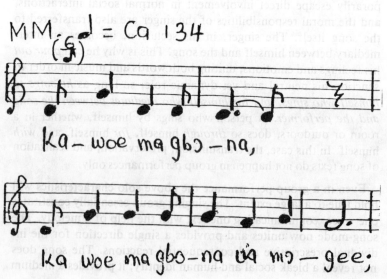

218

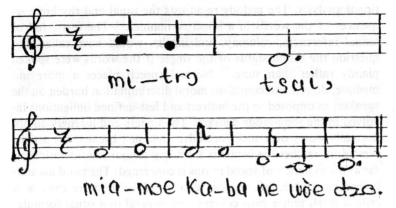

Translation

That is Kawoe coming,
That is Kawoe coming to have sex with penis;
Obstruct her,
To quickly have sex with her and she will go away

Example 4

Mr X has built a house,
He did not have enough material.
He gave a ram with scrotal hernia to Mr B
In exchange for building materials.
All his councilmen were ashamed but Mr X's case is different
His mouth as *lakpa* as that of *henye;*
Mr X with a huge ball-like skull has called for a song,
Kai, I will sing it for him;
Mr X with a long mouth has called for a song,
Kai, I will sing it for him.

It is not enough to say that, "Art . . . . . prescribes polite ways for saying impolite things; it provides ways for expressing the inexpressible"[16] A narrow psychoanalytic explanation is also an easy way out.[17]

The factors of "distancing" and "mediation" earlier described hold special significance in these two cases. The song removes normal and immediate moral responsibilities from the singer, and consequently leaves the singer blameless because of the ontological exemplification of the artistic phenomenon which is beyond functional analysis. The melody re-adjusts the tonal and rhythmic sequences of the words in a sensitive manner.[18] The texts, full of sexual references, calumny, and insults, would have called into question the moral status of the singer if the words were spoken plainly rather than sung.[19] Normal speech places a more immediate, direct, and conscious moral discrimination burden on the speaker, as opposed to the indirect and less-defined obligations involved in the song-mode delivery. The singers and listeners do not normally worry over such forbidden contents, because the artistic dimension rescues the contents from any serious consideration, as far as the violation of social norms is concerned. The mind naturally processes such information at a jovial level rather than at a critical level, unless such contents are integral to a ritual formula. Even when considered within a ritual context the explicit meaning of the contents will also be transferred to that ritual level. The words will assume a more symbolic status, transferring their meaning to something different from the plain literal words or symbols.

I personally witnessed a social incident where, in a social-drinking situation, one person sang a song that was composed to insult another member of the group. The composer was one of the specialists who composed songs for the group, but in this case the song was banned from the repertoire because of the direct attack on a member's image. Despite the unanimous verdict against the singing of the song, one man started singing the song in the presence of the victim who also happened to be among the drinking group. The victim reacted immediately by making an appeal to the group to stop the song in the following words: "You see, you see, he is insulting me". The singer also responded by saying, with an ambiguous smile: "I am just singing a song".

The above situation creates a special conflict that must be resolved in this paper—an artistic practice that is re-interpreted within the core of the social web. The conflict is introduced by the banning of the song and the license taken to sing it. While contextual factors might help in the explanation, it is useful to note that there had been no incident of previous antagonism between the singer and the victim of the song. The drinking situation offers a favourable atmosphere within which liberties are taken to move beyond normal social codes of behaviour. While one may attribute such behaviour to the effects that alcohol has on the conscious mind, neither the singer himself nor the group would cite alcoholic influences as being responsible for this behaviour. As one can infer from the singer's verbal response, he seemed to be protected by the license involved in the artistic mode of song and singing. But does artistic license override special social ruling? The boundaries of social freedom are now poised against the extent of artistic license.

In the case of *halo* songs in which two social factions are involved, anybody who sings a *halo* song after it has been banned is regarded severely by the law (this was the practice when *halo* was in vogue). The same legal procedures are also expected to be followed in this case which involved two persons from the same social group. Although the victim relied on the rest of the group as the final arbiter, they remained neutral, and the case was not pursued further.

The clue to this complex situation is a dramatic one, and can be traced to the supplementary verbal and gestural rationale of the singer. The statement, "I have just sung a song", is valid only up to the point where artistic license no longer holds. The verbal response was given with a smile and underscored by a gentle hand gesture. I believe if the singer were to use adamant and hostile gesture, the group would have been incited to carry the case futher, and artistic license would then have succumbed to the limits of social freedom. The gesture and the smile contained comic ingredients that dampened and restrained audience reaction in pursuit of the law.[20] The verbal statement by the singer was also powerful because it was a spoken form made in relation to a song. No doubt song often draws upon instances of speech, and when such speech forms refer to the song itself, a "meta-effect" is created. The meta-effects help to challenge, verify, and validate the song's artistic license, and the text is endowed with further immunities.[21] The singer was thus able to escape the strictures of a social ruling. A regular offensive song would have been sung without incurring the charge of a social violation, and there would have been little need for supporting statements and gestures.[22] In conclusion, it should be noted that the interplay of body gestures and verbal pronouncements is necessary at certain crucial moments of singing in order to project the authority, affective import, and urgency of the text.

Role of textual adaptation and substitution

Ewe musical practice also allows different texts to be adapted or sung to one melody. The practice is to create new texts to fit the melody and to replace the old text. Sometimes both texts remain concurrent, depending upon the singer's preferences, as the situation demands. The substitution or adaptation is not a fortuitous one, for it helps in the transmission and realization of the texts. When the new text is sung (although the melody is the same), the singer does this with a renewed interest, and sometimes with different accompanying gestures. The listener consequently receives a dramatic change which draws forth the attention necessary for the reception and retention of the text. The effect might however be a little different in the case of a listener to whom both the melody and the text are new. The performance of the new text represents one of those "unusual" events that create excitement, and excitement conditions, fosters, and alters our perceptive and receptive capabilities. While the new text would tend to dominate the memory of the listener, the old text is also recalled and established in the conscious mind. In this manner a single melody is able to create a situation suitable for the communication of two different texts, both simultaneously and retroactively. The old text is communicated in an indirect manner, primarily by means of association, as the melody is originally typical of the old text. It is also possible to adapt more than two texts to the same melody in the same manner. This process always contributes something to the effective transmission, realization, and confirmation of both the old and new texts.[23] Differences in the two texts below are revealed not only in the different words, but also in the contrasted modes of dress-style that belonged to two different periods in the history of the Ewes:

Example 5

Old Text	*Translation*
Daavi taɖetiawo sɔ gbɔ,	Sister the *tadeti* dresses are too many
Yi naɖe avɔgã̃ da ɖi;	
Be taɖetiawo sɔ gbɔ,	Go and remove the big cloth;
Yi naɖe avɔgã̃ da ɖi;	That the *tadeti* dresses are too many,
Be taɖetiawo sɔ gbɔ,	Go and remove the big cloth;
Yi naɖe avɔgã̃ da ɖi aoh!	That the *tadeti* dresses are too many,
	Go and remove the big cloth, aoh!

New Text	*Translation*
Daavi-sukutoe ma gbɔna,	Sister the-school-one is coming,
Baya le megbe nɛ loo;	Has *baya* style at the back;
Be sukutoe ma gbɔna,	That the-school-one-is coming,
Baya le megbe nɛ loo;	Has *baya* style at the back;
Be sukutoe ma gbɔna,	That the-school-one is coming,
Baya le megbe nɛloo aoh!	Has *baya* style at the back aoh!

Role of concrete media and poetics

Song performance in the Ewe context also permits the use of visual or sculptur ed images to reinforce the text. During one of the *Xaisevu* performances in a village called Seva, a sculptural piece depicting an eagle hovering over a turtle was displayed. At one stage during the singing, both the performers and the audience turned to look in the direction of the sculpture. The words being sung at that moment are reproduced here and they are related directly to the images (Example 6). The visual memory of the sculpture will help concretize the text into a more permanent and affective whole. With the visual illustration, the words are less likely to be forgotten, and permanence is consequently achieved.[24]

Example 6

Miawoe nye metsyɔ 'kɔ 'nyi hɔ̃ ʄo na o,
Hɔ̃ la va ʄo mi be fe la 'va klẽ;
Hɔ̃ ʄo klo mekpɔ ɖuɖu ŋuti o,
Numa wo dziku kpɔmee wóle hee;

We are the turtle that does not lie down as prey for eagle,
The eagle will prey on us and its claws will be ruined;
The eagle tried but found nothing to eat,
That is why they are angry;

Song texts are full of proverbs, proverbial sayings, riddles, gossips, euphemisms and personifications: endless examples can be cited to illustrate these linguistic manipulations and proliferations. Apart from being artistic and poetic devices, alliteration, assonance, and parallelism all help in creating pleasurable effects that are necessary in the comfortable and easy reception, recollection, and involuntary evocation of the text. These poetic devices are

223

special forms of word and sound patternings, and, united with the appropriate music and gesture, they appeal to and leave lasting impressions on the minds of the listeners. For instance, all the songs of Mr Klutse Zate (a noted composer from the village of Seva) contain two types of textual manipulation, as far as the use of proverbs is concerned. He quotes or creates his own proverbs, and he elaborates upon them, thus creating an amalgam of proverb and proverbial saying. The other technique is to quote a series of proverbs, a technique which is not usual in the normal speech or conversational mode. One of such songs will illustrate some of these techniques:

Example 7

> Zateglo tsi toŋgɔ,
> Tɔŋgɔ metsi nye zi ha;
> Zate be agbatsɔ ƒea
> De wokpea kɔ na amenɔvi,
> 'Gba menoa tadzi kpea klo hee;
> Xe medoa to de Ɣedzeƒe o,
> Atsiaƒu me miena wotoa fɔ yia
> 'Blotsi o.

Translation

> Zateglo is left beyond the river,
> Beyond the river I am left like this;
> Zate says the place of load makes a friend
> tire under the headload,
> A headload does not tire the knee;
> Sun does not set in the East;
> One does not take advantage of a
> dried-up ocean to walk to
> London.

While the first two lines create a type of cross-parallelism, the remaining lines are examples of a proverb and proverbial sayings. More song transcriptions will also reveal rhyme patterns. In the first line, the composer speaks in the "third" person, but the true "first" person is revealed ("*I* am") in the second line. This underscoring of the "subject" through cross relations and relocation of words attracts listeners' attention. Two different but related means are used to achieve and emphasize one end. The "self-distance" involved in the first line presents the text nearer to the feelings of the listeners, while the second line leads them to reflect longer and more intensively on the text.

Some song texts also contain archaic words, and words whose meanings may not be immediately intelligible. Whether these words are understood or not they are integral to the total linguistic vocabulary of the people. Scholars should, therefore, be careful in thinking that these words are "meaningless" or "incorrect grammar".[25] The Ewes sing appropriately: "The meaning of a song is not immediately understood", and the listener is expected to go home and reflect cautiously and slowly on the texts. This "homework" is indispensable for the establishment of the text in the listener's memory due to the amount of effort involved in the re-collection and re-searching of the text.

Since discussion on this would require a separate paper on the linguistic aspects of song texts, it should suffice to conclude that linguistic devices unite with psycho-musical ones in order to preserve, transmit, and foster the realization of song texts. While most of the findings here would apply to other oral cultures (apart from the Ewe or African cultures), literate and "art music" traditions would need additional tools to explain their systems concerning song communication.

Notes

1. Alan Lomax, *Folk Song Style and Culture* (Washington, D.C.: American Association for the Advancement of Science, 1968). In this work Lomax has demonstrated the universality of song and singing. The human side of singing is also briefly described in Edward Lippman, *A Humanistic Philosophy of Music* (New York: New York University Press, 1977). See chapter on "Form".

2. For example, when you strike me on the head, I may react immediately and furiously by hitting you in retaliation. Or, I may suppress my anger and resentment; such suppression will gain more in terms of internal reaction.

3. "Pseudo-finite" because there is, in theory, no end to the stimulus-response chain; there are constant conditionings from living and non-living things.

4. In performance, sitting arrangements are normally in the form of a circle.

5. There are many forms of the leader-chorus organization. There are complex forms which cannot be discussed in this paper, since they involve detailed musical explanations.

6. Compare Albert Lord, *Singer of Tales* (New York: Athenaeum, 1978). The theories of "individual variation" expounded in this book have limited application in the Ewe context. The Ewe recognize composers who are specialists; songs are taught and learnt at pre-arranged practice sessions, and the goal is toward group performance, except for certain songs whose com-

225

posers are unknown: these songs are known across Eweland, Anlo-Ewe specifically.

7. It should be emphasized at this point that transmission, preservation, and realization can all happen as simultaneous events since they are related to one another.

8. This shows that audience participation in African music has been over-generalized. The next cantor presents the same song.

9. The role of feminine influence is beyond the scope of this paper.

10. Leonard Meyer, *Music, the Arts, and Ideas* (Chicago: The University of Chicago Press, 1973); *Emotion and Meaning in Music* (Ibid., 1956). These concepts of repetition are applied and explained within the scope of "art music" traditions. See also note 5.

11. For example, in singing, extra effort is needed to sing at a high pitch, and varying pitches (and their configurations) therefore involve different qualities of human involvement in singing.

12. "Hatsiatsia" literally translates "selection of song". It is a sectional plan involving the cyclic performance of selected songs. A person who leaves early misses the opportunity of having the song asserted through the repetition cycle.

13. We normally consider a person who talks to himself as "insane" or "mad".

14. The effect of group singing in this context should not be confused with the effects of worksongs that are geared primarily toward greater work output and facility.

15. There was a period in Eweland when songs of abuse were used by different factions as a formalized medium for revengful expressions. These songs are known as "halo" songs.

16. George Devereux, "Art and Mythology: A General Theory" *Art and Aesthetics in Primitive Societies,* edited by Carol Joplin (New York: E.P. Dutton & Co., Inc., 1971.) See also similar comments in Alan Merriam, *The Anthropology of Music* (Evanston: Northwestern University Press, 1964). Chapter on "The Study of Song Texts".

17. The shortcomings of psychoanalytic explanations with regard to art are noted in Lev Semenovich Vygotsky, *The Psychology of Art* (Cambridge: The Massachussetts Institute of Technology Press, 1971).

18. Rhythm is integral to melody.

19. Although Ewe musical aesthetics recognize "good" voice and "good" singing (e.g., clear, resonant, not-too-high, and "sweet" voice), it does not matter here how beautifully the song is sung, once the victim can recognize it.

20. The drinking context is also an occasion for humour and jokes.

21. A subtle example of "preservation" is at work here. The artistic license involved still communicates the forbidden text which would have otherwise been forgotten.

22. The time lapse between the ruling and the event is not prolonged enough to allow social changes that might alter the original significance and force of the text.

23. This technique of textual adaptation and substitution has nothing to do with individual textual and melodic improvizations which are limited in this context.

24. The use of carvings to underscore song texts is also reported among Australian Aborigines. See Richard Waterman, "Music in Australian Aboriginal Culture:

226

Some Sociological and Psychological Implications" *Readings in Ethnomusicology*, edited by David Mc Allester (New York: Johnson Reprint Corporation, 1971), pp. 162-172.
25. See note 12 in the Alan Merriam piece cited above (note 16).

Notes to Transcriptions

Musical transcriptions have been simplified. All the songs are transcribed in the tonic of C. Some of the pitches actually sound a little higher or lower than written. A bell or some other ideophonic instrument normally provides a background rhythmic accompaniment to which the song coheres. In this case regular metric divisions (using bar lines) is not profitable. Broken bar-lines are therefore used to indicate subdivisions and not necessarily the alternation of weak and strong beats.

Standard Ewe orthography is used with some modifications in order to accommodate the musical constraints. Words are translated in a manner that would convey the basis idea. Proper names appearing in the text are replaced with "B" or "X" symbols in order to protect the identity of the persons concerned.

I wish to thank Dr. Gary Wittlich, Professor of Music Theory at Indiana University for his invaluable comments and suggestions in the development of this paper.

Narrative Rhythms in AGiryama *Ngano:* Oral Patterns and Musical Structures

Ronald M. Rassner

I

THE use of a time line (a recurring rhythmic pattern of fixed duration or time span), which clarifies the regulative beat, is a common feature of rhythmic organization in some African traditions.[1]

In drum music, once the essential rhythmic patterns or basic tones which give a piece its identity have been established, other patterns may be improvised by the drummer and linked to them. The basic tones might also be temporarily suppressed and reintroduced, or other configurations based on them may be used. However, all such variations have to be controlled in such a way as to keep the identity of the particular drum piece constantly in view. Any kind of exuberant display that takes the drummer too far away from the identifying rhythms and tones will generally not be attempted by a good musician.[2]

When Kwabena Nketia describes rhythms in African music, as he does above, he is also describing the operations of rhythmic patterns in African narrative. Nketia proposes two inter-related features, the time line and regulative rhythms. The time line is a rhythmic patterning which serves as a means of sustaining the rhythmic motion.[3] This time line is not to be confused with the performance rhythms *per se,* but as an accompanying rhythm with the other multipart rhythmic structures. Do oral narrative performances have time-lines, or repeated rhythmic patterns which clarify the regulative rhythms? And do these narratives even contain regulative rhythms, or "basic tones," which may be varied to some degree (becoming "configurative" rhythms), but maintain an order which must be followed?

228

The answer to both these questions is yes, although with some reservations. A successful narrative performance must be concerned with timing, but not necessarily precision (in the musical sense). Nonetheless, well-structured narratives are composed of regulative rhythms of varying durations; their repeated patterns may be flexible rather than "fixed" (just as a *narrative* time line is not fixed, but suggestive), because they operate imagistically, *extra-verbally,* and not solely at the verbal, auditory level. In other words, cognitive categorization requires linkage (through metaphor and homology, congruency and opposition, etc.), and not precise balance. These regulative rhythms are called narrative rhythms in narrative forms.

Oral narrative performance also has a "time line" which, in a narratological sense, must be defined as an arbitrarily flexible framework for image creation, choice, and juxtaposition. ("Arbitrarily" is used here to encompass traditional frames in respective societies as well as individual talents.) A narrative time line, and perhaps I should suggest the idea here as "image line," is related to Harold Scheub's now discarded concept of *core cliché* (in that one feature of the image line is its being a "dynamic main spring")[4] and Charles Pike's concept of structure determinism.[5] But the image line includes other features, such as retention (back formation or past remembrances) and protention (forecasting or "futuring"). And most importantly, an image line holds force over the duration of an entire narrative performance.

Nketia's idea of control is also central to oral narrative performance. All imagery is linked within boundaries of *both* freedom and order, repetition and variation. In music, the drumming of only basic tones becomes monotonous; "exuberant displays" beyond the tonal model become chaotic. Successful narrative (and music) uses freedom and order simultaneously. It is no surprise to use the term rhythm when explaining the oral narrative process: Plato's definition of rhythm is *kineseos taxis,* an order in movement, or an order in articulation.[6]

Both narrative rhythms and the image (time) line are composed of images in movement (remembering that the image-line is a key narrative rhythm "played" along with the other narrative rhythms). In the perception of music, at any one moment, there is only one beat to be heard. But this beat is meaningful only in its relationship with past beats and future beats. "One beat is not a

229

rhythm; it is the reverberation of a whole set of beats in the mind, all in a certain relationship that constitutes the perceptions of rhythm.''[7] Images in Giryama *ngano*[8] work under similar conditions. For example, in the Giryama narrative, "Nyanje and the Nzembe," as performed by Mrs. Sidi Chengo, the individual image of capturing a gazelle does not become a rhythm until it is patterned with two succeeding images (i.e. capturing another gazelle and capturing the nzembe). One image does not make a narrative rhythm, but several images in juxtaposition, recurrence, and variation compose a rhythm.

II

I recorded "Nyanje and the Nzembe,"[9] on September 27, 1976, in Goshi, Kenya, at the home of Tsaka Gona Maleleo. Mrs. Sidi Chengo, age 50, like all AGiryama, is not a professional raconteur, but has all the attributes of one. She has had no formal education and has rarely left Giryama country. Much of her time is spent either working in the fields or walking several miles a day seeking and bringing back water. Her *ngano* (singular and plural form, oral narrative performance in kiGiryama) are generally concerned with a world of competition and survival, the small and wonderful, the individual versus his society. The *ngano* is as follows:

"Nyanje and the Nzembe"

Chondoni. (*Degeha.*)
There was once a famine, and a man and his son, and famine. They built a rough fence to trap wild animals. They trapped everyday, and everyday they went to check their trap. One day they caught a gazelle.
They trapped, they checked their traps, they caught a gazelle, until one day the father couldn't go, only his son went to check the trap.
The father sent his son, "Go, check the trap;" they had gone to bed that night hungry, and he added, "bring whatever you get, bring it for us to make *mutsuzi.*"[10]
So the child went to check the trap. When he had reached the trap in the bush, he saw an animal in the trap. The child had a hatchet, he took it from his shoulder, he held it aloft to hit the animal on its head, and the animal said, "Save me from the sun, e-e-e-, and I'll save you from the rain." The boy put his hatchet down.
Again he held out his hatchet to hit it, and again it said, "Save me from the sun, friend, e-e-e-, and I'll save you from the rain, e-e-e-."

230

The boy went into the trap, and he freed the animal. And that animal ran off. After he ran away, the boy went home. When he arrived there, he was asked, "Hey, wasn't there something in the trap?" He answered, "Yes, the trap worked, but when I went up to kill the animal, it said, 'Save me from the sun and I'll save you from the rain.' What kind of animal is that?"

"Ha! It's a nzembe,[11] ah! My son, you have freed it. If only you would have killed it, we would be finished with our famine. You caught the animal but you let it go. Oh, well, you know that tonight, again, we will sleep with hunger."

Thus, the boy and father endured the remainder of the day, they slept, and at dawn, the father told the boy, "Come on let's throw down some baobab fruits." He started down the road with the boy until they arrived at a baobab tree. They put in steps, they hammered in steps all the way to the top; then the father and the boy climbed, *vii! up to the top.*

They began to throw down the fruits. They threw them down, they threw them down, until the father began to descend now, and as he descended he took out all the steps, he took out all those steps.

The boy cried, "Father, you have torn out all of the steps, how am I going to get down?"

"Oh, you'll come down, all right," he answered; down, down, went his father until he reached the ground, he finished tearing out all the steps. He gathered up all of the baobab fruits, and he left; he left his son up there.

So the boy remained up in the baobab tree. But near the base of the tree there was a lake at which all the animals drank.

The boy is up there, way up there, until an elephant comes to drink water. When the boy sees the elephant bending down his large neck to drink water, he cries out, "Water and man! Water and man!"

The elephant looks way up there, "Hey, who are you?" the boy sings:

> I am Nyanje,
> A man.
> I am Nyanje,
> A man.
> I freed my father's animal.
> He is called *nzembe.*
> *Guaracha ewe.*[13]
> I am looking for *nzembe.*

Buduga, Buduga,[14] the elephant ran away. So the boy waited awhile, and along came some baboons. He cried, "Man and

water, Man and water!"
"Ah, who are you?"

He sings again:

> I am Nyanje,
> A man.
> I am Nyanje,
> A man.
> I freed my father's animal.
> He is called *nzembe*.
> *Guracha ewe.*
> I am looking for *nzembe*.

"Ah! they ran away too. So the boy waited, and waited,
until the *nzembe* himself came. When it reached the lake, he
bent down his neck to drink water, and the boy said again:
"Water and man!"

"Who are you?"

> I am Nyanje,
> I am a man.
> I am Nyanje,
> A man.
> I freed my father's animal.
> He is called *nzembe*.
> *Guracha ewe.*
> I am looking for *nzembe*.

The *nzembe* bent down, drank that water, he finished and
left-*tiye!*[15] but he didn't run away. He returned to his home,
he arrived. There, at his home there was maize, and it had
already ripened. They have so much millet! and they have
maize! He tells his father, "That person who saved me the
other day, when I thought that I'd be killed, that person who
freed me, I have seen him high up."

"Well, let's go, let's get him down. Where did you see
him?"

"I saw him by the lake. But how will we get him down?"
the son asked.

The elder *nzembe* replied, "Let's go, let's go, let's carry
those ivory tusks, let's go there with these." To his wives,
"Let's prepare plenty of flour for *uji*,[16] because he will be
very, very weak."

The flour was prepared and everything was readied. They
even carried water.

They arrived at the place. The boy was spotted, there, way
up there. Look, "he's as white as a mushroom. Ok, now what
will we do?"

232

The father *nzembe* says, "Let's put these tusks here beneath the tree, they will climb up the baobao tree." So the tusks were beaten upon, and all that remains is that they be sung to. The *nzembe* began:

> Tusks, climb.
> Tusks, you climb.
> Tusks climb.
> Bring Nyanje down.
>
> Tusks, climb.
> Tusks, you climb.
> Tusks climb.
> Bring Nyanje down.

Until they reached the top. They grab him, when they grab him, he is told to hold them fast. He grabbed them and held on. And they begin to return him, to bring him down:

> Tusks return
> Tusks, you return.
> Tusks return.
> Bring Nyanje down.
>
> Tusks return.
> Tusks, you return.
> Tusks return.
> Bring Nyanje down.

Until he is lowered. They catch him, white as a mushroom, his whole body. They cleaned him with corn cobs, they scrubbed his body with corn cobs, until he was completely cleaned, they heated up hot water for him, he drank. They cooked *uji* for him, he drank. He said, "Ok, let's go to my home." They went with him to his compound. When they reached there, the place of his father, there was still great famine. The *nzembe* left him there, with all their food.

Nyanje's father was gone, hunting for food, so Nyanje ordered a feast. Rice and millet were cooked. While his father was wandering about, he saw near the path, a caravan of ants, carrying little seeds, seeds of rice and millet. He says, "Ah!" he grabbed one and tasted it, "It's millet," he thinks, "there must be plenty of food somewhere, wait and I'll follow these ants." He told himself not to go where the ants were going, but rather to go where they had come from.

So he went down the path, *ndeye ndeye,*[17] he and his wife, *ndeye ndeye,* until they came out of the bush, there appeared in front of them----Nyanje!!! He sat, "Is this not my father?" "Is this really you father? Hee. It is really father. And mother. Well, welcome then. Let's sit." They sat down, *wari* was cooked for them, they ate.

233

The mother asked Nyanje, "Your father, do you want him to be saved?"

Nyanje said, "For what my father did to me, I want him to die, but my mother will be saved." "Hee."

His father said, "That's alright, ok." So now dry millet without relish he, the father, ate; rice flour was ground, and he ate; dry sorghum flour he ate; young maize flour he ate. Dry food he ate, so that the man's stomach was bloated. It was so bloated that there was no room for him to breathe that night. "Mama, eee, Nyanje come, heat up water, my son." "Ok, heat up water, my son." "Ok, father, try hard and you will get well."

"Come, heat up water for me, let me drink, I want hot water." Nyanje said, "Ok, father, pray to God."[18]

And so he did drink, until the rooster crowed he drank, *pofu!* he burst, *fwi!* he died.[19]

The boy lived, he continued there with his mother.

My story ends here.

The analysis of oral narrative begins with the rhythm of the narrative. Everything proceeds from rhythm. In Giryama *ngano,* rhythm is created from images. Images, according to Scheub, are actions evoked in the imaginations of the audience.[20] These images occur and recur in patterns, they are repeated in various ways. These patterns of images exist at differing levels: words,[21] single actions, multiple actions, and groups of actions which do or do not follow the linear performance. All of these elements can become images. The repetition of images followed by an image which varies from, or is motivated by, the repetitive pattern, creates narrative rhythm.

Narrative rhythms are related to rhythms of sound, in that their creation begins with the sounds. Note the following example of sound rhythms, from Kadii Katana's "The MuGiryama and the Bird":

*Ni*bwira taratibu,	a
*Ni*bwira taratibu,	a
*Ni*tokapo,	b
Ni mwana wa Biririka,	c
Ni mwana wa Biririkee.	c[22]

(emphasis mine)

In this song, two sound rhythms are evident, the repetition of *ni* in the verses, and the rhythmic patterning of a-a-b-c-c. But the words derived from the sounds, *Nibwira taratibu,* denote action and evoke images; the bird sings to the man, "Catch me with

234

care," and the audience may imagine the MuGiryama gently closing his hand over the speaking bird. This image of capture, when juxtaposed to the next song image (*Nitinya taratibu* — Take me down with care) becomes a narrative rhythm beyond the level of sound, a rhythm which the audience imagines, thinks, and feels. Sound rhythms are heard and may evoke vague images, but these images cannot be as specific as images evoked by word meanings, incidents, and actions. Sound rhythms are movements of organized pitch relationships through time; narrative rhythms are movements of language and its images through time and space.[23]

"The major shaping tool" of these images is repetition.[24] Repetition is a characteristic of oral narrative performance. In the introductory images of "Nyanje and the Nzembe," words, single incidents, and multiple incidents undergo repetition. Words are repeated, as in the first line: "There was once a *famine,* and a man and his son, and *famine.*" Single incidents, or actions, are repeated, e.g., (1) "They trapped every day . . . ."(2) "They trapped." Multiple incidents, including several actions are repeated: (1) "They trapped every day, and every day they went to check their traps. One day they caught a gazelle . . . ." (2) "They trapped, they checked their traps, they caught a gazelle." After these elements are repeated, a change frequently occurs. These changes are variations from, or motivations produced by, the preceding repeated elements. Most of these elements are actions (images) which are worked into patterns. Patterns of repetition and change create narrative rhythm.

Rhythm falls into two broad categories, from the rhythmic organization of syntagmatic units (micro-rhythms) to the rhythmic organization of paradigmatic units (macro-rhythms). "Message" is the result of the interplay between these two categories of rhythm and within the two categories of rhythm—particularly within the macro-rhythmic category.

Micro-rhythms are formed by repetition and variation of flexible speech segments occurring within the syntagmatic chain of narrative actions, i.e., the linear narrative sequence. For example, Sidi Chengo's introductory images become micro-rhythms. The famine image is repeated twice; rather than repeat the word-image "famine" a third time, she introduces the image, "the building of traps". This latter image is related to the "famine" image because it represents a solution to the famine. This is the simplest type of micro-rhythm: the repetition of a word-image that does not itself undergo variation, but instead suggests a change, or a new image.

The trapping image which follows becomes another narrative micro-rhythm: the images of checking the traps, and catching a gazelle are repeated twice, and then varied by the image of catching the *nzembe*. The *nzembe* is caught the same way as the gazelle, but as a different character, it becomes a variation from the preceding images of gazelle. This is the most common type of micro-rhythm occurring in Giryama *ngano*. An image, or a group of imgaes, is presented, repeated and varied. A fully new image is not created; but an alteration in the established image occurs. Another example of this type of micro-rhythm occurs in the following repeated actions:

> The boy is up there, way up there, until an elephant comes to drink water. When the boy sees the elephant bending down his large neck to drink water, he cries out, "Water and man!"
> The elephant looks way up there, "Hey, who are you?" the boy sings:

> > I am Nyanje,
> > A man.
> > I am Nyanje,
> > A man.
> > I freed my father's animal.
> > He is called *nzembe*.
> > *Guracha ewe.*
> > I am looking for *nzembe*.

> *Buduga, Buduga,* the elephant ran away. So the boy waited awhile, and along came some baboons. He cried, "Man and water, Man and water!"
> "Ah, who are you?"
> He sings again:

> > I am Nyanje,
> > A man.
> > I am Nyanje,
> > A man.
> > I freed my father's animal.
> > He is called *nzembe*.
> > *Guracha ewe.*
> > I am looking for *nzembe*.

> Ah! they ran away too. So the boy waited, and waited until the *nzembe* himself came. When it reached the lake, he bent down his neck to drink water, and the boy said again: "Water and man!"

"Who are you?"

> I am Nyanje,
> I am a man.
> I am Nyanje,
> A man.
> I freed my father's animal.
> He is called *nzembe*.
> *Guracha ewe.*
> I am looking for *nzembe*.

The *nzembe* bent down, drank that water, he finished and left-*tiye!* but he didn't run away. He returned to his home, he arrived.

The established pattern in this group of images is Nyanje singing to the animals, all of whom run away. But a subtle variation occurs. Whereas the elephant and the baboons run away, the *nzembe*, according to Mrs. Chengo, does not run away; the *nzembe* runs *to* his home to report to his father. The variation, however slight, creates a micro-rhythm, and it motivates the next group of images.

Repetition by reversal creates another kind of micro-rhythm. It occurs in the following section of the *ngano:*

> Thus, the boy and father endured the remainder of the day, they slept, and at dawn, the father told the boy, "come on, let's throw down some baobab fruits." He started down the road with the boy until they arrived at a baobab tree. They put in steps all the way to the top; then the father and the boy climbed, *vii!* up to the top.
>
> They began to throw down the fruits. They threw them down, they threw them down, until the father began to descend now, and as he descended he took out all the steps, he took out all those steps.
>
> The boy cried, "Father, you have torn out all of the steps, how am I going to get down?"
>
> "Oh, you'll come down," he answered; down, down went his father until he reached the ground, he finished tearing out all the steps. He gathered up all the baobab fruits, and he left; he left his son up there.

Putting up steps and climbing up the baobab tree is paralleled by taking out steps and climbing down. The father establishes a pattern in the first part. He climbs up the tree. Nyanje duplicates this act. The father then reverses the pattern, i.e., climbs down. Nyanje does *not* duplicate this act; he is abandoned in the tree. Within this micro-rhythmic repetition by reversal a variation or imbalance is

237

created; Nyanje's abandonment then motivates the next group of succeeding actions.

III

Through repetition and/or variation, micro-rhythms arouse expectations and motivate succeeding images. They create, resolve and renew tension in the *ngano* plot. They propel the linear, sequential actions forward by an orderly movement. Micro-rhythms have a flexible duration, ranging from shorter images at the word level (famine) to larger image-groups created by multiple actions and songs (Nyanje singing to the animals). Micro-rhythmic patterns, i.e. simple repetition, repetition with variation, and reversal repetition, suggest macro-rhythmic patterns. Macro-rhythms adapt the structural patterns of micro-rhythms; they are also created by repetition, variation, reversion, or inversion. These patterns, however, do not follow the linear narrative performance but may be drawn (in perception) from the narrative performance into paradigmatic categories. Macro-rhythms are more complex narrative rhythms which also produce and resolve tensions. They generally have a longer duration, occurring over the span of an entire performance. They are frequently composed of large groups of images which have rhythmic relations to one another.

The narrative units of macro-rhythms are determined by structural consistencies, persistent symbols and themes, constancy/change in character conflicts/contacts, and in many cases, the movement of micro-rhythms. The five large sections of actions, or narrative units, in Mrs. Chengo's *ngano* are determined by the specific conflict/contact between characters. A narrative unit is created each time Nyanje comes into contact with the *nzembe* or his father. In section 1A, the father orders Nyanje, his son, to bring whatever he can from their traps. It is a time of famine. The boy disobeys, for, in section 1, he frees the *nzembe*. In section 2, the father, furious with his son for letting the *nzembe* go, abandons him in a baobab tree. In section 3, the *nzembe*, who had earlier intoned, "Save me from the sun . . . and I'll save you from the rain," keeps his promise, and rescues the boy from the baobab tree, using the ivory tusks. In section 4, the boy, whose transition to manhood is evidenced by a quasi-ritualistic bathing, avenges his abandonment by causing his father's death.

These "sections" mentioned above are clusters of images, or

image-blocks. The relations of the image-blocks to one another create a simple macro-rhythm. Important images, such as the Nyanje's experiences with his father or the *nzembe*, are particularized and emphasized in the juxtaposition or the comparison of image-blocks through repetition and variation. The succession of image-blocks also develops expectation and feeling. In image-block 1, Nyanje saves the *nzembe;* this act of benevolence causes and emphasizes his father's act of cruelty (image-block 2). The maleficence of the father, exemplified by Nyanje's abandonment, contrasts with the boy's previous goodwill. The tension and expectation in the *ngano* are at their highest point; Nyanje's good act (image-block 1) and his father's bad act (image-block 2) have occurred without any resolution. The audience is left anticipating a resolution of both acts. The resolution comes through repetition and variation in the next two image-blocks. First, the *nzembe* (image-block 3) repeats the goodwill which occurred in image-block 1. Now that the goodwill has been repeated and balanced, Mrs. Chengo performs the final image-block (4), which repeats and balances the maleficence of the father. It is in this way that one macro-rhythm is developed, through the comparison, contrast, and balancing of significant images in the juxtaposed image-blocks. The *ngano* begins and ends with image-blocks (1A and 4) concerning Nyanje and his father. Between these, Mrs. Chengo narrates the *nzembe* image-blocks. The image-block construction is timely and proportioned: father (1A)⎯⎯⎯⎯⎯⟶ *nzembe* (1)⎯⎯⎯⎯⎯⟶ father (2)⎯⎯⎯⎯⟶ *nzembe* (3)⎯⎯⎯⎯⟶ father (4).

Another macro-rhythm which occurs is based on character inversions. Concentrating one aspect of the analysis on the conflicts within the *ngano*, two primary conflicts can be isolated, those between the boy and the *nzembe,* and between the boy and his father. The conflicts undergo exact inversions. For example, in section 1 the boy saves the *nzembe;* and later in section 3, the *nzembe* saves the boy. This conflict inversion may be illustrated in the following schema:

Section 1	*Section 3*
Nyanje	*nzembe*
vs. (saves)	vs. (saves)
nzembe	Nyanje

But this is not the only conflict in the *ngano;* Mrs. Chengo repeats this conflict, but only after contrasting it to the other primary conflict, between Nyanje and his father. In section 2, the father attempts to kill his son, and later, in section 4, the son succeeds in killing his father:

Section 2	*Section 4*
Father	Nyanje
vs. ("kills")	vs. ("kills")
Nyanje	Father

By introducing the conflicts in one way, Mrs. Chengo establishes a pattern which she later inverts. This kind of repetition, inversion, is a narrative macro-rhythm. Inversion is a type of repetition with a "built-in" variation.

In the symbols in this *ngano* another type of macro-rhythm can be discerned. Symbols become rhythmic in their repetition and variation. Repeated symbols are like accents in a musical beat; they become narrative rhythms. The simplest structure in music is the beat; certain beats are accented, and this in turn creates rhythm. In the *ngano* symbols arise as accented beats from the mass of *ngano* details. Because of their importance or uniqueness to the *ngano*, they are remembered by the audience and developed by the performer. For example, one can see that the development of the father and the *nzembe* is not purely arbitrary; they are symbols. The *nzembe*, if captured, would have meant an end to famine, and his compound, as noted later, is full of food. The *nzembe* symbolizes "plenty," whereas the father symbolizes "famine". As long as the father lives, famine remains near him; it is literally the ingestion of food that kills him. The two symbols are in opposition with Nyanje as a mediator. Nyanje, as the only individual who can end famine, is presented with the choice between famine and plenty, symbolized by his own father and an unreal animal. At the symbolic level, Mrs. Chengo creates an ironic inversion. First, the boy frees the *nzembe* (plenty), whose death, according to his father (famine), would have ended the famine. But, ironically, it is precisely the inverse outcome, the preserving of the *nzembe* and the death of the father, that ends the famine. These two symbols are integral to an understanding of the *ngano,* in that the audience must accept a son killing, however indirectly, his father. These symbols are repeated in the *ngano*, and their opposition becomes the variation in the

240

repetitive pattern; they are another narrative macro-rhythm.

IV

The above analysis of "Nyanje and the Nzembe" has elaborated the various types of narrative rhythms in Giryama *ngano*. The micro-rhythms and macro-rhythms all work interdependently, and only through theoretical analysis may one isolate them for study. Continuing the musical analogies forwarded earlier, these narrative rhythms are both regulative (with recurring pattern-like behaviour) *and* configurative (with manipulative and improvisatory rhythm efforts), the latter term covering the range of variations possible. But what about *time line,* or *image line?* What is the image line in Mrs. Chengo's performance? Beginning with the son's violation of his father's interdiction, Mrs. Chengo patterns the entire performance on the *nzembe's* proverb,[25] "Save me from the sun and I'll save you from the rain." It is on the basis of the proverb, and in particular its forecast inversion, that she is able to successfully invert the conflict between the boy and the *nzembe* and the conflict between the boy and his father. The proverb is a time line on which Mrs. Chengo develops her *ngano*. The inherent inversion in the stated proverb "expands" to direct the structure of the conflicts. The sun/rain opposition in the proverb implies the image-block (and symbol) contrasts and juxtapositions. The proverb is also a macro-rhythm, for there is repetition with structural variation, i.e. from proverb to conflict to image-block to symbols, etc.

The important relationship between a time-line and the narrative rhythms can now be examined. The proverb itself is produced by a micro-rhythm; it is a deposited variation/resolution from a preceding repetitive pattern. As a macro-rhythm, it is repeated throughout the *ngano*. A distinct rhythm, it is simultaneously a well-spring for creation, yet interwoven with the other narrative macro-rhythms. And finally, its configurations structurally and thematically recall Nketia's warnings of control, of order and freedom.

The macro-rhythms together help generate the "message" in the *ngano*. The rhythms of the image-blocks present the father and *nzembe* intermittently to the audience. The juxtaposition of the image-blocks creates a metaphor; i.e. an analogy between the good and evil tendencies of man and nature. Through the rhythm of symbols, the poles of good and evil, plenty and famine, are

241

established. The more structural rhythm of the proverb, as well as its meaning, forecasts the character inversions, and introduces the concept of saving as opposed to killing. The rhythm of the inversions clarifies the proverb, and reaffirms the poles of good and evil. Nyanje is a constant figure who mediates between these poles. He disobeys his father's orders, a seemingly bad act. But, in this disobedience, he saves mankind from the famine, an ultimately good act. The development of the macro-rhythms resolves this apparent ambiguity between what is good and what is evil.

The *nzembe,* as a fictitious animal, symbolizes any animal. The irony in the message focuses on this fact. In image-block 1, Nyanje spares the *nzembe's* life at a time when any animal must be eaten for survival. This act of beneficence at a time of hunger and greed becomes the *ngano* message. When the father abandons his son in image-block 2, the effects of hunger and greed are magnified. These oppositions between hunger and goodwill, life and death, fuse into an established macro-pattern that is manipulated through repetition in the succeeding image-blocks. The proverb as time line, character inversions, and symbols clarify and vary the pattern in order to force a mediation. Nyanje, as mediator, partakes of both poles, both worlds. From the *nzembe,* he learns goodwill and receives food; from his father, he learns (and destroys) ill-will and inherits his mother, his people. At the end of the *ngano*, the father has died, the *nzembe* has disappeared, but "the boy lived, he continued there with his mother". Nyanje's survival, generated by the interplay of the four macro-rhythms, is a key to understanding the *ngano* message.

But there are two levels of rhythm operating in the *ngano*. The micro-rhythms contribute to the *ngano* message through their inter-relationships with the macro-rhythms. The impact of the message is not only revealed cognitively through the linear and non-linear rhythms in the *ngano*. The intent of the micro-rhythms is to release the message gradually through the interplay of tension and release, i.e. at the level of emotions. The micro-rhythms create tension and release through repetition, variation, and motivation of the minor elements. These elements are absorbed to create tension and release through the repetition and manipulation of broader elements, i.e. at the level of macro-rhythms. The movement and balance between tension and release is fundamental to rhythm.

Can African oral narrative be better understood, better explained, in the context of musical terminology? How similar can the two art-forms be? Both African music and African oral narrative borrow features from each other. Vocal music provides images through lyric; narrative songs provide images through music. Franz Boas once wrote that "the song and tale are the two fundamental forms of literature found universally which must together be considered the primary form of literary activity."[26] He insisted that in traditional societies, the tale, or poetry, contained a fixed rhythmic form which rarely occured outside a musical context. Music and poetry, song and myth, were rarely separated. With time, a separation has occurred. However, being once composed together, music and narrative share developmental, structural features. And, furthermore, music *and* oral narrative performance occur pervasively as *performing* arts in Africa, requiring audience participation and feedback, as well as a performer's virtuosity and regularity. Nonetheless, the complexity of each of these art-forms makes comparative analysis difficult. Acquiescence to this complexity is simply an acquiescence to one perspective. Can we not, in the manner of a Suzanne Langer[27] or Robert Farris Thompson,[28] go beyond the limits of a single art-form and look for the connective links in the complexity itself? The first step is to assume the role of an aesthetician. Let us look not at one art-form, but at the "fundamental unity of the arts;"[29] let us interpret them as a unified whole. More to the point, let us approach African Art as structuralists, or universalists, and attack (i.e. reduce) the complexity as "strong" critics.[30]

One focus of complexity in African Art is rhythm. A very recent article in *Ethnomusicology* informs us that "Rhythm is probably one of the most profound yet misunderstood aspects of music making in Africa."[31] Rhythm is also a profound feature of oral narrative performance. Narrative rhythm has been defined as the repetition and variation of images, or patterns of images, which induce an effective response from an audience and enhances the communication of "message."

The choice of rhythm as a complex feature helping to explain narrative performance is not an arbitrary one. In an article written 25 years ago, Leopold Senghor chose rhythm as a central focus for explaining African music, dance, art, and literature. He defined rhythm as

> vibrant shock, the power which, through our senses, lays hold of the very roots of our being. It expresses itself by the most material, the most sensual means: lines, colors, volume, in architecture, sculpture, and painting; stresses in poetry and in music; movements in dance.[32]

But Senghor is referring to auditory rhythms in literature, and I have taken his argument one step further. Narrative rhythms may be isolated at the verbal level (through alliteration, rhyme, onomatopoeia, and simple repetition), but more importantly, they exist at the intellectual level, an extra-verbal level by which large groups/patterns of images may be compared/contrasted beyond the linear performance. The analysis above has illustrated these image rhythms of longer duration and thematic intensity.

The parallels between musical structure and oral patterns are obvious and enlightening. In both art forms, a performer can manipulate his/her audience; a raconteur/drummer plays on the anticipations/expectations of the members of his audience. The pattern is the thing. An audience feels a performance through rhythm; aesthetic enjoyment is made up of this multiplicity of excitements and moments of respite, of expectations disappointed or fulfilled beyond anticipation.[33] Lévi-Strauss emphasized the music-"myth" parallels when he wrote:

> It can now be seen how music resembles myth, since the latter too overcomes the contradiction between historical, enacted time and a permanent constant. Like a musical work, myth operates on the basis of a twofold continuum: one part of it is external and is composed in the one instance of historical, or supposedly historical, events forming a theoretically infinite series from which each society extracts a limited number of relevant incidents with which to create its myths; and in the other instance, the equally infinite series of physically producible sounds, from which each musical system selects its scale. The second aspect of the continuum is internal and is situated in the psychophysiological time of the listener, the elements of which are very complex: *they involve the periodicity of cerebral waves and organic rhythms,* the strength of the memory, and the power of the attention. Mythology makes demands primarily on the neuromental aspects because of the length of the narration, the recurrence of certain themes, and the other forms of back references

and parallels which can only be correctly grasped if the listener's mind surveys, as it were, the whole range of the story as it is unfolded. All this applies, too, in the case of music.[34] (emphasis mine)

Finally, Robert Kauffman has written, "when we are aware of the many dimensions of a *cultural time sense,* of musical forms, of rhythmic patterning, and of rhythmic relationships, more possibilities of understanding become available"[35] (emphasis mine). The "cultural time sense" is not unlike Chernoff's rhythm and sensibility linkage proposed in his ethnomusicological data on Ghanaian drumming.[36] And a cultural time sense would relate one art form to another, and perhaps, one culture to another. We could propose the following schema: superimposing the "primordial ritual" upon physiological and psychic rhythm, we could envision art-forms (in Langer's sense as "virtual" life-forms) as centripetal off-shoots from the "ritual" (Lévi-Strauss' "cultural grid") which through a centrifugal (or reductive) analysis, yield rhythm, or repetition and variation. In purely structural terms, then, rhythm becomes the germinal source for art and life, for understanding African music and African oral narrative.[37] What remains to be done is to determine the common denominators between the various types of rhythm.

NOTES

1. J. H. Kwabena Nketia, *The Music of Africa* (New York: W.W. Norton, 1974), pp. 131-132
2. Ibid., p. 243.
3. Ibid., p. 132, and Robert Kauffman, "African Rhythm: A Reassessment " *Ethnomusicology* XXIV (3): 399 (September 1980).
4. Harold Scheub, *The Xhosa Ntsomi* (London: Oxford/Claredon Press, 1975), p. 3.
5. Charles Pike, "The Luhyia Olukano" (Dissertation, Univ. of Wisconsin: Dept of African Languages and Literature, 1977). Chapter 3.
6. Plato, *The Laws,* II, tr. A.E. Taylor (London: J.M. Dent and Sons, 1960), p. 665
7. David Bohm, "Physics and Perception" *The Special Theory of Relativity* (New York: W.A. Benjamin, 1965), p. 209.
8. *Ngano* are the oral narrative performances of the AGiryama (the Giryama people) of eastern Kenya. The Giryama live in the hinterland of the Kenya coast. They belong to a larger group of Kenyan peoples who call themselves Mijikenda, or literally, the nine vallage. The Mijikenda are composed of the AGiryama, ARibe, AKauma, AChonyi, ADuruma, ADigo, AKambe,

AJiboni, and ARabai people. Their population has been estimated at roughly one-half million, with the AGiryama comprising nearly half this total. The nine languages of the Mijikenda belong to the Bantu subgroup of the Niger-Congo family. The majority of the AGiryama live either within forty miles of the coast, or near the all-season rivers, where the land is fertile. My field work (1975-1977) centred around the Galana River, near the towns of Kakoneni, Jilore, Kakuyuni, Goshi, and Marafa.

9. This *ngano* and the comments which follow are based on some of my work in my Ph.D dissertation, "Narrative Rhythms of Giryama Ngano", (Univ. of Wisconsin: Dept of African Languages and Literature, 1980).

10. Relish, a course of food (meat or vegetable) to eat with the *wari,* maize pudding.

11. A make-believe animal; no one was able to tell me more than this.

12. Ideophone, the sound of climbing.

13. KiSanye language. The WaSanye were early inhabitants of Giryama country.

14. Ideophone, running through grass.

15. Sound of leaving.

16. Thin maize (or millet or sorghum) porridge.

17. Sound of walking and time passing.

18. In KiGiryama, the word *mulungu* means the "blue sky," the "heavens," or "God."

19. Ideophones, the former for the noise of bursting, the latter the passing of a life.

20. Harold Scheub, "Performance of Oral Narrative." *Frontiers of Folklore,* ed. William Bascom (Boulder, Colorado: Westview Press, 1977), p. 54.

21. Members of a non-literate society do not imagine a word literally; but rather, a word, such as *famine,* will evoke for them an image.

22.   "Catch me with care,
    Catch me with care,
    Where I come from,
    I am the child of Biririka,
    I am the child of Biririka-ee."

This song is taken from Ms. Katana's *ngano* (No. 15, Tape 1 Side 1: 726-756), performed on August 16, 1976, at Goshi, Kenya, with an audience of 25 people. See Rassner, *op. cit.,* pp. 55-64

23. This idea was taken from a conversation with a colleague at Yale, an ethnomusicologist, Professor Steven Martin.

24. Scheub, "Performance of Oral Narrative," op. cit., p. 54

25. The *nzembe's* proverb is essentially a *cimo,* the proto-Bantu term for crypticism, according to Professor Patrick R. Bennett, linguist and professor of Bantu language, Univ. of Wisconsin, Madison, Wisconsin.

26. *Primitive Art* (New York: Dover, 1955), p. 301.

27. Suzanne Langer, *Feeling and Form* (New York: Charles Scribner's Son, 1953). Also her two volumes entitled *Mind* (Baltimore: Johns Hopkins Univ. Press).

28. *African Art in Motion* (Berkeley: University of California Press, 1979).

29. Langer, op. cit., p. 24.

30. I am referring here to Harold Bloom's dictum from his introductory chapter to *Poetry and Repression* New Haven and London: Yale Univ. Press, 1976, p. 14 ". . . the quest for interpretive models is a necessary obsession for the reader who is strong, since to refuse models explicitly is only to accept other models, however unknowingly."

31. Robert Kauffman, Op. cit., p. 393.

32. "African-Negro Aesthetics" *Diogenes XVI,* pp. 23-38.

33. See Claude Levi-Strauss, *The Raw and the Cooked* (New York: Harper Torch Books, 1975), p. 17.

34. Ibid., p. 16.

35. Kauffman, op. cit., p. 413.

36. John Miller Chernoff, *African Rhythms and African Sensibility* (Chicago: Univ. of Chicago Press, 1980).

37. This idea was jointly conceived with Professor Stephen Martin, the ethnomusicologist, in our 1981 seminar at Yale, *African Rhythms.* Indeed, many of the ideas in this paper are a result of our seminar. For more on the links between music and myth, and a good general discussion of structuralism applied to these disciplines, see Pandora Hopkins, "The Homology of Music and Myth: Views of Lévi-Strauss on Musical Structure " *Ethnomusicology* XXI, (No. 2, 1977) pp. 247-261. She writes that Levi-Strauss concentrates on "human thought (for us, the processes of rhythm) as primordial to its cultural manifestations."

Part Four

Radical Perspectives

Structural and Thematic Parallels in Oral Narrative and Film: *Mandabi* and Two African Oral Narratives

Mbye Baboucar Cham

REVIEWING Ousmane Sembène's film *Mandabi*, in *Cahiers du Cinema*, Pascal Bonitzer makes the observation that ... *d'une certaine manière, tout le film pourrait se lire comme un conte africain de magie*[1] (emphasis mine), if we take into account the fact that *le mandat invisible, impalpable, que le heros-victime ne touchera jamais, est par excellence la force agissant a distance.*[2] Indeed, there seems to be something magical about this invisible, untouchable and elusive piece of paper from Paris which, while quietly sitting in the secure confines of a post office, still manages to set our hero-victim on a quest that will bring him nothing but misery, suffering, dishonour and a resolve, perhaps ephemeral, to become a crook.

The money order does take on the air of a long invisible yet powerfully magnetic hand which yanks our hero-victim from the security, warmth and knowledge of his work community, and thrusts him with reckless abandon into the whims and tricks of bureaucratic and other social wolves who manage a world in which the likes of Ibrahima Dieng are not only struggling misfits, but also fair game. Mr Bonitzer's rapprochement between *Mandabi* and the African oral narrative is indeed revealing, and I propose, in this paper, to take this rapprochement one step further by exploring the affinities that I have observed between the structural lay-out of *Mandabi* and that of two African trickster narratives. I will also demonstrate how, through the skillful use of repetition, these structures function to reinforce the themes of greed and moral corruption in the works considered.

The two trickster narratives chosen are both from West Africa,

251

and variants of these can be found in other parts of the continent and elsewhere.[3] The first narrative, "How Spider Obtained the Sky-God's Stories"[4] (hereinafter referred to as N1), comes from the Ashanti of Ghana, and the second one, *"Les Tours de Leuk-le Lièvre"*[5] (N2), is told among the Wolof of Senegambia. *Mandabi,* Ousmane Sembène's second feature length film, premiered at the Biennale de Venise Film Festival which ran from August 25 to September 7, 1968.

A common thematic thread that immediately emerges from a cursory reading of the narratives and viewing of the film is that of greed and corruption within a social framework where, to quote the charlatan photographer in *Mandabi*, "only scoundrels live well" because of their uncanny, yet perverse ability to ruthlessly and unscrupulously exploit the credulity, generosity, faith and short-comings of their victims for their own narrow self-interest. The readiness with which this common theme of greed and corruption surfaces in these works is a function of the artistic and highly effective use of repetition as a device for structuring. Through the repetition of a structural pattern that sets a protagonist on one pole and 'antagonist(s)' (for want of a better label) on the opposite pole, in a framework of confrontation that centres on a quest for a necessary item or service, not only is the action moved linearly from conflict to resolution (or conclusion), but also the results of the confrontations keep accumulating in a direction that une-quivocally defines a milieu feverishly gripped by a profound political, moral and ethical crisis.

Before proceeding further, it is perhaps appropriate at this point to give a schematic lay-out of the structure accompanied by a sum-mary of the works in question.

N1: How Spider Obtained The Sky-God's Stories
Introduction

Establishment of and agree-ment on conditions to be met in order to obtain desired objective. Success requires a quest,	Kwaku Ananse wants to buy Sky-God's stories.
	Sky-God demands seemingly impossible price: *Onini* the Python, *Osebo* the Leopard, *Mmoatia* the Fairy and *Mmoboro* the Hornets
	Spider agrees on this price and

offers to throw in his mother
too, Ya Nsia, the 6th child.

1st Image-Set
Confrontation:
Ananse Vs Python
Ananse wins = Success
Python loses = Defeat

- Ananse consults his wife and
gets idea on how to obtain
Onini the Python.
- Ananse tricks Onini by tying
him up and takes him to Sky-
God.
- Sky-God: "My hand has touched it; what remains still remains."

2nd Image-Set
Confrontation:
Ananse Vs Hornets
Ananse wins = Success
Hornets lose = Defeat
Repetition of structural model
established in the 1st Image-
Set

- Ananse consults his wife and
gets idea on how to obtain
Mmoboro the Hornets.
- Ananse tricks Hornets by luring
them into a gourd and takes
them to Sky-God.
- Sky-God: "My hand has touched it; what remains still remains."

3rd Image-Set
Confrontation
Ananse Vs Leopard
Ananse wins = Success
Leopard loses = Defeat
Second repetition of structural
model

- Ananse consults his wife and
gets idea on how to catch Osebo
the Leopard.
- Ananse tricks Leopard by luring
him into a pit dug by Ananse
and takes him to Sky-God.
- Sky-God: "My hand has touched it; what remains still remains."

4th Image-Set
Confrontation:
Ananse Vs Fairy
Ananse wins = Success
Fairy loses = Defeat
Third repetition of structural
pattern

- Ananse forgoes advice from his
wife on how to obtain Mmoatia
the Fairy.
- Nevertheless, Ananse tricks
Fairy by luring him onto a
sticky Akua doll. He takes
Fairy, together with his mother,
to Sky-God.
- Sky-God marvels at Ananse's
skill.

253

Conclusion

End of quest.	Sky-God releases his stories to
Conditions fulfilled.	the custody of Ananse.
Ananse obtains objectives =	
Success	

The basic structure of N1 can now be summarized thus:

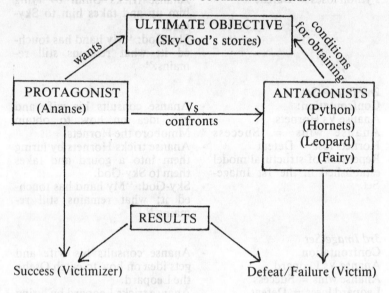

Let us now look at N2, "*Les Tours de Leuk-le-Lièvre*", a narrative from the Wolof of Senegambia.

N2: *Les Tours De Leuk-Le-Liever:*
Introduction

Establishment of and agreement on conditions to be met in order to obtain desired objective.
Success requires a quest.

- Leuk impregnates the King's daughter in violation of the king's injunction.
- After a lengthy search, Leuk is apprehended as the culprit.
- To preserve Leuk's life, the King demands a seemingly impossible price: Leopard skin, 2 Elephant tusks, Lions skin, and the hair of Kouss-le-Butin-Barbu.

1st Image-Set
Confrontation:
Leuk Vs Leopard
Leuk wins = Success
Leopard Loses = Defeat

- Leuk meets Leopard near a river.
- Leuk tricks Leopard into taking off his skin in order to take a bath. Leuk promises to guard the skin.
- Leuk hides the skin, lies to Leopard as to whereabouts of the skin, and recovers it later after Leopard goes away skinless.

2nd Image-Set
Confrontation:
Leuk Vs Elephants
Leuk wins = Success
Elephants lose = Defeat
First repetition of structural model established in 1st Image-Set

- Leuk meets Elephant and his group near a stream.
- Leuk lies to them and tricks them into climbing on top of each other with help from Frog and Turtle.
- Elephants crash down, break tusks, and Leuk tricks them and runs away with the two most beautiful tusks.

3rd Image-Set
Confrontation:
Leuk Vs Kouss
Leuk wins = Success
Kouss loses = Defeat
Second repetition of structural model

- Leuk meets Kouss relaxing under a tamarind tree.
- Leuk tricks Kouss into having his beard shaved so as to look more handsome.
- Leuk shaves Kouss and runs away with the hair.

4th Image-Set
Confrontation:
Leuk Vs Lion
Leuk wins = Success
Lion loses = Defeat
Third repetition of structural model

- Leuk meets Lion near a river.
- Leuk tricks Lion into taking off his skin so as not to get wet, and offers to guard it.
- Leuk tricks Lion into believing his story, and eventually runs away with the skin.

Conclusion
End of quest
Conditions fulfilled
Leuk attains ultimate objec-

- Leuk takes all the required items to Bour the King who now marvels at his exploits.

tive = Success

Bour spares Leuk's life and sets him free.
Attempts by characters humiliated by Leuk's tricks to apprehend him fail.

As in N1, the basic structure of N2 can also be summarized in the following manner:

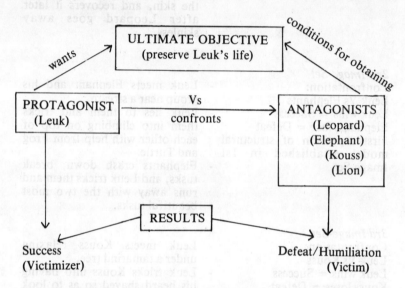

At first glance, it would seem that the structure of *Mandabi* is much more complex and very different from that of N1 and N2, but a closer examination will reveal a structural pattern that very closely parallels that of both N1 and N2. The schema below illustrates this:

Mandabi

Introduction

Establishment
- Routine at Ibrahima Dieng's household and the nature of the relationship between him and his wives are extensively detailed.
- The postman brings the letter

and the money order from Paris.

1st Image-Set
Confrontation:
Dieng Vs Bureaucracy
(Post Office)
Dieng is frustrated = Failure
Bureaucracy Prevails =
Success

- Dieng goes to Post Office to cash money order.
- Dieng needs an identity card in order to cash the money order.
- Dieng is told to go to Police Station to obtain an identity card.
- Dieng leaves the Post Office flabbergasted.

2nd Image-Set
Confrontation:
Dieng Vs Bureaucracy
(Police Station)
Dieng is frustrated = Failure
Bureaucracy Prevails =
Success
1st repetition of structural model established in 1st Image-Set

- Dieng goes to Police Station to obtain an identity card.
- Dieng needs a birth certificate a photograph and stamps.
- Dieng is told to go to City Hall to obtain a birth certificate.
- Dieng goes away flabbergasted.

3rd Image-Set
Confrontation:
Dieng Vs Bureaucracy
(City Hall)
Dieng is frustrated = Failure
Bureaucracy Prevails =
Success
2nd repetition of structural model

- Dieng goes to City Hall to obtain a birth certificate.
- Dieng needs to know his exact date of birth, which he does not have record of.
- Dieng is told to come back when he finds out his exact date of birth.
- Dieng goes away flabbergasted.

4th Image-Set
Resort to an intermediary =
Success, although temporary

- Dieng appeals to a relative Amath, for help.
- Amath fixes him up with a friend at City Hall who can help Dieng get a birth certificate, and gives him a cheque for one thousand francs.

5th Image-Set
Resort to intermediary =
Success, but costly
Repetition of 4th Image-Set

- Dieng goes to the bank to cash the check.
- Dieng is "helped" by a con man who demands a hefty percen-

tage for his "services".

6th Image-Set
Confrontation:
Dieng Vs Photographer
Dieng is frustrated = Failure
Photographer prevails =
Success
Reprise and 3rd repetition of
structural model established in
1st Image-Set

- Dieng has his photograph taken.
- Dieng returns to claim the prints but is told rudely that they were burnt.
- Dieng gets into a scuffle and is beaten up by the photographer's assistant.
- Dieng returns home with a bloody nose and without his pictures.

7th Image-Set
Confrontation:
Dieng Vs Mbarka, the
storekeeper
Dieng is frustrated = Failure
Mbarka holds his ground =
Success
4th repetition of structural
model established in 1st
Image-Set

- Dieng wants additional credit from Mbarka, the neighborhood storekeeper.
- Mbarka is fed up with Dieng's unsettled account, and relays message regarding possible sale of Dieng's house to an interested buyer.
- Dieng reacts furiously and gets into a scuffle with Mbarka. Dieng's two wives join in and threaten to beat up Mbarka.
- Mbaye surfaces and restores calm. Dieng goes home without the credit he wanted.

8th Image-Set
Confrontation:
Dieng Vs Mbaye
Dieng is cheated = Failure
Mbaye prevails = Success
5th repetition of structural
model
Resort to intermediary =
Failure

- Dieng goes to Mbaye and signs a release authorizing Mbaye to cash the money order on his behalf.
- Dieng goes to Mbaye to claim the cash, but Mbaye tells him the money was stolen by a pickpocket.
- Dieng is given a 50 kilo bag of rice, taken home and unceremoniously dumped at the gate of his compound by Mbaye.

Conclusion
End of quest. Requirements

- Dieng resolves to become a wolf

258

are not fulfilled like everyone else.

Dieng does not attain his ultimate objective
Failure/Defeat

- Postman proposes positive action to change the situation -mobilize all forces in the society.
- Dieng gazes at the Postman as images of his recent ordeal flash back into his mind.

A summary of the basic structure of *Mandabi* will look like this:

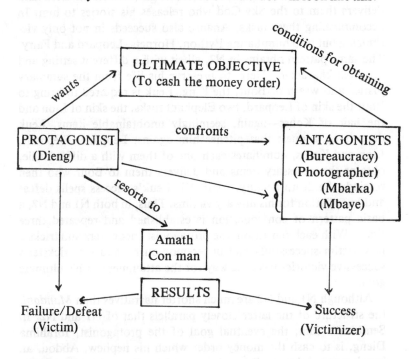

In spite of the differences in detail, as far as setting, character and plot are concerned, it is evident from the analysis of the three works that one is dealing here with one basic, structural pattern. In this pattern, a protagonist sets out to obtain an ultimate objective, but in order to achieve this goal, a number of tasks and conditions (seemingly impossible ones, too) have to be accomplished and fulfilled. The multiplicity of tasks and conditions implies and necessitates repetition of a confrontation between a protagonist, on

259

the one hand, and on the other a possessor of an item or service necessary for the accomplishment of the tasks. The cumulative outcome of the repeated confrontations rounds off the pattern.

In N1, Ananse's ultimate goal is to secure custody of the Sky-God's stories, but the Sky-God will part with these stories only if Ananse brings him Python, Hornets, Leopard and Fairy—tasks which, to the ordinary mortal, seem beyond the realm of possibility. Ananse sets out to confront in turn Python, Hornets, Leopard and Fairy, dupes each one of them with a different trick and delivers them to the Sky-God who releases his stories to him. In accomplishing these tasks, Ananse also succeeds in not only victimizing but also humiliating Python, Hornets, Leopard and Fairy. The same pattern obtains in N2, albeit with a different setting and different characters. Here, to preserve his life from the summary justice and wrath of Bour, the King, Leuk is required to bring to Bour the skin of Leopard, two Elephant tusks, the skin of Lion and the hair of Kouss—again, seemingly unobtainable items. Leuk departs on a quest that pitches him against Leopard, Elephant, Lion and Kouss, humiliates each one of them with a different lie, obtains the necessary items and delivers them to Bour who then rescinds the death penalty. As in N1, Leuk's success spells defeat and humiliation for his unwary victims. Thus, in both N1 and N2, a basic pattern of confrontation is established and repeated three times. With each repetition, the protagonist encounters and tricks a new victim successfully and unceremoniously, and the trickster's successive victories pave the way for the attainment of his ultimate goal.

Although N1 and N2 are much shorter narratives than *Mandabi,* the structure of the latter closely parallels that of N1 and N2. In Sembène's film, the eventual goal of the protagonist, Ibrahima Dieng, is to cash the money order which his nephew, Abdou, an immigrant worker in Paris, has sent him. In order to cash the money order, Dieng needs an identity card, and this he does not have. His immediate task then is to secure an identity card. The quest for an identity card pitches Dieng against an intractable, cold and uncooperative bureaucracy (the Police and City Hall), a charlatan photographer (Ambrose), a neighborhood store owner and usurer (Mbarka), a con man (man at the bank), and a scheming and dishonest relative (Mbaye Saar). Whereas in N1 and N2 the protagonists accomplish their tasks successfully, in *Mandabi* Dieng, the protagonist, fails to accomplish the tasks that will enable him to achieve his ultimate objective.

His initial attempts to cash the money order on his own fail because he does not have an identity card. He then confronts the Police Authority to get an identity card, but here again, he is frustrated because he does not have a birth certificate, a photograph and fiscal stamps. Next he goes to City Hall in an attempt to obtain a birth certificate, but since he does not know his exact date of birth, the attempt fails. After a short-lived relief from frustration and failure—Dieng is aided financially by his nephew Amath who also introduces him to someone who will help in obtaining a birth certificate (which subsequent events imply that he does not claim)—Dieng confronts an impostor at the bank who extorts an enormous amount of money from Dieng for his "help". Dieng's next confrontation is with Ambrose, the charlatan photographer, in an attempt to obtain a passport-size photograph, and this confrontation ends in bloody-nosed failure for Dieng. He then resorts to Mbarka, the neighborhood store owner, for additional credit, but Mbarka's humiliating and impudent proposition —that Dieng should consider selling his house to an interested buyer — brings the two to blows, thus thwarting Dieng's attempt. The final *coup de grace* is delivered to Dieng when he is made to resort to Mbaye Saar for help. Mbaye cashes the money order but keeps the cash for himself, telling Dieng that the money was stolen.

The pattern of confrontation is constant in all three works, but the outcome of these confrontations is not. N1 and N2 are marked by a pattern of success on the part of the protagonist, whereas failure, frustration and humiliation consistently dog the protagonist of *Mandabi*. Ananse and Leuk confront their victims, trick them and humiliate them, but Dieng is cheated and tricked by those he comes into contact with. Sembène establishes the pattern of confrontation resulting in frustration on the part of Dieng in the 1st Image-Set and then repeats this pattern in varying guises five times in Image-Sets 2, 3, 6, 7 and 8. As in N1 and N2, each repeated image-set constitutes an encounter between the protagonist and an antagonist or antagonists, each repetition advancing the plot toward conclusion in a linear fashion. In N1 and N2 the relationship between Protagonist/Trickster and Victims is clearly established and developed with each repetition. In *Mandabi,* it is the relationship between Protagonist/Victim and Tricksters that each repetition explores. Thus, the three works taken together constitute a pattern of relationships between Trickster and Victim, or, by extension, Victimizer/Victimized, Have/Have-not, Exploiter/Exploited. Within the framework of these polarities, certain aspects of society and human behaviour are closely examined, then either upheld as models worthy of emulation and development, or condemned as evils and obstacles to be removed in the interest of the welfare of society as a whole.

With these polarities firmly set in place, it becomes relatively easy to discern the major thematic preoccupation in the three works. This is made easier by the very effective use made of a dominant aspect of the trickster figure who repeatedly employs his wit, cunning and *savoir-faire* to satisfy his own selfish desires at the expense of innocent, credulous and unwary individuals. Unlike some trickster figures who engage in acts of trickery merely for the sake of trickery, those in N1, N2 and *Mandabi* are strongly motivated by greed, vanity, selfishness and lack of self-restraint. These vices in turn tend to compromise and corrupt their moral integrity as well as prevent them from developing any sense of social responsibility and mission. Society for these tricksters is nothing but an arena in which to deploy the full range of their considerable mental astuteness and imagination in the service of greed, vanity and lust. Where this deployment proves successful, as it does in all three works, the results are catastrophic and humiliating for the victims.

Ananse is able to translate his dream of individual glory (and, perhaps, immortality too) into reality by readily taking advantage of the faith and shortcomings of Python, Hornets, Leopard and Fairy. There is nothing altruistic in his undertaking, and no one but himself benefits from his success. By no means ideal social models, Python, Hornets, Leopard and Fairy are nonetheless sympathetically portrayed as unwilling, though stupid, victims of a vicious mind whose profound lack of scruple and obsession with power drive it to commit a most unnatural and anti-social act —throwing in his mother as part of a deal to satisfy a puny desire. By dramatizing Ananse's success with four different victims in four different situations, the performer is able to convey graphically a clear idea of the power of greed and its attendant effects on an individual's sense of self and other. For Ananse, there is no doubt that others function only as tools to be exploited for the advancement of his own self-interest. Every other individual is a potential victim, and, therefore, a potential "resource" for him.

Just as Ananse leaves a trail of demoralized, dejected and humiliated individuals behind him, so does Leuk; and like Ananse, he too is driven by a selfish, albeit understandable, motive to employ his wit to victimize innocent individuals. By duplicating Leuk's initial success against Leopard in the former's subsequent confrontations with Elephant, Lion and Kouss, the performance is able to juxtapose events that reinforce and comment on each other, so that the total picture of Leuk that emerges is one characterized by an absolute disregard and utter contempt for others less endowed. Leuk's total lack of any regard for the welfare of others predisposes him to cheat, lie and trick his way to satisfy his individual desires. For him, the selfish end justifies the consistently ruthless means, and the repetition of the different structural units in the narrative underscores this effectively and appropriately.

Thus, the structural similarity between N1 and N2 is duplicated on the level of theme. The general outline of the thematic concerns of these narratives has been given in the preceding paragraphs, and the parrallels are too obvious to warrant any further treatment at this point. However, it is worth noting that, as trickster figures, Ananse and Leuk tend to inspire two kinds of reaction that may appear contradictory. On the one hand, they may be condemned for moral depravity, selfishness and lack of a sense of reciprocity, but, on the other hand, they may also inspire a mild sense of admiration for their wit, craftiness and ability to achieve the seemingly impossible. Trickster represents what is feared but secretly coveted. Our reluctance to unequivocally condemn Ananse and Leuk is perhaps explained by the distance that exists between our real world and that of Ananse and Leuk. We can afford to indulge in mild admiration of the ruthless and selfish use of wit and craftiness because their world seems too remote from us. This gap becomes a kind of protective shield that shelters us from the potentially catastrophic and humiliating machinations of Ananse and Leuk, hence our willingness to be somewhat ambivalent about them.

If Ananse and Leuk possess some potentially redeeming qualities, Sembène does not allow his tricksters in *Mandabi* any such qualities. These modern-day tricksters are the very incarnation of greed, evil, corruption and reaction, and there can be nothing worthy of admiration in such individuals who, according to

Sembene, constitute the greatest real threat not only to the moral fiber of the masses of society, but also to its material viability. Sembène's tricksters are too close to everyday reality and too adept at their trade to merit any light or favourable treatment. They possess no redeeming qualities and there is nothing in them that inspires the slightest bit of admiration. Their objectives are selfish and anti-social and their methods are crude and vicious. The artist takes it upon himself to systematically expose and denounce these greedy elements in society. He also questions the very foundations —moral and otherwise—of a system that effectively excludes, and is ultimately responsible for, the continued misery and exploitation of people such as Ibrahima Dieng, the so-called "illiterate" majority. *Mandabi* thus becomes both an emotional and perceptual vehicle for provoking a feeling of shock and anger that will contribute to heightening the moral and political awareness and will of people, a vital prerequisite for any form of revolutionary social change.

One of the ways in which Sembene dramatizes the urgency and inevitablity of such a change is by closely scrutinizing the relationship between those forces that exercise control over certain important sectors of society and those forces that do not. Dieng's labyrinthine Odyssey in the world of modern-day bureaucracy becomes an unpleasant, but vital, eye-opening experience, a revelation which Dieng aptly and aphoristically captures, in his observation that "honesty is a sin in this country". If there is any doubt as to the general validity of this statement in the world of N1 and N2 where dishonesty and greed seem to be localized in the person of Ananse and Leuk, respectively, there can be no doubt in the case of *Mandabi* as to its proverbial truth and validity. In *Mandabi,* the oppressive omni-presence of dishonesty and greed baffles and shocks the imagination into an awareness of the social and political implications of a crisis of this nature in society. Everything in the unfamiliar and hostile world of bureaucracy constitutes a blatant assault on Dieng's sense of moral decency, honor and human responsibility. That Dieng, an honest, Allah-fearing and generous man resolves, at the end of his ordeal, to become crooked like all the others is a testimony to the devastating power of the pervasive moral dishonesty and material greed that has so blinded people that the bitter truth embodied in Ambrose's comment that "only scoundrels live well in this country" becomes chillingly clear.

But Sembène does not rely solely on such pronouncements to

convey his message. He imparts it clearly through the movements of Dieng and his confrontations with various bureaucratic and social tricksters. Although these encounters end in defeat for Dieng, Sembène is not thereby conveying a sense of absolute hopelessness nor is he admonishing capitulation to the lure of vice for people like Dieng. On the contrary, Dieng's defeat is as much a diagnosis of what is wrong or is not working in the contemporary neo-colonial society as it is a graphic dramatization of the need for social and political change. Thus, the mailman suggests to Dieng an alternative course of action, one that can contribute to curing, rather than exacerbating, the social and political diseases that presently afflict their society.

As in N1 and N2, repetition dominates in *Mandabi* as a device which the artist skilfully manipulates to carry out a process of social diagnosis in order to lay bare for critical appraisal the typical social forces and trends found in present-day Senegal, and also to suggest possible directions for change. Whereas Ananse personifies greed and dishonesty in N1, and Leuk in N2, in *Mandabi* the twin vices are lodged in more than one character. Whereas in N1 and N2 we follow Ananse and Leuk, respectively, as they successively victimize innocent and honest individuals, in *Mandabi,* we follow Dieng, an innocent and honest individual, as he is successively victimized and frustrated by a motley array of tricksters. He is frustrated by a cold, impersonal bureaucracy and tricked by insensitive individuals whose services he needs in order to attain his ultimate objective.

Frustration, dishonesty, greed—these are the forces that litter every path that Dieng takes in *Mandabi.* They are present in all of the image-sets, except the 4th in which Sembène fleetingly presents a frugal (he drives a "Deux Chevaux") and sensitive member of the élite, Amath, who is the only one with influence to help Dieng without any ulterior motive.[6] Dieng's troubles with the Post Office clerk are echoed in his troubles at the Police Station and at City Hall. His resort to the letter-writer at the Post Office prepares us for his resort to Amath, to the confidence trickster at the bank and to Mbaye Saar. The scuffle, the accusations and counter-accusations of dishonesty between Dieng and the letter-writer at the Post Office foreshadow the same type of encounter—although much more physical—between Dieng and the photographer, and between Dieng and Mbarka. Thus, the Post Office sequence becomes significant in so far as it effectively and clearly forebodes the entire ordeal that Dieng is about to undergo.

The diversity of crooks encountered, and the frequency and consistency with which these crooks and tricksters gang up successfully against Dieng, enable Sembene to juxtapose types of power dishonesty and greed, on the one hand, with weakness and honesty, on the other. Mbarka, the confidence trickster, the photographer and Mbaye Saar are the very incarnation of power (of sorts), dishonesty and greed, and, paradoxically, the guardian of one type of service or another vital to the success of the weak and the honest such as Dieng.

In accumulative fashion, each image-set details the unscrupulous use of power by one of these crooks to satisfy his greed at the expense of Dieng. These crooks are nothing less than bloodsuckers, a fact which Sembène underscores graphically by juxtaposing the shot of the photographer drinking red wine with the close-up of the blood dripping on the sand from the bleeding nose of Ibrahima Dieng, incurred during the scuffle with the photographer's assistant. These modern-day Ananses and Leuks thrive primarily on the blood of the weak and the credulous. Their repeated successes at the expense of Dieng in *Mandabi* make it seem as if Sembène structures the film for maximum 'collision' of opposing forces *à la Eisentien* from image-set to image-set. In this way, he is better able to force the audience to participate in and interpret the events portrayed on the screen. Dieng's repeated failure and humiliation at the hands of social crooks is nothing less than an attempt on the part of Sembène to shock his audience's total consciousness and steer it towards a realization of the power inherent in a unified force of the oppressed and exploited, such as Dieng, his wives, their children and the mailman; a powerful force that is capable of ridding society of elements like Mbaye Saar, Ambrose, and all those modern-day social tricksters who benefit from a system that is unwilling or incapable of serving the interests and welfare of the majority. And, as if to remind the audience of the imperativeness and urgency of such an action and the price of inaction, Sembène uses flashback to recall Dieng's ordeals. He flashes on the screen again for a last time a series of unpleasant images from Dieng's recent ordeal—images which are superimposed on a shot of Dieng flanked by Mety and Aram, with an echoing repetition of his remarks that "honesty is a sin in this country"

Is *Mandabi* a dramatization of the truth of this statement and that of Ambrose—"only scoundrels live well in this country" —in contemporary urban Senegal? Is it possible to look at the film as a "conte moral" as claimed by Bonitzer?[7] The evidence in the film and the manner in which Sembène utilizes repetition—of dishonesty, frustration, greed and failure—to structure the film seem to support this hypothesis. Moreover, if we turn to Wolof oral narrative traditions—a vital source of inspiration and models for Sembène—we will find that there exists a type of narrative that can be labelled 'proverb-narrative', a narrative which is a dramatized illustration, so to speak, of a proverb. A most famous example is the narrative attributed to the legendary Wolof thinker, Kocy Barma[8], that illustrates the truth of the following four proverbs: "A King is neither a relative nor a protector", "Love your wife but do not trust her", "A first child from a previous marriage is not a son, but a perpetual cause of woes",[9] and "An old man is necessary in a country".[10] Sembène, however, is not content with merely enunciating a proverbial truth about society. *Mandabi* is an invitation to political action and morality. Like Kocy Barma, Sembène is a politically conscious black thinker who has managed to identify and capture the rhythm and dynamics of those typical forces within his society into a story that aims to enlighten, teach and provoke action. In *Mandabi*, he reveals the intimate workings of the alienated and corrupt world in which Ibrahima Dieng lives and suffers, and it is now incumbent upon the audience to intervene in the evolution of history by taking steps to initiate change (as suggested by the mailman) in the mechanism of a system and a society whose serious structural and moral defects have been pointed out to it.[11]

African oral narrative traditions have always constituted a seemingly inexhaustible source of inspiration and models for many African artists; and these artists, using various media of expression, have, with varying degrees of success, consistently tapped the resources of their individual traditions at all levels—structure, style, theme—in their creative activities. The examples of Wole Soyinka (in drama), Chinua Achebe, Ngugi wa Thiong'o, Ahmadou Kourouma (in the novel), and Okot p'Bitek and Okello Oculi (in poetry) are only too well known. In film, early efforts to utilize resources from oral narrative traditions tended to be limited to filmed versions of narrative such as Momar Caam's *Sarzan* (1963) and *La Malle de Maka-Kouli* (1969) based on Birago Diop's narratives of the same titles; Paulin Soumanou Vieyra's *N'dion-gane* (1965), also based on Birago Diop's "Petit-Mari"; and the Ghanaian Sam Aryete's *No Tears for Ananse* (1968), modelled on one of the Ananse narratives. Sembène, on the other hand, transcends these limits and goes far beyond filmed oral narrative. with *Mandabi;* a trial which, if followed carefully, may lead us to with oral narrative are to be found in theme and structure, and more specifically, in the skill with which Sembène utilizes repetition —in the manner of N1 and N2—to structure his film for maximum impact of his message on his compatriots about the state and direction of their society.

Ousmane Sembène has indeed blazed a new trail in African film with Mandabi; a trial which, if followed carefully, may lead us to an important fountainhead of African creativity to reveal at the same time the true dimensions of Sembène's commitment to Africa — a total commitment, not only political but also artistic, with profound faith and confidence in the artistic resources of his tradition. Perhaps critics and observers of African film may do well to heed the lesson too. Rather than limping off to Hollywood or to Europe to seek models the minute a Sembène film premieres, the critics would be wise to seek these models at home in the African artistic culture; for it is this culture, its progressive and adaptable dimensions in particular, that constitutes for Sembène a primary source of models. His awareness of the artistic potential of certain aspects of this cultural heritage enables him to go beyond a mere carbon-copy of these models. Sembène invests these models with new life, new experience and a new radical socio-political mission. It is in this respect that Sembène speaks of himself as the equivalent of the *griot* in the society of today.

NOTES

1. Pascal Bonitzer, "Le Mandat " *Cahiers du Cinema,* no. 209, Fev., 1969, p. 58.
2. Ibid., p. 58.
3. See Stith Thompson, *Motif Index of Folk Literature* Vol. 3 (Bloomington: University of Indiana Press. 1956), pp. 456-471.
4. From Paul Radin (ed.) *African Folktales,* (Princeton: Bollingen, 1970) pp. 25-27.
5. Birago Diop, *Lies Contes d'Amadou Koumba* (Paris: Présence Africaine, 1961) pp. 107-117.

6. Compare and contrast with the case of Mbaye Saar who seeks out Dieng in order to 'help' him.

7. Bonitzer, p. 57.

8. A version of this narrative can be found in L.J.B. Berenger-Feraud, *Les Peuplades de la Senegambie* Paris: 1879 (Klaus Peprint, Nendela, 1973), ·pp. 38-39

9. The Wolof original *doomu jiitle du doom, xare bu wafe la* is difficult to render precisely in English. The French translation reads *un enfant de premier lit n'est pas un fils, c'est une guerre intestine.*

10. Other example include Birago Diop's "The Humps", which begins with a proverb: "In the matter of wives two is not a good number," and "The Bone" where we encounter these two proverbs: "If he had his belly behind him, it would drag him into a hole" and "If your greed has not been the end of you, then it is not genuine greed." From *Les Contes d'Amadou Koumba* (Paris: Présence Africaine, 1961).

11. Sembène, like other artists, has continually maintained that he is in no way· obliged to provide concrete answers to the central problems raised in his work. He despises and ridicules people who are pretentious enough to believe that a film or a book can make a revolution. The mission of the African artist, he says, is "not to make the revolution, but to prepare the revolution." The artist's true contribution is realized *par son travail de clarification et d'analyse, de dévoilement et de dénonciation. Il aura innoculé dans les consciences conviction plus claire que la revolution est necessaire et possible.*

Notes on Contributors

Daniel AVORGBEDOR Studied ethnomusicology at the University of Ghana and Indiana (Bloomington). He has done extensive research in African music (with special reference to the musical traditions of the Ewe of Ghana) and has held lectures and workshops on the subject across the United States of America. He has also published articles in scholarly journals like *Percussive Notes*. He now teaches at the University of Ghana, Legon.

Chukwuma AZUONYE teaches in the Department of Linguistics and Nigerian Languages at the University of Nigeria, Nsukka. He has researched extensively and written on the oral epic traditions of the Igbo of eastern Nigeria. His articles on this subject, as well as on African Literature generally, have appeared in journals like *Research in African Literatures* and *Journal of African and Comprative Literature*. He is the editor of *Uwa ndi Igbo: Journal of Igbo Life and Culture* and the *Nsukka Journal of the Humanities*. He is also co-editor of the forthcoming book, *The Hero in Igbo Life and Literature*.

Mbye Baboucar CHAM teaches African Literature and Film in the African Studies Program at Howard University, Washington D.C. His major interest is in the relationship between literature (oral and written), film, and society in Africa and the Third World. He has published in journals like *Ufahamu* and *Ba Shiru*.

Elizabeth GUNNER has worked in the Extramural Division of the School of Oriental and African Studies, University of London. She has published numerous papers on Zulu oral poetry in journals like *Research in African Literatures* and *African Languages/Langues Africaines*. She has also been involved in promoting the teaching of African and Commonwealth Literature, a subject on which she has written articles and a book. She is a freelance writer living in England.

Gordon INNES retired recently as Professor of African Languages in the School of Oriental and African Studies, University of

271

London. He has written numerous articles and books based on his fieldwork among the Gambian Mandinka, the most notable being *Sunjata: Three Mandinka Versions* (1974), *Kaabu and Fuladu: Historical Narratives of the Gambian Mandinka* (1976), and *Kelefa Saane: His Life and Career Recounted by Two Mandinka Bards* (1978).

Edris MAKWARD has taught at the Universities of Ibadan and Calabar and is at present Professor of French and African Literature at the University of Wisconsin (Madison). His areas of research include African and Caribbean literatures in French and English, as well as Wolof oral traditions. He has co-authored a textbook *African Literature* (1972) and written articles in journals like *Exploration* and *Issue*.

Enoch S. Timpunza MVULA teaches Malawian literature (oral and written) in the Chancellor College of the University of Malawi. He has published a play, an anthology of Chichewa (Malawi) poetry, has edited *Kalulu* (a Malawian journal of oral literature), and is at present writing a book on the subject.

Isidore OKPEWHO is Professor of English at the University of Ibadan. He has published two novels *The Victims* (1970) and *The Last Duty* (1976); three scholarly books *The Epic in Africa* (1979), *Myth in Africa* (1983), and *The Heritage of African Poetry* (1985); and numerous articles in the *Journal of Aesthetics and Art Criticism, Journal of American Folklore, African Literature Today, Research in African Literatures, Cahiers d'Etudes Africaines,* and several other journals and books. He is the editor of the *Journal of African and Comparative Literature*.

Ronald RASSNER has done fieldwork in East Africa, taught in the African Studies Program at Yale University, and is at present Director of the World Affairs Center at Beloit College, Wisconsin. His major field of interest is oral narrative theory and documentation, and he has done extensive work on the relationship between the oral literatures and cultures of Africa and the New World (especially Brazil). He has published articles on the subject in the *Encylopedia Brittanica* (Micropedia Project), *Research in African/Literatures,* and other learned journals.

Ropo SEKONI teaches in the Department of Literature in English, Obafemi Awolowo University, Ile-Ife, Nigeria. His area of interest includes semiotics, narratology in both oral and written forms, aesthetics, and literary theory and criticism. He has published in numerous journals like *Ba Shiru, Journal of Commonwealth Literature,* and *African Drama Review.* He is currently writing a book on Yoruba narratology.

275